VAL~~U~~E ~~B~~EYOND MEASURE

VALOUR BEYOND MEASURE
Captain Richard William Leslie Wain V.C.
The Tank Corps at Cambrai 1917

DR JONATHAN HICKS

First impression: 2020

© Copyright Jonathan Hicks and Y Lolfa Cyf., 2020

The contents of this book are subject to copyright, and may not be reproduced by any means, mechanical or electronic, without the prior, written consent of the publishers.

The publishers wish to acknowledge the support of
Cyngor Llyfrau Cymru

Cover design: Y Lolfa
Back cover image: Richard James Molloy

ISBN: 978 1 912631 26 1

Published and printed in Wales
on paper from well-maintained forests by
Y Lolfa Cyf., Talybont, Ceredigion SY24 5HE
website www.ylolfa.com
e-mail ylolfa@ylolfa.com
tel 01970 832 304
fax 832 782

Contents

	Introduction	7
1	The Wain Family	8
2	The Junior Officer	35
3	The Somme 1916	53
4	Messines 1917	73
5	Third Ypres – Passchendaele 1917	92
6	The Battle of Cambrai 1917	101
7	The German Perspective	130
8	The Victoria Cross Award	145
9	The Other Tank Corps V.C. Winners	170
10	The Crew of Abou-Ben-Adam II	176
11	The Other Officers of 'A' Battalion	185
12	The Aftermath	231
13	The Memorials	237
	Epilogue	244

Endnotes	246
Appendix	255
Bibliography	267
Acknowledgements	270

Introduction

AT 6.50 A.M. on Sunday 20 November 1917, the fourth year of the Great War, 350 lumbering steel behemoths left the British front line and slowly began their advance towards the formidable German defences of the Hindenburg Line, east of the French town of Cambrai. Spewing great clouds of exhaust fumes, these machines of the British Tank Corps were closely followed by wave after wave of supporting infantry.

Aboard tank number A.2, with the words 'Abou-Ben-Adam II' painted on its sides, was a young man from Penarth in south Wales. Acting Captain Richard Wain was just 20 years old and was in command of a section of three Mark IV tanks. The crew of the tank in which he was travelling, and the 16 other men in the two tanks on either side of his, were depending on him for success – and survival.

A few hours later Richard Wain and two other members of his crew were dead, three more lives lost in the carnage of the First World War. However, his actions during that intervening time led to him being awarded Britain's highest military honour for gallantry – the Victoria Cross – in recognition of the courage he had displayed that morning.

Over one hundred years later his name is all but forgotten. This is his story.

CHAPTER 1

The Wain Family

RICHARD WILLIAM LESLIE Wain, second child and only son of Harris and Florence Wain, was born at 4 Victoria Square, overlooking Victoria Park, in Penarth, Glamorganshire, on 5 December 1896. His elder sister, Elsie Madeline, had been born earlier that year, on 9 January.

The story of the Wain family during the course of the nineteenth century perfectly illustrates the increased prosperity of sections of British society and the social mobility of the time. Richard's great-grandfather, also named Richard Wain, was born in 1808 in Lincoln and was an agricultural labourer who rose to be the owner of a flourishing business. In October 1831 he married Lydia Sparks, from Horton Kirby in Kent, who worked as a laundress, and together they had ten children.

Disenchanted with life in Britain, and hearing of the Australian Gold Rush, in 1854 Richard Wain and his eldest son Thomas decided to emigrate to the colony to seek their fortunes. They arrived in Melbourne and then sailed on to Sydney aboard the *Antelope*, disembarking there on 15 May. They settled to life in New South Wales, and a year later Richard and Lydia's two eldest daughters, Rebecca and Sarah, joined them; they both subsequently married and settled in Sydney.

On 17 April 1855, Thomas paid £42.10.0 for the steerage passage to Australia of the remainder of the family, plus that of William Black, 35, and Harriett Hatherall, 18.

In 1856 Lydia and six of their children, Alexander, 16,

The Wain Family

Richard Wain senior   Lydia Wain   Rebecca Wain

Interior of similar convict ship

George, 13, Mary, 11, Stephen, 9, James, 6 and Lydia, 3, set sail from Britain aboard the *Robert Small*, and three months later they arrived in Australia. The *Robert Small* was a convict ship that also conveyed paying passengers.

The cabin the family occupied was equipped with only the most rudimentary of items – bunks and mattresses, a washstand, a slop pail, and a lamp. Passengers would supply their own bed linen and other items to improve their comfort for the long voyage. As steerage passengers, they ate the same food as the crew and were segregated from the intermediate and first-class passengers. In periods of rough weather they were confined below decks and ventilation and hygiene would have been problematic. It would therefore have been a great relief to the family when they finally disembarked.

In 1865 Richard was granted the title to 19 acres of land in the parish of Lilliput (named by the land commissioner after its licensee, former convict James Gullifer) in north-east Victoria. He and his sons Stephen and James set to clearing the land of native trees and once this had been done, they built a four-roomed cottage, planted an orchard and reared animals. Eventually they established a vineyard and ran a slaughterhouse. These businesses thrived and Richard and the family prospered.

The only one of the children not to emigrate was their son, also called Richard, who was born in Hawley in the parish of Sutton-at-Hone, Kent, in 1833. By 1851 Richard junior was employed as a groom and lived at Glaslyn Cottage, 57 Forge Row, Llanelli. He appears to have left this employment to work in London, as it was here that he met and married Elizabeth Edmonds from Caerleon on 15 June 1859. He gave his occupation as that of a valet. In 1861 the couple were employed as the butler and housekeeper respectively at the home of

Stephen Wain    James Wain    Richard Wain junior

The Wain Family

John Rowlands, proprietor of iron mines, at Aberystruth, Monmouthshire.

Perhaps in keeping with his new position, Richard now claimed his place of birth to be The Strand, London. He was 28 and Elizabeth was 34. Their first child, born in 1861, was named Madeline Cecelia; his employer John Rowlands had a 23-year-old daughter named Madeline Cecilia.

In 1865 Richard and Elizabeth decided on a change of employment and he began work as the proprietor of the Griffin Hotel at 89 Beaufort Street, Brynmawr, Brecknockshire. In 1867 Richard was elected to the local Board of Health.

Brynmawr had grown from a few scattered farms when the Nantyglo Ironworks opened in 1795. Demand for houses for workers increased as the ironworks swiftly became the most important in the world. The town began to grow commensurately and in 1862 the railway arrived, turning the town into a rail junction.

The Griffin Hotel was probably the finest hotel in the area. It was the main stopping point for the mail coach that ran from Abergavenny to Merthyr, and was frequently used by commercial travellers owing to its proximity to the railway station.

On 7 June 1866, Richard and Elizabeth's only son, Harris Wain, was born.

In the 1871 census Richard now claimed to be 46 years of age but had reverted to being born in Kent. Sometime after 1871 he also took over the running of the Castle Hotel, located on The Square in Brynmawr.

In 1870 the ironworks was sold and the town began to go into decline. Richard Wain sensed this and began to make plans to move his family somewhere more prosperous. On 16 August 1875 it was announced in a newspaper that:

> Mr. R. Wain (for ten years Proprietor of the Griffin and Castle Hotels, Brynmawr), begs to announce that he has completed

11

Beaufort Street, Brynmawr

Painting of the ironworks at Nantyglo by an unknown artist

The Griffin Hotel, Brynmawr

The Castle Hotel, Brynmawr

arrangements with the Cardiff Hotel Company (Limited), and has taken possession of the Royal Hotel, Cardiff, which he will in future conduct. He trusts that the reputation which he acquired as Proprietor, first of the Griffin Hotel, and subsequently of the Castle Hotel, will be an indication of the manner in which he will carry on the Royal Hotel, the Largest and Best Hotel in South Wales.[1]

Cardiff had grown rapidly from the 1830s with the building of a dock which was served by the Taff Vale Railway. Being the main exporting port for the Welsh coalfields, the population of the town grew by 80 per cent each decade between 1840 and 1870, and by 1881 Cardiff was the largest town in Wales.

In the 1881 census Richard once again claimed to have been born in The Strand, London, and gave his age as 57; with Elizabeth being 54. The census shows that he was in charge of a large number of employees and servants, and the hotel was evidently prospering. At this time their son Harris Wain was living at 58 High Street in Oxford and was a scholar, aged 14; he later attended Queen's College, Oxford.

However, tragedy struck the family on 10 March 1882 when their only daughter, Madeline, died of consumption (tuberculosis), aged 21, leaving Harris as their only child. The newspaper report of her funeral stated:

> The cortege proceeded by road to the Rhymney Railway Station, Cardiff, and at 12.25 p.m. the mourners left in special carriages for Brynmawr. Here nearly every shop had been closed as a mark of respect to the deceased, and the funeral procession through the streets was witnessed by thousands of persons.[2]

On 1 January 1886 Richard was initiated into the Windsor Lodge of the Freemasons in Penarth. In 1889 he was listed as the proprietor of the Marine Hotel, which overlooked Penarth Docks, and was also a director of the Royal Hotel Company (Cardiff) Limited. He further extended his business interests

Cardiff Docks

The Royal Hotel, Cardiff

Madeline Wain

The Wain Family

The original Marine Hotel in Penarth, which was rebuilt in 1865

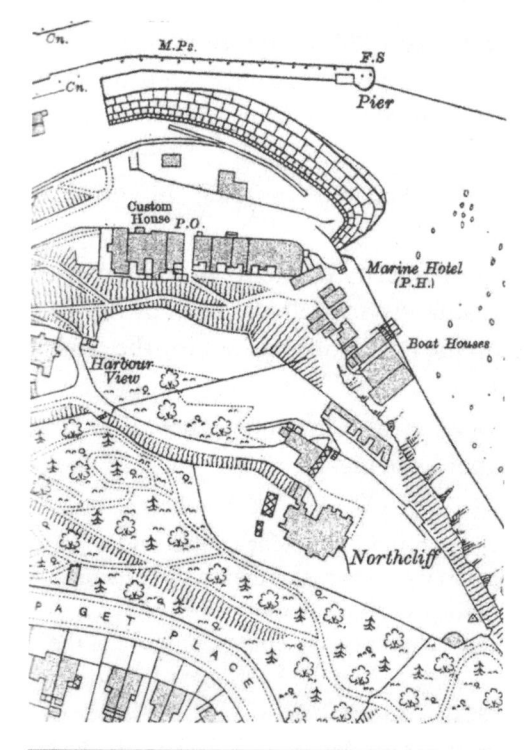

Map of Penarth Docks, showing the location of the Marine Hotel

The Marine Hotel in more recent years, showing its close proximity to the Custom House

15

in May 1889 when he became a director of the wine and spirit merchants Stevens and Son Limited of Cardiff.

By the middle of the nineteenth century, demand for Welsh coal was increasing and, in 1859, a tidal harbour on the River Ely at Penarth was opened. This was linked to the Welsh coalfields by the Taff Vale Railway. Within five years, over 200,000 tons of coal was being exported annually through this harbour. On 10 June 1865 a larger dock was opened and exports rose to 273,996 tons. In 1880 permission was granted to expand the dock further and after this new extension was completed in 1884 over 3,000,000 tons of coal was being exported annually.

In 1851 the population of Penarth was 105; this grew to 2,612 within 20 years.

To reflect the growing prosperity of the town, the Penarth Hotel (later to become Headlands School) was built by the Taff Vale Railway Company on the headland overlooking the docks, at a cost of over £27,000.

The Penarth Hotel opened at Christmas 1869 and was described in one newspaper as being

> pleasantly situated on rising ground, and being contiguous to the sea, commands wide and varied views of the Bristol Channel, extending to the towns of Clevedon and Weston-super-Mare on the opposite coast, and, on a clear day, including a glimpse of the houses and the beach.[3]

Set in 20 acres of landscaped gardens and grounds, the hotel had 50 rooms and had been designed in the latest architectural fashion – the Italian style – by the Cardiff architect C. E. Bernard. The rooms

> are well ventilated, light, and airy, and while the smaller rooms are nicely ornamented, the larger ones are chastely decorated in harmonious colours. The walls are clothed with rich yet delicate paper, the ceilings, especially in the coffee-room, are of a warm

The Wain Family

Penarth Docks

The Penarth Hotel

17

fawn-coloured tint, and the cornices present a graceful blending of gilding and stencil work in various hues.

    The large and handsome coffee-room, surrounded on three sides by windows, and fitted with handsome mirrors; the sitting-rooms, of which there are several, plentifully supplied with lounges, and chairs which seem to invite one to be easy in them; the billiard-room and table, in which the arrangements appear all that could be desired – make the prospect of a visitor a very pleasant one. The winding of the Welsh coast may be followed for a considerable distance up and down the channel, and the Somersetshire shore on the opposite side is always distinct, and sometimes especially clear.[4]

The writer continued:

> The Flat and Steep Holmes, and numerous other points of interest are to be seen from the Hotel, and its proximity to the sea enable visitors to enjoy the excitement of a storm without experiencing the perils and risks that accompany it. Ships with sails spread, as though terror animated them, fly from the fury of the storm to gain the shelter of the roadstead, and now and then the gale seizes an ill-fated bark, and takes the helm out of the power of the pilot, and drives the vessel with all its force upon the sands which dot the channel. These, perhaps, are not of the pleasures the Hotel affords, but they are among its experiences.[5]

Both the Marine Hotel and the Penarth Hotel were owned by the Taff Vale Railway Company, and it appears that Richard managed them on behalf of the company. It was hoped that the Penarth Hotel would be patronised by businessmen and sea captains, but encountered some difficulties at first. A guidebook of 1884 noted:

> At first it did not pay, but now under Mr. Wain's management, the hotel is generally full. Over the roof of the large coffee room is a balcony used for 'kettledrum' parties and dancing in the summer evenings. In front of the garden entrances are fine lawn tennis and archery grounds.[6]

However, the Penarth Hotel did not flourish, and changed hands during the course of the First World War (after Richard Wain's tenure). It was bought by Mrs Gladys Gibbs (née Morel) of the Morel Shipping Company, who acquired it in memory of her late husband, Major John Angel Gibbs D.S.O., 9th Battalion, Welsh Regiment, who was killed in action on 20 September 1917 during the Third Battle of Ypres.[7] Gladys Gibbs presented the building to the trustees of the National Children's Home to be used as an orphanage.

In 1884, after over 30 years in Australia, Richard and Lydia Wain visited Wales and a report of their arrival appeared in a newspaper in May of that year:

A Formidable Excursion.
There have this week arrived at Penarth, on a visit to their son, Mr. Richard Wain, the respected host of the Penarth Hotel, his father and mother, who are both octogenarians. They have made the long journey for the purpose, as they reside 400 miles the other side of Sydney, Australia, and left their home on the 29th of March last. On arriving at Sydney, Mr. and Mrs. Wain proceeded on board the *Chimborazo*, and then sailed for Melbourne, where they made a sojourn of seven days, and afterwards came on in the same vessel to Plymouth, where they arrived last week. They were there met by Mr. Richard Wain, who went out into the Sound in a tender, but he was not recognised by his aged parents. This is not surprising, as they have not met for 33 years – a large gap in the lifetime of a man. The voyage from the Colonies, which was described as a most enjoyable one, was highly appreciated

John Angel Gibbs and Gladys Gibbs after he received the D.S.O. at Buckingham Palace

19

by the travellers, who since their arrival at Penarth have availed
themselves of the opportunity of seeing everything of interest in
the rapidly extending watering place. Mr. Wain, senior, left this
country in 1850 [sic – it was in fact 1854], and proceeded at once
to the locality in which he now resides. He engaged in farming
and the cultivation of extensive vineyards, in which he was soon
most successful. He hailed originally from Kent, and will, before
he returns home, renew his acquaintance with the haunts of his
earlier life. Mr. and Mrs. Wain have left behind them in the land
of their adoption eight sons and daughters, 43 grandchildren, and
six great-grandchildren. We have called attention to this subject
because it is not often to be recorded that parents who have passed
fourscore years in the journey of life travel a distance of between
sixteen and seventeen thousand miles to revisit their native country
and greet once more a member of their family. They have taken
return tickets upon what everyone will admit is a long excursion,
and that they may enjoy themselves and return home the better for
their journey is an aspiration which all will indulge with sincerity.[8]

Richard junior decided to accompany his parents back
to Sydney for an extended holiday, the circumstances and
accommodation being far removed from his parents' voyage a
generation earlier. Upon his return nine months later, he gave
an account of his travels to a reporter.

Nine months ago Mr. Richard Wain, of the Penarth Hotel,
determined to accompany his father – who, along with Mrs.
Wain, sen., had made the long journey from Sydney on purpose
to visit their son, whom they had not seen for many years – back
to Australia and see the country which, though gigantic in its
proportions and wonderful in its enterprise, is still proud to
recognise Great Britain as its 'mother.' Mr. Wain departed with
the good wishes of his friends, and this week, returning from his
long journey, he was welcomed with a cordiality which it is not
likely he will ever forget. Yesterday a representative of the *Western
Mail* 'interviewed' the traveller for the purpose of obtaining some
account of a tour which only the wealthy can make for a holiday.
He found Mr. Wain as pleasant and communicative as ever, and he
elicited the following interesting reminiscences of his travels:

'We started on our voyage,' Mr. Wain said, in the course of several hours' conversation, 'from Tilbury, opposite Gravesend, having taken berths on the fine steamer *Orient*, of the line of that name. We had very pleasant times, the captain and his officers doing everything in their power to conduce to the enjoyment of the large number of passengers on board. The daily menu was princely, and the tables were every day spread with "feasts of fat things." There was plenty of amusement for leisure hours, Shaw's Australian Eleven furnishing a good deal of sport by playing cricket matches on the deck with picked elevens from the saloons.'

'Our first stoppage was at Plymouth, and then we steamed straight away for Port Said, reaching which place Messrs. Cook and Son, of tourist fame, who were with us, kindly organised a party for a trip in Egypt while the vessel was coaling and passing through the Canal. Let me here mention, while speaking of coals, that Capt. Hewinson, who commands the *Orient*, assured me that Cardiff coal was worth twice as much for steam purposes as that obtained in the colonies. The picnic party, if I may so term them, forty-nine in number, embarked in a steam launch, specially chartered for their accommodation, and proceeded to Ismailia, where breakfast was spread under the refreshing shadows of a grove of palm trees, the fruit of which we could pluck and eat as we sat.'

The SS *Orient*

The next section of his account gives an uncanny portent of the future for the Wain family:

'A special train then hurried us on to Tel-el-Kebir, memorable for the battle in which the British were so signally victorious, a walk through the cemetery, with the palms and other trees growing over the graves, reminding us that war has its sorrows as well as its glories. The bodies of many of our brave fellows were lying there, and I was glad to find the place in such excellent order.

'We lunched at Zagazig, and went on by the same train to Cairo, the ride being highly-interesting and enjoyable, not only from the nature of the land through which we passed, but also from its associations. In our progress we crossed and re-crossed the Sweet Waters and the Nile. At Cairo we luxuriated in a bath before dinner, which was most refreshing after the heat and dust of the desert. In the evening we visited the citadel in carriages and on donkeys, and the sentries opened their eyes pretty widely to see their domains invaded by our large party. The night was a lovely one, and all were immensely pleased with what was seen.

'At five o'clock in the morning we were aroused from our slumbers and half an hour after we sat down to breakfast, the early meal being necessary in order to enable us to "do" the Pyramids, twelve miles off. Arrived at these historic piles we climbed, with the aid of the Sheikhs, who ran after the carriages from Cairo, their grim sides, and saw all that was to be seen in the neighbourhood. The drive through an acacia grove was deliciously cool after the furnace-like temperature in the open. Coming back, we turned into the garden of the Khedive, the open sesame being the word of Mr. Cook, whose name is one to conjure with in these parts of the world. The grounds were simply magnificent.

'We reached Suez on the third day, and found our good ship waiting for us, having passed through the Canal. Our next place of call was Aden, where we had a peep at the renowned tanks, which were formerly the only source from which the people could get their water. There are nine of them, holding from five to twelve million gallons each – not a fabulous supply, when I tell you that there has been no rain there for seven years. The tanks are built in tiers, and are cut out of massive alabaster. The inhabitants now obtain a supply by condensing the sea water. After a stay of six hours we sailed out into the Indian Ocean, where we found the heat as much as we could bear. We could not keep a dry rag to our bodies for any time.

'A sail of three weeks brought us to Adelaide, a beautiful city. The railway runs through the magnificent streets from the port to the city, which is one of the prettiest in design from one end of the colonies to the other. After lunch we travelled to Melbourne, 30 hours' distance, which we reached on the 28th of October. I was enchanted with the place, and I really do not think there is another city in the world like Melbourne. The buildings are large and well-built, and signs of commercial activity abound on all sides. The atmosphere is deliciously bracing, although the temperature is pretty high. I found the weather there something like we experienced in this country during the long summer of last year. The outskirts are superb. The Botanical Gardens are immense and are laid out with considerable taste. In the midst of the gardens stands the Governor's house, a fine erection of quite lordly proportions. I here had the pleasure of witnessing the race for the Melbourne Cup – the Australian Derby, as it is called. The course is a grand one, and all the arrangements are perfection. Having spent a week in this charming city, I proceeded to Sydney, breaking the journey by crossing over the River Murray into New South Wales, which was reached on the 12th of November. Thence I travelled overland to Albury, and arrived in Sydney next day. Here I stayed some days, and came across a number of colonists who hailed from the Principality, and who gave me a cordial greeting. I stayed with Mr. Little, whose wife is a sister of Mr. Phillips, the well-known wine merchant of Bristol. He gave me some capital shooting, the game being bears, opossums, hares, and snakes. I shot one of the latter which measured nine feet. I wish, if you would be good enough, to record that I was most hospitably entertained at Sydney, and received a kindness and attention for which I cannot be sufficiently grateful.

'On the 9th of December I left Sydney with my brother-in-law, Mr. Harris, who resides there, and passed over the Pacific Ocean to New Zealand in the steamship *Botomahana*. We reached Auckland after a pleasant passage of six days. I was introduced to a lot of friends, among whom was a director of a large horse-breeding establishment, in whose manager I recognised Major Walmsley, whom I last saw in the pig-skin at

Abergavenny Races as far back as 1849. The grass here grows luxuriantly, and affords excellent fodder to the superior class of horse flesh which is raised on the large station. From Auckland we sailed to Teourangi, memorable for the great battle fought in the locality between the British and the Maories, who are the Aborigines. These latter are a fine race of men, but they are fast dying out in the face of civilisation and the accompanying fire water. They are very fond of trinkets, and I thought they would never tire of admiring my watch chain, for which they manifested unmistakably covetous desires. We afterwards proceeded by coach to various places, our destination, the Hot Lakes, the Pink and White Terraces, the Wairakei Geysers, the Haka Falls, and the Waiwera Hot Springs. The sight presented was an extraordinary one. The terraces were picturesque in the extreme, and the masses of water boiled and bubbled as if heated in some gigantic cauldron by huge subterranean fires. This hot lake district is the great wonderland of New Zealand. About 50 miles south of Ohinemutu are the great hot springs of Wairakei, the greatest wonders of the North Island. The steaming geysers throwing up columns of hot water; the pretty lakelats; the extraordinary variety of thermal springs; the lovely scenery of the Waikato River; the grand beauty of the Huka Falls; the vast island sea of Taupo; the smoking cone of Tongariro in the distance, with the giant form of Ruapehu rising to the region of perpetual snow, all serve to form a marvellous panorama of enchanting scenery which must be seen to be fully realised. We utilised the boiling water by cooking our corned beef and vegetables in it; and we indulged in the pleasures of a hot bath, in which we were joined by the party of native guides who were with us.

'We returned to Auckland by another route, where we spent a very enjoyable Christmas Day in the summer weather. The day following we went to Gisborne and Napier, and thence to Wellington, the capital of New Zealand. From Wellington we took steamer to Christchurch, where we stayed a week visiting all the places of interest within a radius of 200 miles. Here we had the pleasure of meeting with Mr. Alfred Evans, son of Mr. Evans, who was agent to the late Mr. W. S. Cartwright, of Newport. Mr. Evans was very kind and we were greatly indebted to him for the pleasant time he gave us. He drove us one day to a large freezing establishment, where we saw 14,000 sheep killed, dressed, frozen, and shipped to Port Lyttelton, from which the frozen meat finds its way into the markets of the world. We returned to Christchurch on horseback over the Maori Pass by Governors Bay and Port Lyttelton. We also made excursions to the large breeding farm of Mr. Charles King, where pure Shorthorns are raised on an extensive scale; and the large estate of Mr. Evans, where the best trotting horses in the world are trained. We spent a most enjoyable holiday at Christchurch, with its beautiful streets, some of them five miles in length, its public park 580 acres in extent, and it beautiful Botanic Garden, which covers 80 acres of ground.'[9]

Richard Wain's recollections of his travels were to be continued in the next edition of the newspaper, but for some reason this did not occur. Nevertheless, his memories of this extraordinary holiday must have provided hours of entertainment for the Wain family, including his grandson Richard Wain a few years later.

Sometime in 1885, Richard and Lydia returned permanently to Britain and lived with the Wain family at the Penarth Hotel. Lydia died aged 79 in July 1888 and was buried in St Augustine's churchyard. In 1891 Richard now claimed to be 58 and from Sutton in Kent once more, and Elizabeth stated that her age was 65.

In 1891 Harris Wain, aged 24, was by now a boarder in Marylebone, London, and was working as an articled clerk to a solicitor.

In October 1891, Richard Wain junior was involved in an accident.

Harris Wain

Mr. Richard Wain, of the Penarth Hotel, Penarth, met with a serious accident on Wednesday afternoon last. He was passing through the Western Mail-lane, Cardiff, in the direction of the station, when he was knocked down by a hand-truck. He was picked up in a fainting condition, and a messenger was at once sent in search of a medical gentleman, and Dr. Millward was in attendance as early as possible. He discovered that Mr. Wain was suffering from a wound on the head, which he probably received in the fall, and that he had sustained a severe shock. Mr. Wain was placed in bed as soon as he could be removed with safety from one of the bars, and Dr. Rees (Penarth), who afterwards attended, confirmed Dr. Millward's opinion that absolute rest was necessary.[10]

Further details of the accident were provided in another newspaper:

We regret to announce that Mr. Richard Wain, of Penarth, is lying at the Great Western Hotel, Cardiff, suffering from injuries received through a street accident on Wednesday afternoon. It appears that about half-past four o'clock two errand boys were returning to the *South Wales Echo* offices with an empty hand truck from the Great Western Railway Station and, that on turning to the left into the lane leading from the approach, the truck by some means collided with Mr. Wain and knocked him down. Mr. Wain, after being assisted to rise, asked the boys to fetch Mr. George Bowden, of the Great Western Hotel. Meanwhile, with the help of a bystander, the injured gentleman walked into the hotel, where he received every assistance from Mrs. Bowden. Sergt. Damm, who was on duty in the neighbourhood, was then called in. The officer, who is one of the local instructors in connection with the St. John Ambulance Society, perceiving that Mr. Wain exhibited symptoms of concussion of the brain, applied ice pads to the head, and on the arrival of Dr. Millward that gentleman pronounced the treatment as being good. Mr. Wain lost consciousness and remained in that state for some time. Dr. Rees, of Penarth, and Mr. Wain's physician, was sent for and soon arrived, as also did Miss Jackson, of Penarth. Mr. Wain's many friends will be glad to hear that when our representative called at the hotel at a late hour last night he was reported to be rapidly mending.[11]

On 20 October 1891 it was reported that Richard continued on the road to recovery.

> The many friends of Mr. Richard Wain, Penarth Hotel, Penarth, who met with an accident last week by being knocked down by a truck, will be glad to learn that the unfortunate gentleman is now progressing favourably.[12]

Curiously, on 4 January 1892, it was reported that Richard Wain had presented a brown capuchin monkey to the Zoological Gardens, Bristol.[13]

Richard Wain senior passed away at the age of 83. The *South Wales Echo* reported his death on 29 March 1892:

> It is with much regret that we record the death of Mr. Richard Wain, father of Mr. R. Wain, of the Penarth Hotel, Penarth, and formerly of the Royal Hotel, Cardiff. The deceased gentleman had attained to the fine old age of 83, and until within a short time of his death had enjoyed good health. Last Thursday week he came to Cardiff on business, and caught a chill through exposure to the cold winds which then prevailed. Bronchitis supervened, and terminated fatally. Mr. Wain went for a time to Australia, and upon returning about 18 months ago was entertained by his numerous friends at a complimentary banquet. He had since then resided with his son at Penarth. Mr. Wain had a large circle of friends, by whom his numerous excellent qualities were highly appreciated, and the news of his death will be received by them with feelings of the deepest regret.[14]

Two days later the same newspaper reported on his funeral:

> This morning, amid every manifestation of regret, the mortal remains of Mr. Richard Wain, father of Mr. R. Wain, of the

Penarth Hotel, were laid in their last resting place in St Augustine's Church, Penarth. The esteem in which the deceased gentleman was held prompted the many friends to request that his funeral should be of a public character, but it was decided that only a few personal friends should be invited. Mr. Wain had all his life enjoyed robust health, and although of so advanced age, the news of his death came as a shock to his friends in the district. He spent 30 years of his life in Australia, and after settling his affairs returned to this country eight years ago, taking up his residence at Penarth, where he remained until his death. Mr. Wain has four brothers and two sisters living. He leaves behind him in Australia four sons and three daughters, and 90 grandchildren and great-grandchildren. The deceased gentleman's remains were enclosed in a shell, which was encased in an English oak coffin with massive brass furniture. The coffin was conveyed to the churchyard in a State car, the staff of the Penarth Hotel acting as bearers. The service was read by the Rev. C. Davies, after which the coffin, almost hidden by beautiful wreaths and crosses, was lowered into the grave where four years ago Mrs. Wain was laid.[15]

Shortly afterwards, on 5 April 1892, Richard junior's wife, Elizabeth, died, and the following year, in 1893, Richard Wain married his housekeeper, Elizabeth Jackson, daughter of the late Edward Jackson and his wife Emily of Westbury-on-Severn, Gloucester. She was a 59-year-old spinster, and he was 60.

A few months after they had married, in July 1893 it was reported that Richard had retired.

On the occasion of Mr. Richard Wain, until recently the proprietor of the Penarth Hotel, retiring into private life, a few of his friends thought the opportunity a fitting one to show him in some tangible manner the regard and esteem in which he was held by them. A small committee was formed, and a dinner was given to Mr. Wain at the Penarth Hotel about two months ago. It was intended to present him that evening with two handsome pieces of plate in the form of a soup tureen and a ladle of solid silver. These articles, however, did not come to hand in time, and on Saturday afternoon several friends of Mr. Wain assembled at the Royal Hotel, Cardiff, for the purpose of making the formal presentation.[16]

Harris Wain was present at the event and heard his father described as a man who:

> had maintained the traditions and dignity of the trade in which he had been engaged, and had done much to justify its existence in the eyes of those who respected liberty and who felt that a very difficult trade could be conducted honourably to the man in whose hands it was placed and to the benefit of the entire community.

Richard had been a licensed victualler for 33 years and the speaker hoped that all who were in the trade would have the good fortune to do as well as he had done.[17]

The following year Richard's retirement was interrupted by an appearance in court, which nevertheless gave his son Harris an opportunity to demonstrate his legal skills:

> Several cases were heard at Penarth Police Court on Monday last against persons in the district for keeping dogs without licences. Mr. J. Beer, the superintendent of inland revenue in the district, stating there was a large number of cases of evasion of the excise at Penarth and the neighbourhood, which was infested with unlicensed dogs. One of the summonses heard was against Mr. Richard Wayne, Plymouth-road, and late of the Penarth Hotel, who had neglected to take out licences for three dogs in his possession. Mr. Wayne, jnr., appeared, and admitted the offence, stating there was no intention on his father's part to defraud the revenue. Colonel Guthrie: 'There is no excuse whatever for a gentleman like Mr. Wayne; he ought to have known better.' Fined 7s. 6d. and costs.[18]

There was another family marriage on 15 November 1894 when Harris Wain married Florence Emilie Tucker of Abergavenny in her hometown. She was the daughter of Emily Jackson and the late William Tucker, of the Greyhound Hotel in Abergavenny. The couple made their home at Claremont in Cathedral Road, Cardiff.

Coincidentally, Emily Jackson's father was also an innkeeper. William's parents were John and Ann Tucker. Emily married again in 1885 – to Thomas Harrell Tompkins, a corn merchant's cashier.

After Richard Wain retired and was living at Plymouth Road, Penarth, he commissioned the design of a house to be built on Cog Road in Sully. Completed after two years' work in 1901, The Knoll bears his monogram over the entrance doorway, showing his pride in his rise from the son of an agricultural labourer to the owner of a grand Victorian villa.

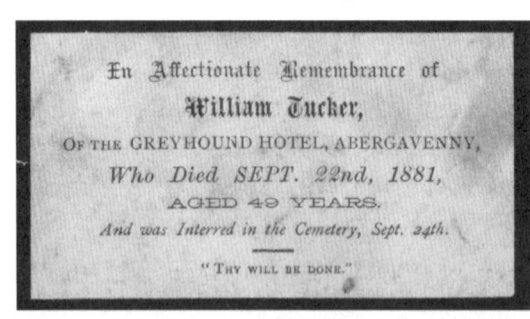

In Affectionate Remembrance of
William Tucker,
OF THE GREYHOUND HOTEL, ABERGAVENNY,
Who Died SEPT. 22nd, 1881,
AGED 49 YEARS.
And was Interred in the Cemetery, Sept. 24th.
"THY WILL BE DONE."

Memorial card to William Tucker

John Tucker

Ann Tucker

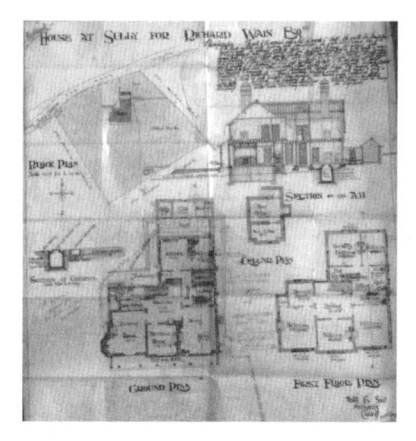

Drawing of the floorplan of the house   Monogram

Map of Cog Road showing the semi-rural location of The Knoll

The Knoll

In the 1901 census Richard gave his occupation as that of a retired hotel proprietor and stated that he had been born in Hawley in Kent. Also living with him and Elizabeth were Harris Wain, by now 34 years of age, his wife Florence and their children: Elsie Madeline, aged 5 and Richard William Leslie, aged 4. Their servants were a cook, a housemaid and a parlour maid.

On 22 May 1903 Richard Wain passed away, aged 70, at their home in Sully, just two years after it had been completed. His second wife Elizabeth died on 3 March 1909. Curiously, the date of death on her headstone is incorrect.

Richard William Leslie Wain lived with his parents and grandparents at The Knoll from 1901 to 1906. His father was working as a solicitor at the Bank Buildings, 97/98 St Mary Street, Cardiff, and was also a manager at Sully National School when Glamorgan Council took over the running of the school in 1905.

As Harris's career developed, the family moved from The Knoll to a succession of rented houses: in 1911 they were at 7 The Green, Llandaff; Hillside in Llanishen by 1914; then 22 Plasturton Avenue in Cardiff in 1916; 94 Newport Road, Cardiff in 1917 before finally, later that year, buying Woodside, 4 The Avenue, Llandaff.

The Green, Llandaff

Elsie was educated at Howell's School, Llandaff, and Caldersyde Girls' School, Seascale, Cumberland, just along the coast from St Bees where her brother was studying.

She also served her country during the Great War. Elsie was working as a clerk in the Employment Department of the Ministry of Labour when she joined the Women's Army Auxiliary Corps during the Great War. She enlisted on 20 July 1918 and was assigned to the 534th Agricultural Company Cardiff (Labour Corps). She was described as an 'immobile' meaning that she could only work in a place that was near her home, rather than be posted anywhere in the country – or even abroad.

Elsie worked at Ely Racecourse, Cardiff, as a General Clerk and would have worn a military uniform with brown coloured inserts in the shoulder straps to indicate that she was working in the Clerical Section. After just short of twelve months' service she was discharged on termination of her engagement on 10 July 1919.

In 1920, at Llandaff Cathedral, she married John Thomas

Caldersyde Girls' School

Elsie Wain's signature

Victor Webster D.S.O., from Londonderry, a Lieutenant-Commander Paymaster in the Royal Navy, who had served aboard HMS *Cardiff* during the Great War. Three years later she gave birth to a daughter, Pamela Mary Wain Webster.

The Wain family had seen a considerable change in their fortunes throughout the nineteenth century. They had prospered at home and abroad, and had travelled to the other side of the world. Richard and his sister were born into a comfortable middle-class home, far removed from the family circumstances at the start of the century. It was now his turn to make his mark on the world and to leave his own legacy.

CHAPTER 2

The Junior Officer

RICHARD WAIN ATTENDED the Cathedral School, Llandaff, on the opposite side of the village green to the family home, until 1911. A school had existed in Llandaff since the ninth century but in 1880 the Dean of Llandaff established a school for 50 boys on Cathedral Green. There are no existing records of Richard's time there.

After attending the Cathedral School, Richard was sent to St Bees, a prestigious independent school in Cumberland, and was educated there from 1911 to 1914.

Founded in 1583 by Edmund Grindal, the Archbishop of Canterbury, the school expanded rapidly during the nineteenth century. In 1903 the Officer Training Corps was formed there and by the start of the Great War the school had 300 pupils on roll. Three Old Boys of the school would be awarded the Victoria Cross during the war[1] and 184, including four masters, would be killed.

The holder of a House Scholarship, which he had won while at the Cathedral School, Richard Wain progressed into the Sixth, joined the Officer Training Corps and passed the Higher Certificate, Oxford and Cambridge Joint Board. Intending to go to Oxford University, like his father before him, his plans were halted by the events of the summer of 1914.

He returned home and on 30 September 1914, at the age of 17 years and 9 months, he attested in Cardiff for the Territorial Force. His home address was Hillside, Llanishen, Cardiff. He

Cathedral School, Llandaff

St Bees School

St Bees School OTC cap badge

The Junior Officer

stated that he had served for two and a half years in the Officer Training Corps at St Bees School. Richard joined the 7th (Reserve) Battalion of the Welsh Regiment, a Territorial Force Cyclist Battalion which never saw active service, and was given the service number 1654.

Richard served in the local area and the pre-war orders for the Barry Company give some idea as to the routines Richard would have undergone:

> 7th Battalion The Welsh Regiment (Cyclists)
> Lieutenant-Colonel C. Wilson (Commanding)
> Barry Company Orders for the month of August 1910.
>
> Drill (with Cycles) at Barry Island every Tuesday and Thursday, commencing August 25th at 7.30 p.m. Dress, drill order.
> Every Saturday, Drill (with Cycles) at Barry Island at 2.30 p.m. Dress, drill order.
> All men are reminded that they must make themselves efficient before October 31st, the end of the Territorial year.
> Rifles – All rifles to be returned thoroughly cleaned to Headquarters on Monday evening, August 29th.
> Musketry – Musketry will, probably, take place each Saturday afternoon. Supplementary orders regarding this will be issued later and will be posted at Headquarters. All ranks are expected to make themselves acquainted therewith.
>
> Ernest E. Green, 2nd Lieutenant
> Officer Commanding 'C' Company
> Barry Headquarters,
> 1, Canon Street
> Barry

When war began the following notice appeared in a Barry newspaper:

> Welsh Regiment, 7th Battalion, Welsh Cyclists Reserve.
> Men who wish to join this Regiment can apply at the Recruiting Office, Barry. Only men who own Bicycles can be enlisted. Over

37

Valour Beyond Measure

The Wain family

The 7th Cyclist Battalion at Llantwit Major

The 7th Cyclist Battalion in training at Tenby

The Junior Officer

200 excellent Recruits have already joined at Cardiff, and all those in the Barry district who wish to join should do so as soon as possible.[2]

Richard Wain was, however, discharged from the Territorial Force on Christmas Day 1914 as being medically unfit. His service had lasted for just 87 days. The reason for this is unclear from the records.

Undeterred, on 28 December 1914, Richard presented himself for a medical examination in London with a view to enlisting in the Regular Army. He gave his birthplace as Penarth and his age as 19 years and 1 month – which was incorrect as he was barely 18 at the time, but in common with so many young men he lied about his age in order to enlist and serve abroad. He stated that he was of independent means, did not have a trade or occupation, and was still living at Hillside, Llanishen. His height was measured as six feet and his weight at nine stone and ten pounds. He had a 35-inch chest and his physical development was considered good. He possessed a vaccination mark from infancy on his left arm and his vision test scored six out of six.

Two days later, on 30 December, he enlisted in the 16th Battalion of the Middlesex Regiment, the Public Schools Battalion (based on his time at St Bees). The battalion was raised in London on 1 September 1914 by Lieutenant-Colonel J. J. Mackay. They trained at Kempton Park racecourse before moving to Warlingham in December, which is where Richard joined the battalion.

Richard Wain's signature

39

A new recruit was put through three months of basic training in order to build up his physical fitness and confidence, to instil discipline and obedience and to teach him the basic skills required of an infantryman.

The soldiers were awoken at 5.30 each morning by the bugle call of Reveille. After dressing and tidying their quarters, they would have a cup of tea. An hour later they would parade in order to work on their fitness. Breakfast began at 8 a.m. and was followed by drill on the parade square.

Lunch was taken between 12.15 p.m. and 2 p.m., followed by more drill until 4.15 p.m. Some men would take part in fatigues or work parties, but the majority would then clean their kit in preparation for the following day.

After a few weeks of this routine, training would become more advanced. The infantryman would learn the basics of movement in the field and would experience night operations and route marching. Once these were mastered he would be trained in weapons handling, musketry and the digging of trenches and fortifications.

Richard was discharged from the 16th Middlesex on 30 June 1915, without serving overseas, as the result of his receiving a commission in the Manchester Regiment on 3 July 1915.

During the Great War the number of officers in the British Army grew from 12,000 in 1914 to 164,000 by the time the war ended in 1918. Richard would have found Officers' School to be crowded with young men such as himself, all intent on making the grade as an officer. Cadets had such comforts as a servant and a mess

Richard Wain

room. Their day started at 6.30 a.m. with a drill or a lecture and then continued through a variety of routine tasks, such as scrubbing floors, map work, studying *The Manual of Military Law*, and other preparation for the examinations in musketry, reconnaissance, drill and military law. From 7.30 p.m. to 9.30 p.m. each evening Richard spent his time cleaning, polishing and preparing his uniform and kit for the following day.

A second lieutenant was paid ten shillings and sixpence a day. At the end of the war he was entitled to a gratuity of 31 days' pay for each year or part-year of service during the war. If he was unfortunate enough to be wounded, he was entitled to a wound gratuity of £100 plus a wound pension of £70 per annum, a widow's pension (should his wound lead to his death) of £8 p.a. and a child's pension of £15 p.a. for each child. Shellshock and gassing were not classified as wounds.

From his pay, £9 was docked for his Officer Cadet uniform. Lodging was two shillings a day if not in quarters; fuel and light (if not laid on) was seven pence a day in winter and four pence in summer. Field accommodation was two shillings and sixpence per day if under canvas. Travelling was three shillings and sixpence per day, or fifteen shillings per night, and, finally, ration was one shilling and five pence per day. The Outfit Allowance was £50 and included field kit, which comprised:

Folding bedstead
Pillow
Waterproof sheet
Folding tripod washstand with basin and bath
Folding chair
Bucket
Valise or holdall

The battalion that Richard now joined, the 17th Battalion of the Manchester Regiment, was formed in Manchester on 28 August 1914 by the Lord Mayor of Manchester, Alderman Sir

William McCabe. It was the second of the Manchester City or Manchester Pals battalions.

There were a number of Pals battalions raised during the Great War and they served with distinction. They were especially constituted to enable men who had enlisted together in an area recruiting drive to serve alongside each other in a distinctly local battalion, rather than being subsumed into another battalion or regiment or branch of service. Friends, neighbours and work colleagues would thus join a battalion with a unique regional identity. The idea had come from General Sir Henry Rawlinson, who believed that men would enlist in greater numbers if they knew they could serve together. He appealed to the stockbrokers of London to set an example by forming a battalion consisting of men who worked in the City of London. This idea was such a success that over 1,600 men enlisted in the 10th (Service) Battalion of the Royal Fusiliers in just one week in August 1914. This battalion was then given the name 'The Stockbrokers' Battalion', in recognition of its recruits.

Just a few days later the Earl of Derby developed the idea by proposing the raising of a battalion of men from Liverpool, and within two days 1,500 men had joined up. Derby had written:

> It has been suggested to me that there are many men, such as clerks and others engaged in commercial business, who wish to serve their country, and would be willing to enlist in a battalion of Lord Kitchener's Army if they felt assured that they would be serving with their friends, and not be put into battalions with unknown men as their companions.[3]

Over the next few days three more Pals battalions were formed in the city.

Given the success of the initiative, Lord Kitchener, the Secretary of State for War, expanded the scheme to cover the whole country, and by the end of September 1914 over 50 towns and cities had formed Pals battalions.

The Junior Officer

Troops boarding a train at Amesbury

After completing their training at Larkhill on Salisbury Plain, the 17th Battalion of the Manchester Regiment was posted to France in November 1915. They left Larkhill on 7 November and travelled by train from Amesbury to Southampton where the advance party embarked for the crossing to Le Havre. The following day the remainder of the battalion crossed to Boulogne via Folkestone.

For the next few days they made a series of route marches in order to arrive at the village of Bertangles on 18 November. Here they remained for ten days and took part in further training. There followed a march to Montrelet for training in trench warfare. On 9 December they moved into the front line near Foncquevillers.

On 12 January 1916 the 17th Manchesters relieved the 16th Manchesters and moved into the second line trenches at Maricourt Wood. The remainder of the month was spent alternating between periods in the trenches and out of the line.

43

Soldiers of the 17th Battalion of the Manchester Regiment

The notion of 'trenches' is here somewhat of a misnomer as part of their defences were built into the cellars and ruins of damaged houses and the water table was so high in the area that some defences were breastworks built up of sandbags.

February saw the battalion alternate between periods of front line duty and their billets at Sainte-Suzanne. Even this period out of the line was not entirely peaceful, as the town itself was shelled on a number of occasions.

On 12 March 1916 Second Lieutenant Richard Wain joined the battalion, along with Second Lieutenants J. J. Ilett, H. Haslam and R. M. Calvert. Of these four young men, who had travelled over to France together, only John James Ilett, later wounded in action, would survive the war. He lived at Headingley Mount in Leeds.

Herbert Haslam, from Tamworth Street in Oldham, had been promoted through the ranks. After a period of time serving as an infantry officer, he transferred to the Royal Flying Corps and trained as a pilot. He was killed on 16 September

1917. At 3.55 p.m. that afternoon he had taken off in his RE8 on a photo reconnaissance mission and was later shot down by *Oberleutnant* Oskar Gustav Rudolf Berthold of *Jasta* 18 over Swannhoek. His body was never identified and he is commemorated on the Arras Flying Services Memorial.

Robert Mayson Calvert was the son of Robert and Fanny Maria Calvert of Burgh-by-Sands, Cumberland. He too had been educated at St Bees School alongside Richard Wain. He was a Hastings Exhibitioner at Queen's College, Oxford, having been awarded a scholarship, but stayed for only one term in the autumn of 1914 before enlisting. Killed on Sunday 9 July 1916 during the attack on Trônes Wood, he was buried in Serre Road Cemetery, Number 2, aged 20.

From March 1916 these four young men began to adapt to the duties and responsibilities of an infantry officer. The routine for the battalion continued until the evening of 18 March when it was relieved and the men marched to Grovetown Camp, close to the town of Albert, for a period of rest. April saw them provide working parties at Bonnay, Heilly and Morlancourt,

Herbert Haslam

Robert Calvert

until they moved to billets at the village of Saint-Sauveur, west of Amiens, for a fortnight of intensive training. This included bayonet practice, Lewis gun training, bombing practice, as well as sports competitions. A route march to the front line at Vaux Wood followed at the start of May.

The next few months were spent on guard duties, forming working parties taking supplies up to the front line and repairing trenches and barbed wire. Here Richard would have learnt the practical duties of an infantry officer in a war zone.

Going over the top was a rare experience for a soldier. Most of the time that he spent in the trenches was a period of unrelieved boredom, interspersed with short periods of action. However, that is not to say that the very real feeling of anxiety was ever far away. A section of the front line such as this one was an active one, and the Germans were capable of springing a surprise assault at any time. There would have been just one man holding each seven yards of trench and, as an incoming officer, it was Richard's job to survey the stretch of trench his unit of the battalion had taken over. He was required to make detailed notes on the state of the trenches and any repairs that were necessary. Richard would have established how many listening posts had been set up and where they were located. The condition of the barbed wire in front of the trench would be ascertained in order to determine if any gaps needed to be filled. Also under his remit would have been the trench stores, the Lewis machine gun posts, the telephones, ammunition store, bomb store and the latrines. *The Trench Routine* was a publication that set out 25 areas that the incoming officer needed to check until he was satisfied. He would also conduct an inventory the following day, initialling his name against each item on the list. He thereby became responsible for each item's location and condition, and thus the relief was completed.

The front-line dugout that Richard came to was one of the rudimentary sort that the British constructed, never meaning to stay in them long. It would have been no more than six feet

The Junior Officer

high, and water would have covered the makeshift floor. Damp and cold, conditions were miserable. For his rest he lay on lousy straw on a narrow wooden bunk six feet in length and some two foot in width, sprung with chicken wire, with light being provided by flickering candles. The bunks were built two or three high, with just a small central gap to pass through. A few postcards would be pinned to the walls or on the wooden bunks. The other ranks, meanwhile, slept on groundsheets, and in winter they were allowed to take their greatcoats with them to use as blankets. Officers like Richard were invited to choose their own servant from amongst the men of the battalion. There was no shortage of volunteers, as servants were excused from sentry duty. He would have been struck by the harassed look on the officers' tired and haggard faces as he entered the front-line dugout for the first time.

Rats were constant companions, as were lice. The men soon adapted to having vermin scuttle over them, inhabiting the dugout as they did, but lice were more of an irritation. The constant scratching would lead to men of all ranks removing their uniforms and burning the lice out of the seams, which gave only temporary relief until the next infestation.

The days were times of routine duties, meals and a time to snatch some rest. During the daytime he would have slept (if he could) in the dugout, while his men slept on firesteps or in 'funk holes' dug out of the sides of their trench. Movement during daylight was limited, with the constant threat that a careless peep over the parapet could result in death from an enemy sniper. But the long nights were another matter.

What were his thoughts that first night, staring into the blackness of no man's land through a loophole, well aware that the German infantry in the trenches opposite was well dug-in, supported by machine guns and artillery? From that moment onwards Richard became nocturnal. Under cover of darkness most of the routine work occurred and the men were kept constantly busy. If he was not leading a patrol there were working parties to organise, with men bringing up sleepers, duckboards, and everything else needed to maintain a trench. The weather made little difference – work continued regardless. The men repaired the parados and parapet, the sides of the trenches, and replaced the duckboards that ran along the bottom of the trench. These were slatted wooden paths built above the water level to keep their feet as dry as possible. They filled the sandbags they had carried into the front line, and revetted the trench walls with wooden planks.

Then they would have turned their attention to digging saps – shallow trenches just deep enough for a soldier to crawl along – which projected out from the front line at 90 degrees towards the enemy lines. These were manned at night in order to provide safer access to the listening posts where men spent periods of time in no man's land observing the German lines.

The tensest time was at dawn, the time when most attacks began. Half an hour before dawn came 'Stand To'. The officers and soldiers manned the firestep for a half an hour either side of dawn until 'Stand Down' was called. For most men the only light relief during Stand To was provided by the issue of the rum ration. The rum issued was 59 per cent proof and warmed the cockles of the heart of many an infantryman standing on the parapet in the freezing dawn. It arrived in an earthenware jar with 'SRD' stamped on the side. The tot was an eighth of a pint and it was Richard's duty to issue it. By contrast, he and his fellow officers would often have whisky to drink in their dugout.

After 'Stand Down' the men would wash and shave, and then Richard would carry out a general inspection of rifles and ammunition. As it was difficult to bring ammunition into the front line, each round had to be accounted for. The men would state to him how many rounds they had fired since the previous day's inspection and why they had fired them. The condition of the rifles and revolvers was also inspected and any found to be less than scrupulously clean would result in

The Junior Officer

Richard placing the owner on a charge. This was essential as mud in a weapon could lead to it misfiring or jamming. After this, gas helmets, feet, socks, iron rations, field dressings and trench stores were inspected before the men were dismissed. Breakfast would then be taken at 9.00 a.m., some hours after 'Stand To'.

Breakfast often consisted of bread, boiled bacon and tea. It was served in the men's mess tins. After breakfast had been eaten, the sentries would be posted. The rota was two hours on and four hours off. To men who had been awake all night this would have proved a trial, but although they craved sleep they were forced to stay awake, as a court martial would result for the unfortunate soldier if Richard had found one of his men asleep whilst on sentry duty.

For the men not engaged on sentry duty, there would be more trench repairs – drainage improvements and any damage to the officers' dugouts would also be repaired. The dugout that Richard and his fellow officers would have been housed in was far less salubrious than its German equivalent. This inequity was caused through British military thinking which held that this was a war of Allied advance and thus to make officers dugouts, or indeed soldiers' trenches, comfortable would lull the men into thinking that an advance was a chore. On the other hand, the Germans were, by and large, fighting a defensive war, and therefore set out to ensure that their men were accommodated as comfortably as possible, thereby ensuring that they were well protected from artillery bombardment and were in better physical condition to resist any Allied attacks.

There were frequent meetings of the officers to discuss schemes, maps, instructions and all the other elements of trench life. One of his other jobs was censoring scores of letters each day. Each of the officers would have taken turns to be Orderly Officer of the Day, and when it was Richard's turn he stamped all the battalion's letters – an onerous task which would have taken him some time. Given the casualties that occurred he also wrote the letters home to the families of the dead.

One of his less thankful tasks was foot inspection. Boots and socks were removed and he inspected the condition of the men's feet and watched as they rubbed them with whale oil. Trench Foot was a serious condition which could incapacitate a fighting man and it was therefore vital that good hygiene was maintained in order to ensure as many front-line soldiers as possible were available for duty.

Smoking was a comfort to the men in the front line; it quelled nerves, and chain-smoking was common. It was a drug that relieved stress but was dangerous in the dark and gave rise to the 'third light' superstition. (A sniper would see a match, take aim at the approximate area of the second soldier lighting up, and fire at the third one when the match indicated his exact position.)

An officer inspecting his soldiers' feet

Lunch was served at midday. It generally consisted of a stew made of bully beef, bread and a mug of tea. After this the men not involved in sentry duty would sleep for three to four hours until tea at 4.00 p.m. This was likely to be bread, butter and plum and apple jam. There was another equipment inspection at 4.30 p.m. and then preparations began for the night's activity. Richard once more organised the fighting and listening patrols and the barbed wire repair party. Tea was served at midnight in order to warm the men up. They brewed tea themselves, heating the water over candles, though care had to be taken as a light in the darkness would draw enemy sniper or artillery fire.

Water supply was a real difficulty. If they were lucky the men were supplied with water from a nearby well. Otherwise, it was from a bowser brought up to the front line by nightly carrying parties in petrol cans, which left the water with a taste the soldiers would never forget. The water bottles they carried were filled before they went up to the front line, but these could be drunk from only when given the order by an officer. Water for washing was usually at a premium and men often delayed washing until they were out of the line. Shaving was accomplished by using the last dregs of a cup of tea. Whether an officer such as Richard washed depended on water supply and his relationship with his men. Often if the men had no water to wash then the officer desisted too.

Parcels from home were a welcome relief from the misery of life in the front line. A highly efficient system was established with letters and parcels being delivered within three days of posting, in either direction. Officers ordered hampers from Harrods and Fortnum & Mason. After passing along the trench on a filthy night, with body parts protruding from the walls, it would have been bizarre for officers such as Richard to enter, dirty, tired and dishevelled, a dugout wherein a hamper had just been delivered from home, containing provisions incongruous to the situation outside the dugout.

Before the war began cocaine was a common ingredient in medicines and tonics. It was considered as harmless as tobacco. Harrods was fined in 1916 for supplying cocaine and morphine to soldiers when it offered small packages of the drugs, complete with a syringe and spare needles, and was sold as, 'A useful present for friends at the front'. There is no evidence that Richard himself participated in this, but it is certain that he would have been aware of some of his fellow officers using cocaine or morphine.

In addition to his uniform, he wore a steel helmet, a buff coloured leather jerkin, gauntlets and rubber waders, which reached up to his hips. This offered some protection against the mud. Prior to 1915 an infantry officer carried a sword into battle, but in that year this was substituted by the standard British rifle, the Short Magazine Lee Enfield (SMLE). This was a bolt-action repeating rifle, firing a .303-inch bullet up to 2,500 yards, though its effective range was about 600 yards. With training, it could be fired accurately 15 times a minute, though five was the norm.

At points along the trench system were placed the battalion's machine guns. These were of two designs: the standard machine gun was the Vickers .303 with a range of 2,000 yards and a rate of fire of 250 rounds a minute, and the other was the Lewis light machine gun which had become available in 1915; it fired 600 to 700 rounds a minute.

This was the world that Richard Wain was now part of: a squalid, dangerous, stressful existence with periods of extreme violence and death mingled with extended periods of hard physical work and routines. It was to be endured, survived and feared, and the unknown was always present.

On 11 June the 17th Manchesters moved to Maricourt in preparation for the great attack that they knew was coming – the Battle of the Somme was just a few weeks away.

CHAPTER 3

The Somme 1916

IN DECEMBER 1915 a military conference took place between the Allies at Chantilly, Oise. They agreed to launch a series of offensives, with the major thrust on the Western Front being made by the French and British forces against the German lines in the area of the Somme. However, the German assault on Verdun on the River Meuse, which began on 21 February 1916, meant that the French diverted a number of divisions from the Somme to reinforce their lines around Verdun. The burden of the Somme offensive now fell primarily on the shoulders of the British.

The Battle of the Somme has become synonymous with the slaughter of the Great War. It began on 1 July and was finally halted on 18 November. More than a million men were killed or wounded during that time and the British casualties of 57,470 on the first day of fighting made it the bloodiest day in the whole history of the British Army.

On the evening of 30 June 1916, the 17th Battalion of the Manchester Regiment moved into the assembly trenches north-east of Maricourt. Second Lieutenant Kenneth Callan Macardle (who was killed on 9 July) wrote:

> We had a comfortless night in the assembly trenches, for they were very crowded and there was no room to sit down. It was cold and the morning broke with a chill white mist on the ground over which the sun shone turning the white and yellow balls of shrapnel all pink.[1]

53

Kenneth Macardle

The attack was preceded by an enormous artillery bombardment which had begun on 24 June. Over 1,730,000 shells were fired on the German lines, though it has been estimated that 30 per cent of these failed to go off.

Richard Wain and 'A' Company watched as, just prior to 7.30 a.m. on 1 July, the British artillery barrage intensified. Sixteen Vickers machine guns behind them opened fire over their heads and the 19th Manchesters and the 17th King's Liverpool Regiment left their trenches and advanced across no man's land.

An hour later, at 8.30 a.m., 'A' and 'B' Companies of the 17th Manchesters left their assembly trenches and advanced towards the German lines as part of the second wave, with orders to capture the village of Montauban. Macardle wrote:

> The German shells littered the battlefield with dead and wounded: all around us and in front, men dropped or staggered about. A yellow mass of Lydite shrapnel would burst high up and a section in two deep formations would crumple up and be gone. 'A' Company was in front of us, advancing in sections, with about 20 paces between blobs, in perfect order at a slow walk. Next came a carrying party of Scots and then our Company. Montauban was a mile and a quarter away and in between us and that heavily wooded village every inch of the ground was churned up and pitted with shell holes. It was impossible even to locate the enemy's front line; his second was an irregular ditch, all craters and newly turned earth. We advanced in artillery formation at a slow walk, guiding our sections in and out of the stricken men who were beyond help

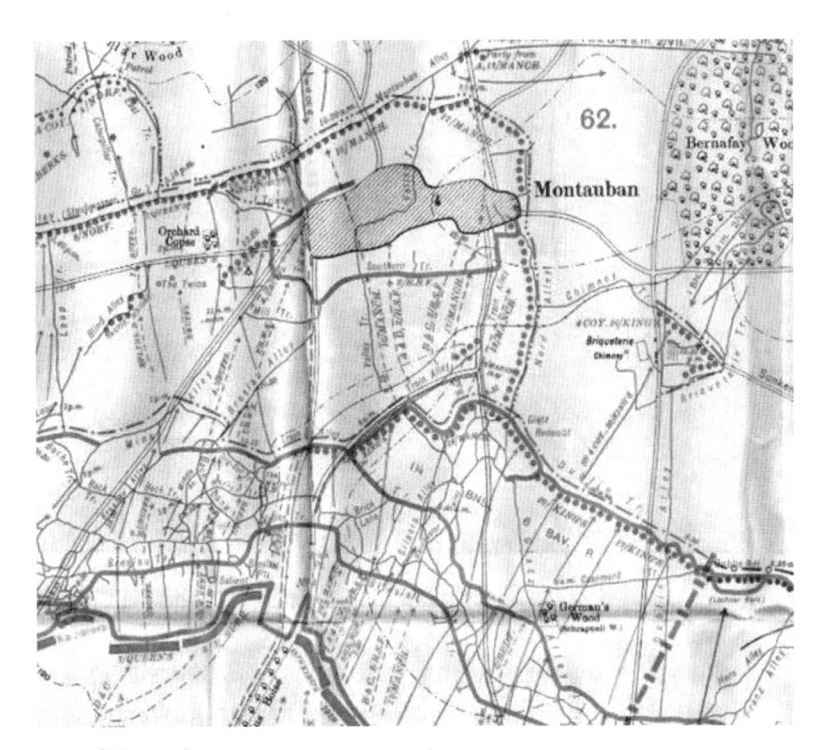

Map of Montauban

or whom we could not stop to help; it seemed callous but it was splendid war. Men crawling back smiled ruefully or tried to keep back blood with leaky fingers. We would call a cheery word or fix our eyes on Montauban – some were not good to see.[2]

The casualty toll eventually meant that the attack ground to a halt. Macardle again:

> The ground was so rough and broken with shell holes that when I lay down under our barrage, I found myself ahead of the first line – I had four men left. The 17th had advanced too quickly. We had done it all at the slowest walk and been quite unchecked – so we lay down for forty minutes, under the shells, waiting. Waiting is hard. We were to rush the village at 9:56.
> The time came. I was watching 'A' Company to see them rise and the seconds ticked on. I hailed a serjeant and asked him,

Contemporary illustration of the advance

shouting in his ear, where his officers were. 'All gone, Sir!' he shouted back.

I caught a glimpse of young Wain, his face haggard with pain, one leg soaked with blood, smoking a cigarette and pushing himself forward with a stick. His voice was full of sobs and tears of pain and rage. 'Get up you bastards. Blast your souls – get up.' I waved to him and he smiled and dropped – he knew it was not absolutely up to him any longer. We of 'B' Company took over, for he was the last of 'A' Company's officers and their Serjeant Major was also killed. We were enfiladed from our left (where another battalion had failed to advance) by machine gun and rifle fire.[3]

The war diary of the 17th Manchesters described the events of that morning:

> Slight shrapnel and indirect machine-gun fire met with 100 yards in advance of Assembly Trenches... The leading waves were held up by our own barrage... Rear waves closed up to shorter distance and became to a small extent intermingled. During this check the advance was harassed by rifle and machine-gun fire from left flank. Shelter was taken in trenches and shell holes... Shells were still falling short of Montauban on our left flank during the advance up the southern slope.[4]

Second contemporary illustration of the advance

Montauban was entered but what met the soldiers bore little resemblance to the town it had once been:

> The town was practically deserted and was completely in ruins. It was almost impossible to trace even the run of the streets. All enemy met with surrendered immediately.[5]

Once they set about fortifying their new positions, it was evident that the German artillery had targeted the village:

> Hostile machine-gun fire was opened on the village immediately on our entry and about 2 p.m. a heavy bombardment of 15cm. and 77mm. was opened on the town, which continued almost without cessation until the battalion was relieved about 40 hours later... The digging of trenches was very difficult owing to the fact that the village was a mass of shell holes and loose crumbling earth. The total inadequacy of trenches in such a soil was abundantly proved in the next 48 hours... Practically no dug-out shelters were available for the men and casualties were heavy from the commencement of the bombardment.[6]

Richard was by now unable to walk and was evacuated back

to a Casualty Clearing Station via the Regimental Aid Post and a Field Ambulance. The Regimental Aid Post was situated in the front line and its purpose was the immediate treatment and triage of casualties. The Field Ambulance was a mobile medical unit which formed an intermediate step between the front line treatment and assessment and the Casualty Clearing Station, which was situated well behind the front line, out of range of the German guns.

On 4 July his parents received a telegram informing them of his wounds:

> Wain 22 Plasturton Avenue, Cardiff
> 2 Lieut R. W. L. Wain, Manchester Regiment, was wounded on July 1st – further news will be sent when received.[7]

The wound to his leg was so serious that he was evacuated back to Britain, where he spent time recovering from his injuries.

During the attack on Montauban by the 17th Manchesters, eight Officers and 340 Other Ranks became casualties. Two of the dead officers had connections with St Bees School.

Captain Reginald James Ford was 28. He was leading 'A' Company when he was shot and killed. A former master at the school, he was the son of James and Lois Kate Ford of Radcliffe, 36 Warwick Street, Oxford. The St Bees' Roll of Honour recorded:

> Captain R. J. Ford, who was killed in action near Montauban on July 1, 1916, was captain of a gallant Manchester Regiment for which he helped to win undying fame by the fresh vigour and splendid originality it set up as an example to the new formations of the British Army. His work began in the choir school of Queen's College, Oxford, then at the College itself, and then he came as a master to St. Bees. Here his development came rapidly, and when, one by one, masters were called off from varied duties to fulfil the privilege of this generation, it was Ford who took up their work

in the Science School, in the charge of the Foundation, and of the O.T.C., until his own call came and he too went as cheerfully as to any privileged office.[8]

His father received the following letter from Major John James Whitehead, Commanding Officer of the 17th Manchesters:

Dear Mr. Ford,
It is with the deepest regret that I have to write and inform you of the death of your son, Captain Ford, who was killed on Saturday morning, July 1st, while gallantly leading his company (A Company of this Battalion) into action. Briefly, we had taken the German trenches and were advancing on a village 600 yards in rear (A Co. forming the first wave), when Captain Ford fell, shot in the head and body, by machine-gun fire. He was a most painstaking officer, and had done excellent work in the Battalion, and was beloved by all ranks. We shall miss him so much. All the officers of his Company were either killed or wounded, and his gallantry and example were most praiseworthy. He leaves a record of which any officer could feel proud. The Brigadier has thanked and complimented the Battalion on its excellent work in taking the trenches and turning the enemy out of the village and holding it. He especially paid a compliment to the behaviour of the Battalion in the advance, saying that 'they advanced across the open and into the village as if on parade.' As Captain Ford commanded the leading company, we feel we owe much to his gallantry, and mourn him as a true friend. You have the heartfelt sympathy of his brother officers, believe me.[9]

Reginald Ford

On 13 July Colonel Herbert Johnson, the Commanding Officer of the 17th Battalion on the day of the attack, wrote to James Ford:

> Dear Mr. Ford,
> Major Whitehead tells me he has written to you, but I feel I must send you a line to tell you how much I sympathize with you in the loss you have sustained. I was wounded myself early on Saturday and did not hear anything about your son for some days. He was a very good officer and his whole heart appeared to be in his work. I had a long talk one day recently with him as to whether he fancied the idea of going into the army as a regular profession (we had a proposal sent us by the War Office) and he said 'I will wait and see how this battle comes off'. I deeply feel the loss the Battalion has sustained.[10]

Captain Stanley Kenworthy was aged 32. The son of the famous portrait painter John Dalzell Kenworthy and his wife Dinah Toweson Kenworthy of Seacroft, St Bees, he had entered St Bees in 1895 and left in 1903. He fell while leading 'D' Company in action.

The *Whitehaven News* reported:

> The death of Captain Stanley Kenworthy, the elder son of Mr. and Mrs. J. D. Kenworthy, of Sea Croft, St. Bees, who was killed in action on July 1st, the first day of the British advance in France, was telegraphed to Mr. Kenworthy on Friday. After the outbreak of war Captain Kenworthy was one of the first to offer his services, and having been accepted, he

Self-portrait of John Dalzell Kenworthy

The Somme 1916

was shortly afterwards gazetted as second lieutenant in the 17th City Battalion, Manchester Regiment. He soon proved himself to be a very capable and smart officer, and was promoted to the rank of lieutenant, and then to that of captain. Since he had been in France he had seen a good deal of fighting, and his name appeared in Sir Douglas Haig's list of those who had distinguished themselves in the field, which was published on June 16th last.

Educated at St. Bees School, Captain Kenworthy obtained Fox and Grindal Exhibitions to Queen's College, where he graduated M.A., and when war broke out he was a master at Merchiston Lodge, Edinburgh. As an athlete he had always taken a prominent place both for school and county, having played football and cricket for Queen's, and football for Cumberland and Cheshire. He was also an enthusiastic golfer, and well-known at Seascale, where a few years ago he won the cup for the final in the medal competition. He was popular not only in the field of sport, but as an officer, and his death is deeply regretted, not only by his comrades in the field but by his many friends and acquaintances in this district, where his manly cheerful presence was so familiar. The deepest public sympathy with Mr. and Mrs. Kenworthy is everywhere expressed, with sorrow, for they, with so many others, have suffered the bitterest loss that war can inflict on parents – that of the eldest born.[11]

Stanley Kenworthy was a classical scholar at Queen's College, Oxford, and after graduating taught at Normanton School, Buxton, before teaching at Merchiston. He enlisted at the start of the war and was promoted to the rank of captain early in 1915.

Both men are buried in Dantzig Alley British Cemetery, near Mametz.

Stanley Kenworthy

Having that connection to St Bees and serving the same company would have brought Richard Wain and Reginald Ford closer together, and one cannot help think how his demeanour that morning was affected after seeing his fellow officer and friend killed.

While Richard was on leave recovering from his wounds, he visited his old school, St Bees. No doubt he was able to tell the staff and pupils about the fate suffered by Reginald Ford and Stanley Kenworthy.

After making a full recovery, Richard was transferred to the Heavy Branch of the Machine Gun Corps on 2 January 1917 and was posted to 'A' Battalion, joining them on 23 January in France where he underwent training in the new weapon: the tank.

By the start of the previous year, 1916, it was apparent that the situation on the Western Front was one of stalemate. The Germans were dug in along a line stretching from Switzerland to the North Sea coast and the First Battle of Ypres in the autumn of 1914 had effectively meant the end of open warfare. What was needed was a breakthrough. Quick-firing field guns and defensively-sited machine guns meant that Allied attacks were doomed to failure – and costly loss of life.

Recruiting for this new arm began at the end of March 1916. Volunteers came from men who in civilian life had mechanical

Postcard of St Bees from 1916, with text showing how many former pupils had died in the war by this time

The Somme 1916

skills, other were already drivers in the Army Service Corps. The majority of recruits, around 700 other ranks, came from the Motor Machine Gun Service – a branch of the Machine Gun Corps.

In addition, certain officer cadets of the M.G.C. and the 18th, 19th and 21st Royal Fusiliers with engineering experience were asked to volunteer for what they were told was an experimental armoured car unit. After being interviewed by Colonel Ernest Swinton, the Commanding Officer of the new arm, and Lieutenant-Colonel R. W. Bradley of the M.M.G.S., the successful volunteers were granted temporary commissions in the M.M.G.S. and posted to two new companies – 'K' and 'L' Companies.

Basil Henriques, who was later to command a tank in the first tank attack during the Battle of the Somme, described the interview process:

> Our interview with Colonel Swinton was short. He told us that a profoundly secret new unit of the Machine Gun Corps was being formed, but he gave us no hint as to its purpose.
> 'What do you know about motor-cars?' he asked.
> 'Nothing at all, sir,' I replied.
> 'What machine guns can you use?' was his next question. I mentioned one, having just returned from a special course in musketry.
> 'That is the only one we don't use,' he said. 'Do you know the Lewis?'
> The reply was in the negative.[12]

Despite this apparent lack of suitability, Henriques was selected.

As further reinforcements arrived, these companies were formed into a battalion and after Easter 1916 training began at M.M.G.S. headquarters at Bisley in Surrey. Here instruction was given in the use of Vickers and Hotchkiss .303 machine guns and later in the Hotchkiss six-pounder naval gun. Being a

63

rifle range, the guns could not be fired safely here, so the men were sent to Larkhill Royal Artillery Range on Salisbury Plain, and to the Royal Navy's gunnery schools on Whale Island at Portsmouth and to Chatham. By the early summer of that year the personnel were proficient in the use of all three weapons.

The title of this new unit began to pass through a number of guises. Initially known as The Tank Detachment, in April 1916 it became the Armoured Car Section of the Motor Machine Gun Service, and the following month the Heavy Section, Machine Gun Corps. This was then altered to the Heavy Branch, Machine Gun Corps in November.

In June 1916 a dozen officers, N.C.O.s and men were sent to Lincoln and other centres to view the first tanks being produced there. William Foster and Company of the Lincoln Metropolitan Carriage, and the Metropolitan Carriage, Wagon and Finance Company at Wednesbury, were given an initial order to produce a hundred tanks, but in April 1916 this was increased to 150. Further orders were to follow. Foster's produced 37 male tanks, while 113 tanks – 38 males and 75 females – were produced at Wednesbury. Production was swift and the first tanks were ready for deployment in August 1916.

The remaining crews were moved to Lord Iveagh's estate near Thetford in Suffolk, where a specially-constructed training area had been produced, guarded by six lines of sentries, three rows of barbed wire and cavalry patrols. Secrecy was paramount.

The Heavy Section was organised into six companies, nominated 'A' to 'E'. Each company was made up of four sections of six tanks, plus one tank to be held in reserve – 25 tanks in all. The company was commanded by a major and each section was led by a captain. An individual tank was commanded by a lieutenant or second lieutenant. The rest of the crew comprised an N.C.O., a driver and five men classed as 'gunners'.

The Mark I tank weighed around 28 tons and was just over 32 feet in length, which included a wheeled stabiliser that also provided an aid to steering. There were two types: male and female. The male tanks carried a six-pounder gun in a sponson on each side, plus three Hotchkiss machine guns; the females had two Vickers machine guns on each side and a Hotchkiss machine gun at the front.

Four men were required to start the engine by turning the crank handle. When the engine fired, the driver engaged the first or second gear and instructed the gearsmen to do the same. Every 30 minutes the gearsmen were required to squirt grease over the gears to prevent them wearing out or jamming, to tend the engine, and, during a battle, hand ammunition to the gunners.

Owing to the cramped conditions inside the tank, the gunner could not stand up or sit down while serving his six-pounder gun but had to crouch over it to take aim and fire. Adjustments were made using his body weight and while the tank was moving the vibrations meant that accurately sighting a target through the crude telescopic sight was impossible. The machine gunners in a female tank did not face the same degree of difficulty and could saturate a target with bullets.

There were three Hotchkiss air-cooled machine guns in the male tanks. One was located in the front and operated by the commander or driver, and one in each sponson to the rear of the six-pounder gun; these were operated by the loader or gearsman. The empty brass shell cases from the six-pounder were dropped through a hole at the bottom of the door in the sponson. Three hundred and thirty-four shells were stored inside the tank, while the female tank carried 24,320 rounds of .303 ammunition.

Basil Henriques wrote that his tank crew had to find room for iron rations, 16 loaves of bread, 30 tins of food, plus cheese, tea, sugar and milk to sustain the crew. In addition, there was a spare drum of engine oil, one of gear oil, two drums of grease and three water cans. A first aid kit, two boxes of ammunition for the revolvers, a spare Vickers machine gun, four spare barrels for the Vickers guns, one for the Hotchkiss, two wire cutters and three signalling flags were all crammed inside the tank.[13]

Each crew member had two gas helmets – which were in effect hoods – a pair of goggles, a leather helmet to protect his head from impact injuries as the tank lurched about, plus his standard kit of field service cap, water bottle and haversack. Each man was also issued with a revolver carried in a leather holster on a leather belt. This could be fired through the loopholes scattered around the tank and also afforded personal protection should the tank have to be abandoned, though crews were instructed to remove the light machine guns if possible.

Once the tank was underway, conditions inside soon became appalling. The noise from the engine was so loud that even shouts could not be heard and all communication was by signal. The temperature could reach 50 degrees Celsius and the exhaust fumes from the engine would make the crew ill, confused or even unconscious. Vision was challenging as the rudimentary periscopes offered little clarity once the tank was on the move. The slits dotted around the front and the sponsons were protected by glass prisms but these soon smashed once combat began. The hinged loopholes gave better vision but left the user exposed to enemy fire.

At the end of June 1916 the first Mark I tanks began to arrive, being detrained at a special railhead within the area. As training tanks, their armour was boilerplate instead of hardened steel. Training now began in earnest. As time was short, this consisted of four main essentials: the crews were trained in operating the tank, in using its armament, in teamwork, and in visual training in order to find their objectives.

One officer who underwent this intensive training wrote:

The Somme 1916

We felt a terrific pride in our Company and Section, and also as a Tank crew against other crews. There was always healthy competition, and this competition carried us right out to France... Besides that, Tank Commanders had the very great advantage of training their crews themselves... We knew our men thoroughly.[14]

Once training was completed the companies began the move to the Western Front. On 13 August 1916 the first 13 tanks left Thetford by rail for Avonmouth Docks. The addition of the sponsons meant that the machines were too wide for the British railway system, so these had to be removed prior to being loaded onto railway wagons.

Once loaded aboard ship, they were ferried to Le Havre. Entrained once more, they were moved to Abbeville for training with the supporting infantry. Once this was complete they were again taken by rail to The Loop, a railhead close to Bray-sur-Somme where they were readied for action.

The British tanks first saw action on Friday, 15 September 1916. That date was the opening day of the Battle of Flers-Courcelette, which saw 49 tanks deployed. Of these, many did not even make it to their starting points; some lost their way in the dark or became caught up in other traffic, while others simply broke down.

The objectives were the two villages of Flers and Courcelette. At 5.20 a.m. male Tank No. 765, under the command of Captain H. W. Mortimore, moved forward alone. His two supporting tanks were delayed, a scenario not unique that day as, of the 49 tanks due to be deployed, only 32 were now available. Five soon became ditched in trenches or shell holes, a further nine broke down as they advanced, and another nine moved so slowly that they were left behind. The remaining nine broke through the German lines and caused great damage. Basil Henriques' tank was one of these and he commented that the enemy machine gun bullets penetrated the steel walls of the tank, killing

67

Valour Beyond Measure

Tanks on railway wagons and being loaded on to ships

or wounding his crew. The glass prisms in the vision slits shattered under fire, sending glass shards into the eyes and face of the observer.

An extra item of equipment was issued to the tank crews in an effort to protect their faces from the effects of machine gun fire but it was not a popular piece of kit. One Tank Corps man recalled in later years:

> The Germans would play a machine gun up and down the outside of a Tank and as far as they could see where there were little loopholes and what have you. They didn't always pierce the loopholes, but they would splash lead pieces from the bullets and the little splashes would often come through and get into your eyes. This is why the crews would wear protective masks but these obscure your vision so much that you couldn't always tell what you were supposed to be doing. You couldn't really see through them because if you had it low enough to stop the splashes you couldn't see what you were doing. What you used to do was try to shield your eyes with your hand and just put up with it.[15]

The following day, 16 September, three tanks saw action by stopping a German counter-attack near the village of Flers. All were eventually hit and put out of action.

These two days gave a glimpse as to what might be achieved with this new weapon and, four days after the first battle, Sir Douglas Haig, the British Commander-in-Chief, sent an order to London for a thousand more tanks.

On 26 September, near Gueudecourt, the infantry were held up at a German position known as Grid

A chainmail mask

Trench. A single tank, commanded by Second Lieutenant Charles Ernest Storey, advanced on the strongpoint and captured a substantial number of prisoners. Storey was awarded the Distinguished Service Order and Haig wrote, 'I consider this to be the best tank performance up to date'. The citation stated:

> For conspicuous gallantry and initiative when in command of a Tank. He took his car up and down the enemy trenches, working until all his petrol was exhausted and only two of the crew were unwounded. He is reported as having been responsible for the taking of between 200 and 300 prisoners.[16]

This action gave a clear indication as to what could be achieved by a tank against enemy trenches and gave hope that a breakthrough might, at last, be possible.

The tanks were used in small numbers throughout October without a good deal of success and the deteriorating weather conditions and a shortage of available machines meant that another breakthrough was impossible at this stage. One notable action did occur on 13 November though when female tank No. 544 of 'A' Company, commanded by Lieutenant H. W. Hitchcock, advanced. The two tanks supporting it failed to get into action and his tank became bogged down in a shell hole and Hitchcock was mortally wounded. The subsequent citation for the Military Medals later awarded to his crew took up the story:

> Corporal A. Taffs, Lance Corporal R. Bevan, Lance Corporal S. A. Moss, Gunner F. Ainley, Gunner A. Tolley. These men formed the crew of a tank operating against St. Pierre Divion on November 13, 1916. Brought up under very difficult conditions, theirs was the only tank to start, and penetrated to the second enemy support line. Here for more than an hour they maintained their position without assistance, their infantry having lost touch owing to the heavy mist. The officer in charge was killed while endeavouring

to establish touch. Corporal Taffs then took command and Lance Corporal Bevan drove on another 200 yards, when the tank was ditched in a German dug-out. The crew worked under fire for over two hours, endeavouring to extricate it. Finding this impossible, they attached themselves to a battalion of the Black Watch and assisted them in mopping up the position.[17]

Lieutenant Herbert William Hitchcock was 22 years old and was the first Bristol Grammar School pupil to win a Classical Scholarship at Balliol College, Oxford. The school magazine stated that:

> his death cuts short what would almost certainly have been a very distinguished career. He had great powers of concentration and clear thinking, and a powerful English style: at the Bar he would probably have won great success.[18]

Buried alongside him in Mill Road Cemetery, Thiepval, is another member of his crew – Gunner William Joseph Miles from Birmingham. The accompanying photograph shows their tank A.13, with two white crosses top right. It is probable that Richard Wain and the two men of his tank who were killed with him would have received similar burials, laid to rest some distance from their wrecked tank so that their graves would not be lost when the tank became the target for German artillery fire, as it may have housed observers.

William Joseph Miles

Tank A.13

CHAPTER 4

Messines 1917

HAIG'S ORDER FOR more tanks meant that the Heavy Section, Machine Gun Corps, needed to be expanded, with many more crews required. An additional one hundred tanks were supplied on which to train these new crews, and a larger training ground was also needed, as the current camps at Bisley and Elveden were too close to populated areas. A huge camp at Bovington in Dorset was chosen. With rolling downs and woods, it was similar to the topography of the battlefields of the Western Front. As importantly, the area around it was deserted, so the new weapon's development and the training of its crews could take place without observation. In addition, a complex trench system had been created prior to 1916, which was vital for training for attacks.

At the end of September Lieutenant-Colonel Hugh Elles of the Royal Engineers took over command of the Tank Corps and on 20 October it was formally announced that the arm was to be expanded, with the companies now being enlarged to form battalions.

Hugh Jamieson Elles had served as a second lieutenant in the Second Boer War and was posted to the staff of the 4th Division in August 1914. He took part in the early battles of the war before being wounded during the Second Battle of Ypres. After recovering from his wounds he served as a liaison officer before being sent back to England in January 1916 by Haig to investigate the early development of the tank. He attended the first trials and reported back favourably.

Hugh Elles

As the new training tanks were not intended to see battlefield action, it was decided to make them of mild steel (boilerplate) and not full armour. They were built in equal numbers of male and female tanks and were designated as 'Mark II'. A slightly narrower cab, to permit wider tracks, and a replacement for the manhole hatch on the top of the hull were the major differences, plus the discarding of the steering tail wheels.

Despite the fact that they were ill-designed for combat, 26 Mark II tanks were sent to France and took part in the Battle of Arras which began on 9 April 1917. Although their armour was thin, they, and the Mark I tanks, had been upgraded by the replacement of the Vickers and Hotchkiss machine guns by the air-cooled Lewis gun. By the time the Battle of Arras ended on 16 May, 60 tanks had seen action: 25 Mark II males and 20 Mark II females, plus seven males and eight females of the Mark I design.

On 11 April tanks of 'D' Battalion attacked in support of Australian infantry, but the snow that had fallen during the night meant that the white guide tapes could not be made out, so the tanks lost their way. Against the white background they were also clear targets for the German field guns and many were lost.

The sections became scattered. In the centre, one section was ordered forward without any infantry support. These 11 tanks crossed the Hindenburg Line trenches but then ran into trouble. One was hit and disabled after using up all its ammunition; another reached Bullecourt village but broke down; a third was hit by a shell in its petrol tank and caught fire immediately; a fourth received two direct hits from German field guns and blew up. In all, nine tanks were disabled by shellfire. The remaining two entered the village of Hendecourt but were never seen again. Captured by the Germans, they were probably used later against Allied troops.

Fifty new tanks were now produced, designated as 'Mark III'. Again they were unarmoured, so were clearly assembled for training use. A new type of female sponson was introduced to accommodate the Lewis guns. In addition, upgraded escape doors made abandoning the tank much easier if it caught fire.

What was required though was an improved model of tank that incorporated the lessons learned in battle, particularly those absorbed at the Somme. The result was the 'Mark IV', of which over 1,200 would be built.

Though it did not differ materially in design from the Mark I, there were some significant improvements. Its armour was of better quality steel, which gave it some resistance to the German armour-piercing bullet. The two sponsons, which up to that time had to be removed whenever the tank was moved by rail, were now constructed so that they could be pushed in to narrow the width of the tank. Much more robust track

A Mark II tank

A captured British tank at Arras, 11 April

A Mark III tank

A Mark IV Tank

rollers and links were introduced in response to difficulties faced in the previous design. The petrol tank was moved to the outside and to the rear of the tank, and was protected by special armour-plates. Other improvements were made to the armament and the overall weight of the tank was reduced.

The crew of eight each had a specific role. Sitting alongside the Tank Commander at the front of the tank was the driver, often called the 'first driver'. In reality, the driver required the assistance of three other members of the crew in order to operate it. Two brakesmen sat at the rear of the tank and were responsible for operating the gear levers on each side of the machine and for loading the six-pounder guns. A gunner was assigned to each of the tank's two Lewis guns and each six-pounder gun had a gunlayer.

The four-man driving system was wearing and inefficient, and in trials in March 1917 Lieutenant Walter Wilson's new gearing system proved to be successful. This allowed the tank to be steered by just one man. It was, however, too late to be accommodated into the Mark IV, production of which was begun that month at an initial rate of 20 tanks per week.

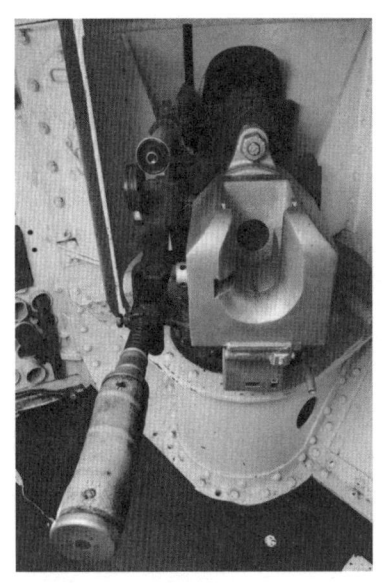

A new six-pounder gun was designed with a barrel length over four inches shorter than the original, meaning it was less likely to become clogged with mud if the tank leaned over too far, and could avoid obstacles more easily. The adoption of the Lewis gun was less successful. Being an air-cooled gun, the tank's cooling fan drew the air away from the

The six-pounder gun mechanism

gun and the fumes from the muzzle were drawn back into the gunner's face every time he fired.

That winter, training took place in the Bermicourt area, with the core of veteran tank personnel from the initial use of tanks at the Somme in September 1916 being supplemented by volunteers from other units, either already in France or from home. There was no shortage of recruits, as the idea of fighting in a tank was popular and Richard Wain therefore found himself amongst men wearing a range of uniforms and badges, as the recruits were permitted to wear the dress of their original unit, including bonnets and kilts, riding breeches and naval blue.

New recruit Serjeant Harold Aylmer Littledale, a pre-war journalist who lived in Pontypool and who later won the Pulitzer Prize, wrote:

> We came from the infantry, from the cavalry, from the artillery, from the Machine Gun Corps, the Motor Machine Gun Corps, the Flying Corps, the Army Service Corps, and even from the Navy.[1]

Within a week men had mastered the basics of the machine gun, while a further two weeks' training saw them familiar with the principle of the internal combustion engine and the mechanism of the tank.

The lessons learned on the Somme were put into practice and time was spent training more instructors, owing to the expansion of the branch. In addition, the ground over which the new crews trained was more akin to the realities of the battlefield in Flanders. Harold Littledale again:

> There is not one of us who will ever forget his first ride – the crawling in at the sides, the discovery that the height did not permit a man of medium stature to stand erect [Littledale was 5' 6". Richard Wain stood 6' tall], the sudden starting of the engine, the roar of it all when the throttle opened, the jolt forward, and

the sliding through the mud that followed, until at last we came to the 'jump' which had been prepared. Then came the downward motion, which suddenly threw us off our feet and caused us to stretch trusting hands toward the nearest object – usually, at first, a hot pipe through which the water from the cylinder jackets flowed to the radiator. So, down and down and down, the throttle almost closed, the engine just 'ticking over', until at last the bottom was reached and, as the power was turned full on, the Tank raised herself to the incline, like a ship rising on a wave, and we were all jolted the other way, only to clutch again frantically for things which were hot and burned, until at last, with a swing over the top, we gained level ground. And in that moment we discovered that the trenches and the mud and the rain and the shells and the daily curse of bully beef had not killed everything within, for there came to us a thrill of happiness in that we were to sail over stranger seas than man had ever crossed, and set out on a great adventure.[2]

In February 1917 individual courses came to a close and unit training began. The Heavy Branch Machine Gun Corps was now some 9,000 men strong and from this three brigades, each of three battalions, were formed. Each battalion was allotted 72 machines in four sections, supplemented by a Headquarters Section and a Battalion Workshop, plus miscellaneous support – from tailors to clerks.

A large area between the River Ternoise and the Hesdin to Saint-Pol road was allocated to the Heavy Branch and Colonel Elles set up his new headquarters at the village of Bermicourt, in the centre of this area. Twenty-four acres were taken up with workshops and stores; there were huts for a staff of around 1,200 officers and men, a theatre, a hospital and a compound for 500 Chinese labourers. The area soon became known as the 'Tankodrome'.

From nearby Érin Station, 11 rail lines with 10,500 feet of sidings led into the main camp. Nearby was a driving and mechanical school. Every one of the 3,000 tanks sent to France arrived at Érin via Le Havre, where it was tested, kitted out and

79

Tanks behind the lines

then issued to the respective unit. Every machine recovered from the battlefield was sent to Érin to be repaired and restored to fighting condition.

The training that Richard Wain would have received to become a competent tank officer was thorough. In just a few months a tank officer was required to understand the workings of the tank mechanism and was instructed in driving and unditching the tank; courses in map-reading and compass work taught the navigational skills required. In addition, there was the knowledge Richard would already have acquired as an infantry officer: platoon and company drill; rifle, revolver and Lewis gun practice; bombing and the use of gas appliances. Artillery was studied so that an officer was familiar with the workings of the tank's six-pounder gun. He became proficient in signalling by lamp, flag and semaphore, and how to use carrier pigeons. Tank tactics were also taught.

The first Mark IV tanks were now beginning to arrive in France and a section of old trenches at Wailly, close to Arras, was converted into use as a driving school.

From 17 April, Richard spent ten days on leave in Paris. Leave posed a logistical challenge to the British Army because the priority for the railway network was, of necessity, the transportation of men and supplies to the Front. Conditions for the servicemen travelling by rail on leave were therefore very poor. They were often required to travel standing up in slow-moving, poorly lit, unheated trains. Officers were allowed one leave every three months, while other ranks were permitted a leave every fifteen months. If a soldier wished to return to the U.K. to visit his family, he was at the mercy of submarine warfare, and could often be sent back to the Front having never crossed the English Channel at all as his boat had failed to show up. Transportation time was also included in the period of leave, so men from the northern part of Britain were discriminated against.

Soldiers arriving in Paris on leave would have arrived at the Gare du Nord or the Gare de l'Est, and Richard would probably have obtained accommodation in one of these areas. There was a high demand for entertainment, which resulted in the revival of cafés and restaurants, which had seen a decline since the start of the war, as well as cinemas and theatres and, naturally, a huge increase in prostitution.

He returned from leave on 27 April and proceeded to the forward area in Belgium where preparations were underway for the great battle of Messines.

The Battle of Messines was in no sense a tank battle – the success of the Allied forces was due to the role played by the artillery, the tunnelling companies and the infantry. It was fought from 7 to 14 June 1917 and the tactical objective was to capture the German defences on the Messines Ridge which ran from Mont Sorrel in the north, through Messines and Wytschaete to Ploegsteert Wood in the south. This would deprive the German Army of the high ground south of Ypres, paving the way for a larger British operation that summer – the advance to Passchendaele Ridge and thence to the Belgian coast.

By now promoted to the rank of acting lieutenant, on 7 June, the first day of the attack, Richard Wain led his tank crew into action across marshy ground – totally unsuitable for tanks. His tank was A.5 No. 2690. He was part of 1st Company, No. 1 Section which was led by Captain Richard Hampden Hobart Dorman, who was just 20 years of age. Dorman fought at Cambrai, survived the war and remained in the Army.

Tank A.1 was commanded by Second Lieutenant Richard Thomas Cronin, whom Richard was to command at Cambrai on 20 November. Tank A.3 was commanded by Second Lieutenant Frederick Bertram Keogh, who was to win the Military Cross at Messines, and later a bar, serve at Cambrai and lose his life in the final year of the war. The final tank in the section, A.4, was commanded by Second Lieutenant Thomas Oswald Atkinson from Stratford.

Richard's orders were to wait at the Haringbeek before proceeding to the Mauve Line. His tank and Atkinson's were to move to Polka Estaminet, down Odour Trench to the Wambeek, then to follow the railway line to Oosttaverne Wood.

The section left Lyonsberg between 8.00 a.m. and 8.09 a.m., and all four tanks reached the Haringbeek without incident by 10.20 a.m. They were then ordered to the Mauve Line. During this advance Captain Dorman was wounded and Lieutenant

Thomas Atkinson in later life

Duncan, who was to fight alongside Richard Wain in the same tank at Cambrai, took command of the section. He ordered the tanks to stop to refuel and then set off again at 12.45 p.m. Richard's tank reached the Mauve Line at 2.15 p.m. He could see no infantry, so he turned the tank south for half a mile along the Mauve Line in search of them. His tank crossed the Wambeek and then a piece of shell from a British artillery barrage struck the side of his tank and wounded one of the crew. He turned the tank back through the barrage and met up with the advancing British infantry, leading them to Odonto Trench. North of Polka Estaminet his tank manoeuvred behind three German machine guns located in concrete emplacements and silenced them. He then headed north-east and reached the Oosttaverne Line in the area held by infantry of 19th Division. Some snipers were holding up the advance, so Richard gave the order to open fire on the hedge in which they were hiding. At 6 p.m the tank left the Oosttaverne Line and headed to the rallying point, which it reached at 7 p.m.

The official history of the battalion stated:

> On the afternoon of the 6th a message was received from Brigade that the Zero hour would be at 3.10 a.m. on the 7th. No. 1 Company being in reserve, all the Tanks of Nos. 2 and 3 Companies were in position and the battle opened with what was probably the finest barrage of the war, and the blowing up of a great many mines under the enemy's front line. The Tanks moved off to their various objectives, i.e. a line running approximately East of the village of Oosttaverne. Owing to the extraordinary sticky nature of the ground, several of the Tanks got ditched, but rapidly overcame their difficulty and followed up the attack at full speed. When the Tanks reached the top of the ridge they saw the enemy in full retreat and followed them up as fast as possible.
>   Orders were received by No. 1 Company, which was standing in support at 8 a.m., to move forward to a line on the other side of the village of Wytschaete. All the Tanks reached the Hospice, and stopped to refill at noon. They then received orders to proceed to a line on the East side of the village of Oosttaverne.

At this point there was a check as to the progress of the Tanks which were being hindered by the observation of two enemy balloons. Word was sent back to the R.A.F. [sic, this would have been the Royal Flying Corps] and in the short space of half an hour both of these balloons were brought down in flames. Six Tanks reached the line East of Oosttaverne and four of these were ditched but remained in the forward position. During this action Captain Dorman was wounded and Lieut. Duncan took command of his Section. These Tanks got into action and found no great resistance.[3]

The War Diary of the 1st Battalion contains the report that Richard later made:

Tank Operations with Second Army on 7th June 1917: Report by 2/Lieut. ROBERT [sic] LESLIE WAIN, Tank A.5.
At 8.5 a.m. orders were received to start for the MAUVE LINE. The Tank started at 8.8 a.m. At 12 noon we reached a point O.19. d.1.6. S.E. of WYTSCHAETE where we refilled. The ground between the German Front Line and this point had been very difficult owing to marshy bits and heavily crumped ground.
While we were refilling I tried to find out the time of the new Zero for the MAUVE LINE, but nobody now knew, and the only information I received was that 33rd Bde were attacking at 1.10 p.m.
At 1.15 p.m. I left the refilling point making for my objective as quick as possible, and reached the MAUVE LINE at 2.15 p.m. I had seen no Infantry, British or German after passing the BLACK LINE, so in reaching the MAUVE LINE I proceeded south for about ½ mile to try and find some but without result. Thinking that they had already attacked I went on and crossed the WAMBEEK about O.21.d.8.4. All shell holes here were full of water and the going was very bad. At this place about 3 p.m. I was caught in our own barrage. A piece of shell came through the side of the tank and wounded one of the crew. We turned round and came back and met the Infantry behind the barrage and proceeded a few yards in front of them to the ODONTO TRENCH. North of POLKA ESTAMINET we got behind about 3 German Machine Guns in a concrete emplacement and put the teams out of action. Going

North East we reached the OOSTTARVERNE LINE with the 19th Division. I asked them if we could do anything and they asked if I could dislodge some snipers in a hedge about 300 yards in front. We went forward to about O.22.b.1.9. up and down the hedge and fired but saw no snipers. At 6 p.m. I left the OOSTTARVERNE LINE and arrived at the Rallying Point at the South West Corner of OOSTTARVERNE WOOD at 7 p.m. Two Pigeon messages were sent, one from ODONTO TRENCH and one from the OOSTTARVERNE LINE.[4]

Tank A.10, commanded by Second Lieutenant Reginald Liles, also took part in the battle. Liles wrote a letter to his parents a week later outlining his part in the action:

14.6.17
Dear Mother and all,
Seven days have elapsed since the last show and I have only now been able to call sufficient time my own to write and tell you anything about it.
 The papers of course have given you a lot of the news but I will just tell you my own experiences.
 The evening of the sixth we crept up after dark to within 300 yards of our own front line about 400 from the bosche, and then lay snug and quiet until 3.10 a.m. on the seventh when the earth opened with fiendish roars and the artillery opened a bombardment, such as has never before been used in any battle. We had 16% more artillery than had ever before opened in any previous battle so you can imagine what fury was let loose.
 40,000 shells were poured over in the first ten minutes and then the creeping barrage went on and so did the infantry and us.
 The top of the ridge was taken with very little opposition – through the green line, through the black line and on to the mauve line by 1.30 p.m. and the prisoners were thick by then.
 Now these positions were consolidated and at 3.10 p.m. we started the whole show again (fresh infantry having been brought up) straight through another village and a huge wood to the new green line.
 All the time we had been doing ordinary work, helping the Infantry through with any hard spots they came to. Now our own

stunt came. We had to go on without the Infantry to farms ahead of the last line taken by us and tackle the Hun guns.

This came off all right when we returned to the line which the Infantry had now consolidated and waited for the counterattack. From here on read my report on the show which you will find enclosed in another envelope.

When we reached the wood we met Officer commanding No. 1 Company and he gave orders to abandon the tanks and return to the rallying point.

Now we are waiting a chance to go and salve them.

No more news Ma for the moment.

Love to everybody.

Yours.

Reg.[5]

In his official battle report Liles wrote:

Report by Commander of Tank A 10, 2nd Lt R W Liles

Tank No A10 reached mauve line at 2.55 p.m. and went forward with Infantry about 3.10 p.m. according to orders.

We reached Oostaverne line about 4.15 and found it very lightly held by the 52nd Batt A.I.F

Tank A8 which had been my escort to this point branched off to Van Hove farm and I pushed on to Joye Farm and satisfied myself that it was not held by the enemy.

This fact I reported to the Capt. i/c A.I.F who stated his intention of throwing outposts round the farm.

I then proceeded to Van Hove farm and unditched Tank A8. The two tanks then retired, in accordance with orders, behind the Oostaverne line to await until the line was consolidated.

6.30 p.m. Tanks A3 and A4 were now in the vicinity of the line and everything seeming settled movement was made to return to the rallying point but my engine broke down owing to two big ends working loose so I made arrangements with Tank A4 to tow me if possible.

Tanks A8 and A18 returned. Tank A3 now received orders from its section commander to proceed once round Joye Farm to make everything certain that the enemy were not there but the ground being swamp it got ditched.

Tank A4 was sent to unditch same and as I knew the ground I took this tank and unditched Tank A3 but got A4 ditched in the process.

Now A3 tried to unditch A4 and both got ditched owing to it being absolutely impossible to swing the cars out of the bog.

It was now getting dark and we, the three Tank commanders, decided that as the Infantry had not yet put posts round the farm that we should stay with the tanks.

Tank A4 was at an angle that made habitation very uncomfortable so I started back with this crew to put them into Tank A10 when we were fired on by our own and by enemy machine guns wounding one man badly.

Seeing it was not possible to go on we went back to Tank A4 and there I took dressings and called for a volunteer to go out to the wounded man.

Corporal Clements came with me and we dressed the man and tried to draw the attention of the Infantry who were entrenched about 50 yards away.

This I eventually did by shouting during a lull and was told to advance with my hands up and I was met by Capt. Maxwell A.I.F

He then tried to get a stretcher bearer for the wounded man but it was not for 5 hours that this was possible and Corporal Clements lay with him all this time.[6]

Lincolnshire Regiment now arrived to join up with the A.I.F and they put a post of six men and 1 NCO between the farm and the two tanks in front.

Nothing much of importance happened until dawn when the enemy shelled Tank A10 and I decided to leave tank and take Lewis guns into the trenches in front.

We had done this when I saw the enemy Infantry massing on the ridge and also in holes about 100 yards from the trench.

I opened fire with six guns and sent word to the nearest Infantryman in the trench. Tanks A3 and A4 had also seen the enemy and opened fire with their guns.

The enemy dropped into shelters and opened sniping fire and it was difficult to get back to tank for ammunition but I asked for a volunteer to accompany me and Gunner McCoy volunteered but we had no sooner got over the top when we were forced to take shelter in a shell hole.

On trying to get to the tank McCoy was shot through the head[7]

and Sgt Brash[8] took his place and between us we got ammunition and also dressed McCoy's wound and took him into the trench but he died in an hour.

The Artillery then put a barrage on to the ground and the enemy tried to return to the ridge but suffered many casualties from the 14 Lewis guns taken from the tanks and the Infantry.

The South Staffs came down from the left and the line was made very much stronger.

At 2 p.m. things were quiet and the tank crews had worked like n******s and were exhausted so I talked over with Lt Duncan, who was i/c Tanks A3 and A4, the idea of returning with the men and leaving the guns with the Infantry. At 2.30 this was done and we returned by crews to Oostaverne Wood.

Receipt received for the six Lewis guns from Tank A.10 attached herewith.

R. W. Liles, 2nd Lieut. No. 2 Sec[9]

From 9 June onwards the tanks were brought back to Courage Camp for the necessary repairs. The crew rested and reinforcements from the depot arrived. For the remainder of the month the crews and reinforcements underwent training.

A report was produced in late June entitled *Notes on Tank Operations April – June 1917*. The first section looked at the limitations of the tank and its crew:

Reginald Liles and his tank crew. Sergeant Brash is seated to his right.

The main limitations of the tank are:-
(a) Its weight which mitigates against its going over heavily shelled wet ground.
(b) Its speed which over heavily shelled ground is 10 yards a minute over unshelled ground from 1 mile to 5 miles an hour.
(c) The difficulty of maintaining direction on account of limited visibility.
(d) The exhaustion of the crew due to heat and the difficulties of driving.

From these limitations experience has led to the following conclusions:-
(a) If the ground over which the tanks are to proceed has been heavily shelled, they will cross it slowly but if it is also soaked with rain the majority of them will not cross it. Consequently to employ tanks on such ground is to throw them away (e.g. Tanks with First Army operating against Vimy Ridge 9-4-17).
(b) Tanks cannot keep up with the infantry until the zone of heavy bombardment has been crossed. This zone is approximately 3,000 yards deep. To expect tanks to co-operate in initial attacks in this zone is to expect the impossible (e.g. Tanks with Second Army operating against the Damm Strasse 7-6-17).

The following observation in pace during the Battle of Messines were made:-
(i) Up to our old front line (good going) 30 yards per minute.
(ii) Between enemy's front line and blue line ground badly shelled 10 yards per minute.
(iii) Between Blue and Black lines (firm ground moderately shelled) 18 yards per minute.
(iv) Beyond Black line (firm ground lightly shelled) 20 yards per minute.

(c) Tanks cannot with any certainty proceed during the dark or in twilight over ground which is intersected with trenches or which has been shelled unless this ground has been reconnoitered.
Mist and smoke will bring tanks almost to a standstill; so will dust, not only dust thrown up by shells but that picked up by the tracks and blown into the face of the driver. (Motor goggles should be provided for the driver and officer.)

(d) On a hot day the temperature in the tanks will rise to 120 degrees in the shade. This excessive heat causes vomiting and exhaustion. Eight hours continuous work is about the limit of a crew's endurance, after which the men require 48 hours' rest.[10]

The companies moved to Mountain View Camp, beginning on 21 June, and throughout the following month the tanks were prepared for action and the new unditching gear arrived and was fitted. This was the fascine, a large bundle of wooden sticks which was carried on top of the tank and then released once a wide deep obstacle was encountered. The tank would then drive over the fascine.

On 22 June, Richard was promoted to the rank of acting captain and began preparing his tank section for the upcoming offensive at the Third Battle of Ypres (Passchendaele). His pay would have increased from 9s. 6d. per day, plus 2s. 6d. field allowance as a lieutenant, to 13s. 6d. per day, plus 3s. field allowance as a captain.

The Battalion War History described the preparations:

> Training was now started, as was also the Reconnaissance for the big attack which was to take place at the end of July. In this attack starting points were to be selected by Company Commanders themselves, and this entailed a more extensive reconnaissance. On the 2nd of July two Sections proceeded to the St. Omer area where a practice was carried out with infantry of the 2nd Army, over ground similar to that on which the attack was to take place. On the 8th preliminary instructions were received and that afternoon the Battalion was issued with a new unditching gear which was to prove so useful on the boggy ground in front of Ypres.
>
>   At this time parties of Officers and men were being sent weekly to Merlimont to undergo courses in Gunnery, and on the 17th Tank routes for use in the coming offensive were prepared by the 84th Tunnelling Company, Royal Engineers. A general reconnaissance was then carried out by R.O.'s and Company Commanders. Tank Commanders and first drivers started their reconnaissance of the forward area on the 19th, and work on the

routes was being carried out. The new unditching gear was then tested and was found to be very satisfactory.

No. 1 Company moved to Coxberg on the 28th and went on to Elton Point on the night of the 29th... Crews were then taken back to Camp on motor lorries, and rested most of the day. On the 30th all Crews proceeded to their Tanks ready for action and stayed by them till Zero hour. One Tank received a direct hit here and was unable to go into action.[11]

Richard Wain's No. 1 Company was allotted to the Reserve.

On 27 July 1917 the Heavy Branch became the Tank Corps. A new cap badge was introduced and the motto 'Fear Naught' was adopted. Sometime between the end of the Battle of Messines and 31 July, 'A' Battalion adopted names for all its tanks. Richard's tank, No. 2690, was christened 'ABOU-BEN-ADAM'.

CHAPTER 5

Third Ypres – Passchendaele 1917

THE THIRD BATTLE of Ypres, more commonly known as the Battle of Passchendaele, began on 31 July 1917 and finally ground to a halt on 10 November that year. It was fought in order to drive the Germans from the ridges east and south of the Belgian city of Ypres. Field Marshal Haig gave the orders for the attack to his commanders a week after the conclusion of the Battle of Messines, but he did not receive final approval for his plan from the War Cabinet until 25 July.

Once again the ground was unsuitable for tank deployment. The soil was composed of sand, silt and clay, and was drained by a series of ditches, streams and canals, though the fighting in Flanders since 1914 had destroyed much of the drainage system.

Captain Daniel Edward Hickey of the Tank Corps gave the following description of conditions in the Salient:

> The awful nature of the Salient gradually became apparent. Now the copses and fields gave place to a horrid waterlogged swamp, and the ground was shell-pocked, boggy clay, with not a blade of grass nor a tree that had not been torn to pieces by shell-fire.[1]

The artillery bombardment had begun 11 days earlier and on 31 July the ground attack began. While there were many

Third Ypres – Passchendaele 1917

advances initially, the tank assault was only a partial success. The advance of the tanks of No. 2 and No. 3 Companies was thwarted by the ground conditions and the fierce resistance put up by the Germans. The *Battalion War History* commented:

> Several Tanks were ditched, as in places the ground was hopeless to cross, being churned up by the intense shell fire. Some of the Tanks unditched themselves five or six times during the day.[2]

Around this period tank officers set aside their usual canes and began to adopt a longer stick, known as an 'ashplant', which they used to test the ground if possible before their tank advanced. This, of course, could be suicidal. Despite the use of this new aid, more than 70 tanks ditched on the first day of the battle alone. Even where the ground was firm, in following each other they made perfect targets for the German artillery.

There were some successes, however. On 19 August nine tanks took part in the capture of the village of Saint-Julien. Two bogged down crossing a stream but the remainder destroyed the German strongpoints and drove the enemy out. Five of the tanks were able to drive safely back to the British lines.

The training routine continued for the other crews throughout the month of August while the great battle for Passchendaele Ridge raged in the distance.

The War Diary of 'A' Battalion gives an indication of the difficulties faced by the tank crew in such trying conditions when they finally began their advance on 26 August:

> It commenced raining very heavily at 8.30 p.m. and continued for about two hours. Some difficulty was experienced in reaching Clapham Junction owing to the state of the ground.[3]

Eventually the tanks reached their starting point. The artillery barrage began at 5 a.m. but all communication with the supporting infantry had been lost, owing to the telephone lines having been cut. In addition, visual signalling was impossible and the runners were finding it difficult to make their way across the terrain. Very heavy rain had continued throughout the night and at 4 a.m. the Germans brought down a barrage on the sector of the line where the tanks were. Conditions were now horrendous:

> At about 4.45 a.m. Tanks attempted to move forward, but had sunk in most cases up to the Sponsons, and beyond, and it was impossible to open the doors. The leading tank (Lt. J. C. Brown 'A' Battalion) managed to move forward a short distance, but received a direct hit on the track. The crews stood by their Tanks and attempted to unditch them, until it was seen to be impossible… At about 5.30 a.m. an Infantry Officer came to Brigade H.Q. and reported all Tanks were ditched, Section Commander Killed, Thirteen of the Crews wounded, and that the Infantry had failed to materialise.[4]

The Section Commander was Captain Marcel Vardy, aged 21, the son of Epam and Mabel Vardy (step-mother), of 27 Randolph Crescent, Maida Vale, London. He was killed by the German artillery barrage. A native of Greece, he had enlisted in the 18th Battalion Royal Fusiliers and had served on the Western Front since 14 November 1915. He was commissioned into the Motor Machine Gun Corps on 25 April 1916.

The War Diary continued:

> Five attempts were made by various officers to get forward from Brigade H.Q. and clear up the situation, and in each case they were unable to get further than the Hooge Gap owing to the enemy's shelling.[5]

The tanks were now helpless. Marooned in the mud, they were a sitting target for the German artillery.

> The Tank Crews were met by Major Butler, and told to take cover. They remained there until about 9 a.m. when Lieutenant A. F.

Kidd and Lieutenant G. H. Monckton ('A' Battalion) returned to Ypres.

An attempt was to be made on the night of the 27th to unditch Tanks, but after a conference with the Officer Commanding 2nd Brigade and the Officer Commanding 'A' Battalion, the attempt was abandoned. All Lewis Guns, Clocks, Compasses, Maps etc. were brought back by the Crews.[6]

After this disastrous deployment, the tanks of 'A' Battalion were in action again the following month:

During the early days of September, intensive training was carried out in the Battalion and Tanks were prepared for action. On the 18th No. 1 Section of No. 1 Company under Captain R. W. L. Wain moved to Leinster Farm and on the following night No. 8 Section of No. 2 Company under Captain K. Skelding moved forward as wireless Section. The Officers of No. 6 Section were engaged in supervising the bringing up of guns on gun-carrying Tanks. These officers remained with the gun-carriers until the end of the month. On the 20th Captain Wain's Section went into action with

A destroyed British tank

the object of proceeding down the Menin Road to the Blue Line, and if required by the Infantry Tanks were to go on to the Green Line objectives. During the approach march one Tank broke down and the other was ditched. The remaining three Tanks started at Zero down the Menin Road where they engaged and knocked out some machine gun emplacements. The Infantry did not require the assistance of the Tanks at the Green Line, and consequently they returned, two receiving direct hits on the journey. The casualties resulting from this operation were:-
Lieut. Atkinson. Wounded.
2/Lieut. Liles. Wounded.
Three other ranks Killed and six Wounded.[7]

Tank A.1 of Richard Wain's section was commanded by Lieutenant R. T. Cronin, as at Messines, who wrote in his report:

> At 10.30 p.m. on the night of 19th–20th September we moved Tank from Leinster Farm to proceed to Starting Point. The route was rather difficult going past Hooge and through the Hooge Gap but everything went well until we reached a point about 150 yards from the Starting Point. Here a very large shell hole was on our track and the leading Tank had difficulty in getting across. My Section Commander [Richard Wain] sent word back as how to pass safely. His orders were to swing to the Right – as we afterwards learned – but the message when we got it was to swing to the Left. This brought us safely past the shell hole, but brought us into marshy ground. Finding ourselves in marshy ground we tried to come out in reverse, but the engine could not pull out.[8]

Try as they might, the crew could not get the tank free of the marshy ground and, at 2.45 a.m., they began to dig the tank out. During this, one of the crew lost the top of his thumb and was sent to a Dressing Station. To add to their travails, at 4.30 a.m. a German artillery barrage came down. Lieutenant Cronin was knocked unconscious when a shell burst beside him but he recovered his wits after a few minutes. By 5.15 a.m. Cronin decided that their task was hopeless so he ordered the crew of

Third Ypres – Passchendaele 1917

A.1 back to Leinster Farm and reported to Richard Wain that his tank was ditched. The tank could not be unditched, so A.1 was left where it was to sink further into the marshy ground. The second tank in Richard Wain's section was A.2, 'Abou-Ben-Adam', now commanded by Lieutenant Christopher William Duncan, who later wrote in his report:

> We started from Clapham Junction at zero in very bad light, and on account of this and the smoke, slightly lost direction... Got on to the fringe of the attack and fired at snipers... Advanced with Infantry at 9.55 a.m. (zero plus 255) intending to get through Gap in bad ground... but got ditched... At 11.4 a.m. Officer Commanding No. 1 Section [Richard Wain] arrived and told me to return... got into a hostile barrage which was spreading from Inverness Copse to Glencorse Wood. While in this the Car was slightly ditched. I sent three Gunners ahead with some of the Guns and proceeded to unditch. The Car was hit on the top by a shell which threw off the unditching gear and punctured the Radiator.

I attempted until 3.30 p.m. to unditch, but as the shelling became more heavy and water was leaking freely from the Radiator, I decided to leave the Car there and accordingly removed all Guns, Maps etc. Clock and Compass, closed up Tank and came back, arriving at Camp at 5.30 p.m.[9]

He noted one suggestion for future operations:

> I suggest that in future a light be fixed so as to shine on to the Compass. This would have been invaluable in the smoke of the first barrage at dawn. The Radium markings did not show up and the Compass could not be used.[10]

The third tank in the section, A.3, commanded by Lieutenant J. H. Cross, broke down when the teeth were shorn off the rear sprocket wheel. He was ordered to take another tank instead but had only gone a short distance when the left track broke. James Henry Cross was born in Watford but the family moved to Abersychan in Monmouthshire, where his father gained employment as a colliery fireman. James himself worked underground in the local pit after leaving school and when the war began he enlisted in the Royal Fusiliers. After gaining a commission in the Welsh Regiment, he volunteered for the Tank Corps and eventually rose to the rank of captain.

Cross sent his crew back to Leinster Farm and he himself went forward to find Richard Wain, whose contribution to the day was noted by Major J. C. Tilly, Commanding Officer of No. 1 Company, 'A' Battalion:

> After two attempts to reach Torr Top and being stopped by heavy and continuous barrage, also on learning that direct communication between 68th and 69th Brigades had been cut off, and that they were communicating with one another by Lamp through Yeomanry Post Signal Station, and also as I could keep in communication by Lamp with the 9th Yorks Battalion H.Q. which was also the Headquarters of Capt. R. W. L. Wain, Section Commander, I decided to make Company H.Q. at Yeomanry Post Signal Station for the night.
> About 8.30 p.m. Capt. Wain, who had been to tape the route, reported that the Menin Road at the point where the Tanks got on to it was choked with Lorries and Limbers. After a good deal of trouble this was cleared about 10 p.m.
> On the way up to the Starting Point it was extremely dark and raining, and the route difficult to follow. In my opinion the Tanks were very well led by Captain Wain.
> At 5.15 a.m. the enemy put down a very heavy barrage. After Lieut. Cronin had been blown in the air and the crew were pretty severely shaken, Capt. Wain ordered him to leave his Tank and take cover, afterwards reporting to me at Leinster Farm as soon as he could get through the gap. He was ordered to lock up his Tank and leave the Guns there as they might prove useful later. These guns were fetched back afterwards.[11]

Gefreiter Johann Müller of the 2nd Battalion Infantry Regiment 60 was in the opposing German lines and he

Third Ypres – Passchendaele 1917

described the appalling conditions in which the fighting was taking place:

> The whole area is always shrouded in dust and smoke. And the craters here are five to six metres in diameter; one after another; some deeper than others. Torn up railway tracks and sleepers, parts of the wrecked embankment, wagons from the narrow gauge railway piled up higgledy-piggledy: it is a scene of utter confusion and it is hardly possible to pick a way through it, even by day.
>
> When you see the position, you would think it almost impossible to be able to get through such a desolate crater field. The shelling never ceases... The companies, including the officers, spend the whole time in the open, in shell holes. Normal command is impossible. Everyone has to huddle down in a crater, stay hidden and do what his neighbour does... Throughout the night the shells continue to rain down... Only in the morning does the shelling ease up. The the stretcher-bearers go out with Red Cross flags and collect the wounded. When the Red Cross is shown, there is no firing from either side. The way the positions are entangled can be seen from the fact that our stretcher-bearers bring in masses of British wounded and the other way round. Apart from that, nobody dares show his face by day.[12]

On 26 September Harris and Florence Wain received a telegram informing them that Richard had been wounded for a second time:

> Wain, 94 Newport Road, Cardiff
> 'Beg to inform you Captain R. W. L. Wain, Tank Corps, was wounded September twenty second but remained at duty.'[13]

The circumstances surrounding this are not clear as nothing is noted in the Battalion's War Diary. He seems to have been classified as having been 'wounded at duty' i.e. he was treated on the spot and did not need to leave his unit. It is possible that the date stated is incorrect and that he was wounded in action on 20 September, which accords with the narrative above. The war history notes that on this day, after they had knocked out the machine gun emplacements: 'The infantry did not require the assistance of the Tanks at the green line, and consequently they returned, two receiving direct hits on the journey.'[14]

On 10 October, Richard oversaw the work of No. 1 Section in moving the Company Stores to Ouderdom. The following day the company entrained at Ouderdom for Wailly. Richard was not present though, as on the same day he was granted leave and travelled home to recover from his wounds. By now the family were living at 4 The Avenue, Llandaff, Cardiff.

It was the last time his family would see him alive. He travelled back to the front on 21 October and rejoined his section in the field the following day.

Tank No. 2690, 'Abou-Ben-Adam', seems to have been taken out of front-line service at this point as it was replaced by tank No. 2399, which was soon christened 'Abou-Ben-Adam II'. The origin of this name is a poem by Leigh Hunt that Richard would have known, though the spelling is slightly different.

Preparations were now finalised for the second major battle of the autumn of 1917 – the Battle of Cambrai. During this action the tanks were to play a leading role and Richard Wain was to display the valour that would earn him the Victoria Cross.

CHAPTER 6

The Battle of Cambrai 1917

THE TOWN OF Cambrai was located some seven miles behind the Hindenburg Line. It had been in German hands since the first year of the war and was a major communications centre, with four railway lines, several main roads and waterways converging on it. The railway lines in particular were essential to the Germans in that they allowed the swift supply of men and materiel to this sector of the front.

The Hindenburg Line defences were several miles deep and had been constructed to make the best possible use of the topography of the region, with high ground being used to its greatest advantage. The three main lines of trenches had been dug up to 16 feet wide to prevent British tanks crossing easily. Concrete fortifications staffed by machine gun teams, miles of thick barbed wire and extensive artillery support all meant that infantry alone had little chance of penetrating these robust defences.

The area was described as being:

> ... excellently fortified, with very broad and deep trenches, protected by exceptionally strong and wide wire entanglements. The various lines were furnished with numerous concrete machine-gun emplacements; each bay was pierced by the shaft of a deep dug-out – though some were still unfinished – and in places the dug-outs were joined up by tunnels running forty feet below ground. Walls and roof of shafts and dug-outs were timbered and the dug-outs were always dry.[1]

To enable the tanks to cross the wider trenches of the Hindenburg Line an ingenious invention was required:

> The actual trenches themselves were deep and approximately about 15 feet wide, but a Mark IV tank could not cross a trench more than 10 feet in width. In the passage of a wider obstacle, when the tank is about half way over (but not yet balanced on the parados), the tail would leave the parapet and drop to the bottom of the trench; the machine would then be at an angle so near to the vertical that the tracks could not grip against the dead weight below and the tank would become 'ditched'. To surmount this difficulty the Staff of the Central Tank Workshops at Érin (near St Pol) devised a huge brushwood fascine (8 feet long and 5 feet in diameter) for each tank to carry into action on its cab, and this bundle was to be dropped into the trench over the nose of the machine by means of a release mechanism operated from inside the tank. The fascine was to assist the tank when faced by the wider trenches of the Siegfried position; it was not intended to be used as a bridge, but to keep the tail of the tank from dropping so far that the machine would be unable to recover. Naturally these huge bundles were to be used sparingly; weighing over one and a half tons a tank could carry only one fascine, and once dropped it could only be picked up again with great difficulty.[2]

Tank with fascine on railway loader

The Battle of Cambrai 1917

The region surrounding Cambrai had seen very little fighting so far, and the ground was therefore relatively unspoilt. Lieutenant-Colonel John Fuller proposed this as an ideal area in which to launch a tank attack.

Fuller's original plan was to conduct a major raid, its purpose being to destroy or capture German troops and guns – not to take ground. His initial proposal met with a lukewarm response until General Julian Byng, commander of the Third Army, lent his support, though what had begun as a raid gradually became a major assault, with the capturing of enemy territory becoming the main priority.

In mid October Field Marshal Haig gave his support once it became clear that Third Ypres was grinding to a halt, which meant that the ground conditions were now not as favourable as they had been earlier in the autumn.

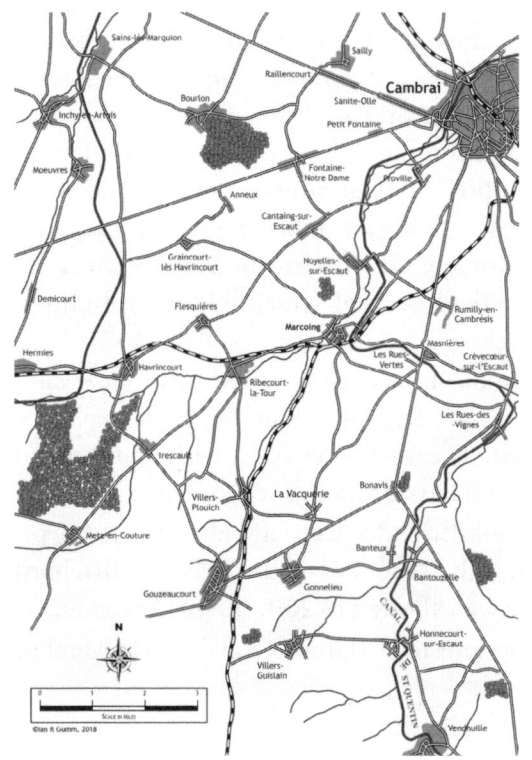

Map of the Cambrai area

Byng's plan was to use tanks to break through the formidable German defences along a six-mile front from the Canal du Nord on the left flank to the Canal de L'Escaut on the right. Three brigades of Mark IV tanks would be supported by six infantry divisions, with more held in reserve. The main geographical features to be captured were the ridges of Flesquières and Bourlon. Once this had occurred five divisions of cavalry would ride forward and isolate Cambrai. The advance would then continue north-eastwards towards Valenciennes. In support would be over 1,000 artillery guns and 14 squadrons of the Royal Flying Corps.

The tactics for the advance of each tank section were new. The first tank would crush the German wire, then turn left once it reached an enemy trench and drive parallel to it, machine gunning the occupants. The second tank would drop its fascine into the trench, cross over it, and then turn left to attack the trench from the rear. The third tank would advance to the second line of trenches, drop its fascine and deal with the enemy. Meanwhile, the first tank would advance to the third line of trenches and attack the enemy infantry therein. The infantry was to follow in close support and special wire-pulling tanks fitted with anchors would drag the barbed wire away in preparation for the advance of the cavalry. All told, 474 tanks were to be deployed, of which 376 were fighting tanks.

In October 1917 male tanks were issued with case shot which was to prove more effective than the high explosive round previously used. The shell was filled with small metal balls which would wreak havoc amongst enemy infantry.

Second and 3rd Tank Brigades were attached to III Corps, which comprised the 6th, 12th and 20th Divisions. Richard Wain's tank company was allotted to 20th (Light) Division.

Preliminary Instructions to 'A' Battalion on the 13 November 1917 noted:

The Battle of Cambrai 1917

On a date and at an hour to be notified later, the III Corps, in conjunction with other troops to the North, is carrying out a surprise attack on the enemy's front... the 20th Division in the centre. Subsidiary attacks and feints will be carried out along the remainder of the Army front.

The object of the operation is to break the enemy's defensive system by a coup de main between the Canal de L'Escaut at Banteux and the Canal du Nord, West of Havrincourt, and to pass the cavalry through the gap thus made with a view to operating in a north-easterly direction.

The success of the operation will depend on our ability to seize the crossings over the Canal de L'Escaut at Hasnieres and Marcoing, break through the enemy's last line, namely the Masnieres-Beaurevoir Line, and pass the cavalry through before the enemy can bring up his divisions to counter-attack or organise a new defensive system.

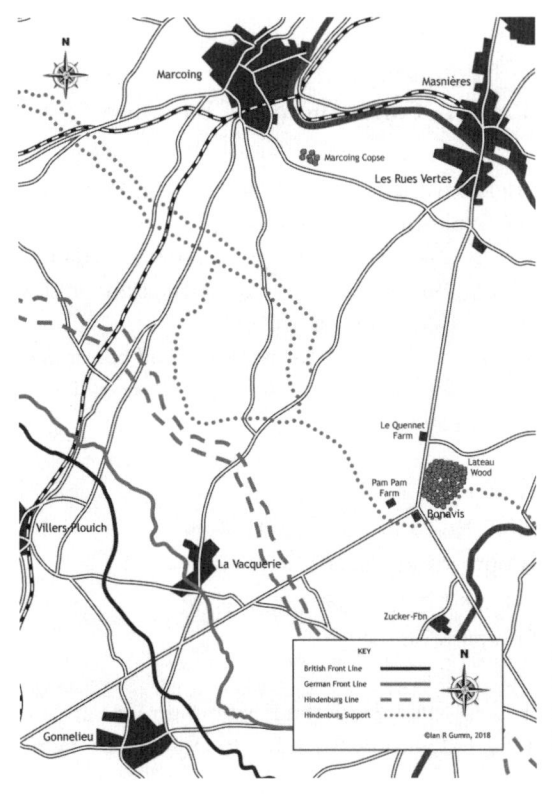

Map of the 20th (Light) Division Area of Operation, 20 November 1917

105

> There will be no preliminary bombardment and no wire-cutting by Artillery, except in one or two places, prior to Zero. The attack will be preceded by waves of Tanks, and will be covered by standing barrages which include smoke. Those barrages will lift from objective to objective as the attack progresses.
>
> The intention is to overwhelm the enemy with a sudden rush of Tanks and to penetrate the first line before he has time to realise the nature or locality of the attack. Celerity is therefore all-important.
>
> It is also necessary to impress upon all ranks the importance of Secrecy. Operations are not to be discussed in Officers or other Messes, or over the telephone.
>
> Nos 1 and 2 Companies are allotted to the 60th Infantry Brigade, 20th Division. The allotment of No 3 Company will be notified later... The Battalion has been allotted Dessart Wood as a Lying-up Place until X/Y night, when the Battalion moves to Villers-Plouich.[3]

On 16 November Operation Order No. 4 was issued to Lieutenant-Colonel P. Lyon, Commanding 'A' Battalion:

> The 60th Infantry Brigade will attack in two waves, with 18 Tanks in the first wave and 6 Tanks in the second wave.
>
> The attack on the first objective (Blue Line) will be carried out by the 6th Bn. Oxford and Bucks Light Infantry on the right, and the 12th Bn. King's Royal Rifle Corps on the left.
>
> The attack on the second objective (Brown Line) will be carried out by the 6th Bn. King's Shropshire Light Infantry on the right and the 12th Bn. Rifle Brigade on the left.
>
> Tanks are allotted as under:-
> 1st Objective: 3 Sections No 2 Company on the right
>   3 Sections No 1 Company on the left
> 2nd Objective: 1 Section No 2 Company on the right
>   1 Section No 1 Company on the left
>
> The first wave of Tanks starts from the Forming-up Line at Zero minus 10 Minutes, followed by the Infantry attached to them.

A distance of 75 yards will be maintained between the Tanks and their attached platoons, and 50 yards between the remaining Companies of Infantry...

As soon as the 18 Tanks of the first wave have carried out their original task, i.e. the capture of the first objective, they will immediately advance and threaten the second objective.

The second wave of Tanks, with its Infantry, will follow the first wave at a distance to be given later, and will proceed straight to the second objective.

After the capture of the Brown Line 6 tanks of No 1 Company and 6 Tanks of No 2 Company will proceed in the direction of Marcoing without waiting for Infantry support.[4]

More than 36 trains, each carrying a dozen tanks, were required to transport the tanks to the detraining centres behind the British front line. In addition, huge quantities of petrol, grease, ammunition – both six-pounder shells and small arms ammunition – and stores were moved forward. To preserve secrecy, this was all accomplished at night. From their detrainment stations the three tank brigades moved to

British tanks captured later by the Germans being moved by train

their lying-up areas of Havrincourt Wood, Dessart Wood some two miles further south, and in and around Villers-Guislain and Gouzeaucourt. Fortunately, during this assembly period a dense mist covered all movement.

The War History of the 1st Tank Battalion described the final arrangements:

> November opened with the arrival of new Tanks drawn from Érin to complete the Battalion establishment, and the following week the Battalion busily engaged in preparing these for action, the fascine making its first appearance at this time, the art of using it being frequently demonstrated; how well these lessons were learnt was proved by the astonishing results obtained at the Hindenburg Line a fortnight later. Tanks in cooperation with infantry formed part of the Battalion training at this period.
>
>   On the 11th all three Companies with Tanks entrained at Beaumetz for Plateau [a huge marshalling yard], which they reached on the following day, Headquarters remaining at Wailly. Tanks detrained and were camouflaged in a wood close to the siding, personnel proceeding to an old infantry camp in the neighbourhood of Bray. The next five days were spent in improving the fighting condition of the Tanks and demonstrations with infantry, one in the presence of Sir Douglas Haig, were practised. On the 16th the railway journey to Ytres was accomplished, and from there the Tanks were driven to Dessart Wood where a rough camp was prepared, the Battalion Headquarters moving directly from Wailly to the village of Equencourt. A further move forward from Dessart Wood to Villers-Plouich was undertaken on the 18th by Nos. 1 and 2 Companies, No. 3 Company following the next evening. This journey was made on low gear with reduced throttle to diminish noise, and instructions issued to prevent swinging, thus suggesting the presence of tractors should the route come under the eye of the ever-watchful enemy aircraft. The previous two days had been devoted to reconnaissance and taping of routes to the jumping-off line, by R.O.'s and Section Commanders. It was along these tapes that the final trek was made on the night of the 19th and 20th.[5]

Plateau Railhead

Section commander Captain Daniel Hickey of 'H' Battalion described the approach:

> At about five o'clock, after darkness had fallen, on Monday the 19th of November, we left Dessart Wood on our 'approach march' to Beaucamp. A white tape, about two inches wide with a black line along the centre, had been laid over the whole distance. The officer walked in front of his tank to be able to see the tape and direct the driver, guiding him by the glow of a cigarette. A tank was not allowed to go astride the tape for fear of ripping it up... It was quite impossible to direct the tanks by the lie of the country, for the night was pitch black and no landmarks were visible.
>
> About midnight we reached our jumping-off place, taking up a position behind a hedge. The four miles of approach march had taken seven hours – an average speed of little more than half a mile an hour! The rollers of the tanks were greased up, and the tanks were left ready for action, while the men turned in to snatch a few hours' sleep inside the tanks.[6]

Captain Francis Robert Jefford described the hazards of this task:

> The tank commanders went out on foot under cover of darkness and laid white tapes through the maze of trenches to the points behind the front lines. The tanks reduced speed so that the engines were just ticking over by the time the starting point was reached. It was a dangerous operation for the commanders, who had to walk in front of their tanks to guide the drivers. The greatest hazard was barbed wire, for if a commander got caught up in this the chances were that he would be crushed down by his own tank. In fact, we lost several officers in this way before the battle started.[7]

The attack was preceded by an artillery barrage laid down by over 1,000 guns and howitzers – over 300 of these were heavy guns. The barrage began at Zero Hour without any prior registration which would have given the Germans notice that an attack was imminent. After wreaking havoc on the front-line trenches, the barrage made three jumps to the first objective and remained there for 20 minutes. At zero plus 105 minutes it made three jumps to the second objective and remained there for another 25 minutes. The shells fired were high explosive and shrapnel, while 4.5" howitzers laid down a smoke barrage on the right flank on Welsh Ridge, Premy Chapel Ridge and Flesquières Ridge.

One tank officer described the effect:

> Suddenly, the air itself seemed to reel under a tremendous blow. A dull and curiously mellow roar broke forth and continued with a peculiar rhythm. The atmosphere became alive with the scream of shells. On the opposite slope we could see them bursting on the German trenches, while behind these there was a huge black curtain, thrown up by our smoke shells. As they landed they gave the effect of the embers of a burning haystack. Splinters of flame were on every side like exploding stars in the night sky. The Germans were sending SOS rockets from their trenches all along the line. They shone out vividly against the black curtain beyond.[8]

The Battle of Cambrai 1917

The Third Army had extensive air support from the aircraft of the Royal Flying Corps. One hundred and thirty-four fighters were assembled to support the advance of the tanks and infantry; opposing them were just 20 Albatros DV fighter of *Jasta* 5.

The German fighter squadron at Estourmel, south-east of Cambrai, had been forewarned of the attack. At 11 p.m. on 19 November, the Commanding Officer was in bed when he heard the telephone ring. He was told that the British were to launch an attack the following morning and that his fighters were to be ready to take off at 7 a.m. This was not the first time he had received news of an impending attack and most of the time nothing happened. The weather showed no signs of improving and he was not minded to believe this report, so he went back to sleep. A few hours later the roar of the artillery barrage woke him.

The low cloud and mist hampered the efforts of the British pilots. The bombing tasks were almost abandoned and night bombing could not take place at all.

Lieutenant Arthur Gould Lee of 46 Squadron wrote:

> It was a ghastly morning – low cloud, mist, occasional rain... It was 6.30 before we could see to take off in formation, when we were immediately in the clouds. How [our C.O.] found the way, I don't know. Nearly forty miles across country in mist and rain, and never more than 100 feet from the ground.[9]

He described the sight as he flew over the advancing tanks:

> A few seconds later we passed over the deep wide trenches of the dreaded Hindenburg Line, with its vast belts of wire, through which the first waves of tanks had crushed hundreds of lanes. From then on the mist was made denser by the smoke-screens laid in front of the advancing tanks which still hung around. We pass over the rear wave of the advance, reserve and supply tanks, field

111

artillery, support troops and so on, then quickly catch up the first wave

...

I see the ragged line of grey diamond-shaped monsters, thirty to fifty yards apart, stretching into the mist on either flank, rolling unevenly forwards, their tracks churning round, their exhausts throwing out blue-grey smoke. I see, behind each tank, a trudging group of infantry, casually smoking, looking up at us. Other knots of infantry stroll along a little in rear, between the tanks. To a flank, I see a disabled tank, flames leaping up, the troops standing helplessly around. A chance shell bursts between two tanks, knocks down a small bunch of soldiery like ninepins.[10]

The squadron that suffered most was 3rd Squadron which began the 20 November assault with a series of dawn raids to bomb and strafe the enemy aerodromes at Estourmel, Carnières and Caudry. When the Sopwith Camels arrived over Estourmel at around 7.30 a.m., they saw 12 enemy fighters readying for take-off. Only two succeeded in doing so but they managed to shoot down Second Lieutenant George Wilfred Hall from Shelburne, Ontario. The weather was overcast; the mist still persisted and a slight drizzle was falling. In the poor light two other British aircraft collided with trees and crashed.

Second Lieutenant George James Taylor Young was flying an RE8 two-seater with Second Lieutenant Alan Lindsey Wylie M.C. as his observer when they were attacked by German fighters and shot down in flames. Young was born in Brome, Quebec, Canada, in October 1890.

George Young

His widowed mother lived in Montreal and he had two sisters, and was an only son.

Wylie had served as an able seaman in the Royal Navy at the start of the war before transferring to the Royal Field Artillery and being commissioned in September 1915. The citation for his Military Cross appeared in January 1917:

> For conspicuous gallantry in action. He fought four trench mortar guns in a forward position with great courage and skill under very trying circumstances.[11]

His family lived at Ruvigny Mansions in Putney, London, and he had been previously mentioned in dispatches.

Both men are buried in the same row in Fifteen Ravine British Cemetery, Villers-Plouich.

Another R.F.C. casualty that day was Second Lieutenant Harold Partington Ledger of 3rd Squadron. He was 23 and from Canterbury in Kent. The son of a schoolmaster, he was educated at Christ's Hospital School, Horsham, before joining the Holt and Company Bank, Whitehall Place, London. He enlisted in the Royal Fusiliers and was commissioned into the Royal Flying Corps in 1916. Initially reported as missing, his body was later recovered and identified; he is buried in Marcoing British Cemetery.

There are several airmen who have no known grave and they are listed on the Arras Flying Services Memorial. One of these is Second Lieutenant William Clifton Vernon Higginson of 3rd Squadron.

Harold Partington Ledger

Originally from Leicester, he was a medical student at St Bartholomew's Hospital, London, before enlisting. He was attacking field batteries around Lateau and Vaucelles Woods when he was shot down. His body was never identified. Nineteen days earlier his brother John Thomas Gordon Higginson had been killed in a training accident and he was buried in Crewe in Cheshire.

An obituary stated of William Higginson:

> Mr. and Mrs. Higginson's eldest son, Second Lieutenant William Clifton Vernon Higginson, R.F.C., who has been in France since September 24th, a flying officer, is now reported missing on the 20th inst., and they are very distressed indeed. This son was a medical student at St Bartholomew's Hospital and an undergraduate of London University, matriculating in 1915, and taking his M.B. (first examination) in July, 1916. He joined the R.F.C., and was commissioned in April last, being previously in the London University Officer Training Corps (Medical Unit) and afterwards Inns of Court O.T.C.[12]

Richard Wain probably never met any of these airmen but they were flying over the battlefield on the first morning of the battle, risking their lives to provide air cover for the advancing tanks.

At dawn, Richard's tank section moved forward from its concealed position around the village of Gouzeaucourt, using

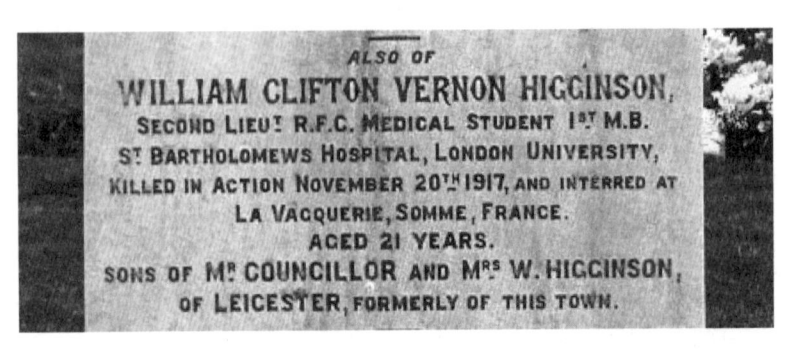

Headstone of the family grave

The Battle of Cambrai 1917

low gears to reduce the noise. The German troops were terrified by the approach of these lumbering machines emerging out of the early morning mist.

Captain Francis Jefford, who in 1953 was awarded the M.B.E. for his work as the Chief Sanitary Officer for Cheltenham, later recalled conditions inside his tank:

> I finished up with only the driver and myself conscious due to the escape of exhaust gas in the pipe from the engine. The crew were so badly affected that they were sent straight back to England. The driver and I escaped the gas, having the advantage of fresh air coming through the front flaps. At one stage of the battle I was faced with the rest of my crew unconscious, the engine stopped, and the enemy firing on my tank. It required four men to work the starting handle, so I had to shake three of the crew alive to get the engine started so we could drive back to safety.[13]

Captain Daniel Hickey described his role:

> A section commander's job was to be where he could be of most use to the infantry while still keeping control of his tanks... The noise inside... was deafening: it almost drowned the noise of the barrage, and speech was practically impossible. I was in the left gangway to keep in touch with Hardy, the tank commander. The rattle of the tracks and machinery produced the illusion of tremendous speed; but we were not moving faster than a mile an hour.[14]

Second Lieutenant Wilfred Bion, a Tank Commander with 'B' Company who won the Distinguished Service Order for his work at Cambrai, described the thrill of the initial advance of his tank and the effect of enemy fire against it:

> I raced my tank – in those days four miles and hour – towards my objective... The firm ground made it easy and exhilarating. The ground sloped upwards to an enemy strongpoint. As we came nearer I could see how formidable was the barbed wire – at least six

feet high and ten yards thick surrounding the fortification proper. As a routine I closed my flaps and plunged into the wire; for a moment I felt a slight tug as it gripped us. Then we broke through and over wire which at Ypres would have held fast for weeks any attack no matter how powerful the artillery support, and probably for as long as we cared to go on hanging our corpses on it.

I still had not got over my exhilaration when an appalling din broke out. It was probably only one gun left out of the depleted garrison, but there may have been as many as two. It sounded, each bullet, like a sledgehammer stroke against a sheet of cast iron held against one's face. There was no way of seeing anything. Taking control I drove the tank so that the bullets struck in front of me; they could do no harm against our amour, and I argued that so long as the bullets were striking on the armour in front of me we must be heading straight for the machine-gun. As each bullet struck off a red-hot splinter from the armour, we had an improvised direction finder provided by the bullets themselves.[15]

Richard Wain was in the leading tank of 'A' Battalion, No. 1 Section, which consisted of tanks A.1, A.2 and A.3. His tank, A.2 'Abou-Ben-Adam II', was commanded by Lieutenant Christopher William Duncan. Their orders were to proceed in the direction of Good Old Man Farm towards Marcoing and assist the infantry in their advance.

A crew member of another tank stated later:

It seemed almost too good to be true, this steady rumbling forward over marvellous going, no craters in the ground, no shelling from the enemy, and our infantry following steadily behind. Emerging out of the gloom, a dark mass came steadily towards us – the German wire. It appeared absolutely impenetrable. It was certainly the thickest and deepest I had ever seen, stretching in front of us in three belts, each about 50 yards deep. It neither stopped our tank nor broke up and wound round the tracks as we had feared, but squashed flat as we moved forward and remained flat. A broad carpet of wire was left behind us, as wide as our tank, over which the infantry were able to pick their way without any difficulty.[16]

Wilfred Bion

Good Old Man Farm today

Conditions inside the tank were extremely challenging:

> Nothing could be seen outside, nothing could be heard, while inside one half shaded lamp gave an eerie, murky glimmer in the stygian gloom. The walls represented the limits of one's world and the crew of eight – and the three carrier pigeons – the population. One was completely isolated. Existence depended on the driving skill of the driver and the wits of the officer. Tanks on the left and tanks on the right might be seen through the tiny peepholes in the armour plate, but they existed merely as other worlds. Once we started there was no co-operation between the tanks, no tactics, no external command.[17]

Francis Jefford noted:

> Firstly, we used the periscope to judge the effect of our firing. Secondly, by lifting the shutters of the peep holes, we could watch the fate of other tanks next to us, which wasn't pleasant when they were hit. It was also important to watch the visual compass in order to know one's direction if it became necessary to get out of difficulties quickly. It was extremely difficult to concentrate the gunners on the required target when under shell or machine-gun fire. The gunners on the six-pounders had vertical gaps through which to aim their telescopic sights, but inside the tank, when

machine-guns sprayed our armoured plating, it was like the sparks flying around in a blacksmith's forge. When I was using my forward machine-gun, it was impossible to sustain firing for any length of time, as the hot sparks hit my hand and wrist. My skin was mottled for days afterwards.[18]

Private George Brown of 'H' Battalion served in tank H.50 'Hurricane'. He later described the first minutes of the advance:

When we moved off... it seemed a long time before we were given the order to open fire. At first we were just firing in the general direction of the enemy lines. Even at this early stage, the atmosphere inside the tank was beginning to get unpleasant: the fumes from the engine, the cordite fumes, the heat from the exhaust pipe, which was now red-hot. The noise was terrific: the rattle of the Lewis guns, the empty cartridge cases landing on the floor of the tank, and the driver banging onto the engine cover signalling to the secondary gearsmen. Sometimes the two gunners on one side of the tank were not in a position to see any targets on which to fire; this enabled them to relax and perhaps have a drink from their water bottles.[19]

In the event of a tank being unable to continue its advance the orders were clear:

Tanks that have become ditched or are put out of action will not be abandoned by their crews. If in the opinion of the Tank Commander it is unnecessary for the whole of the crew to wait with the Tank, a sentry and his relief will be posted over the Tank. In all cases the signal 'Broken down' must be left on position and the Tank camouflaged. A message will be sent in as soon as possible giving the number of the Tank, map location, and the extent of the damage so that the Section Commander may take immediate steps to get the Tank in action again.[20]

Captain Douglas Gordon Browne wrote of the advance of the first wave:

The Battle of Cambrai 1917

In the centre of the six-mile line, in a tank called the 'Hilda' of H Battalion, General Elles was leading into the most revolutionary battle of the war the corps which had made it possible, and which he had controlled almost from its infancy. It was not the ordinary post for the commander of a large organisation, but this was not an ordinary occasion. It was the consummation of two years of struggle and disappointment. There can have been little doubt in his mind, or in that of any other man in the 350 tanks, as to what the result would be now that the adventure was fairly launched.

The immediate onset of the tanks inevitably was overwhelming. The German outposts, dazed or annihilated by the sudden deluge of shells, were overrun in an instant. The triple belts of wire were crossed as if they had been beds of nettles, and 350 pathways were sheared through them for the infantry. The defenders of the front trench, scrambling out of dugouts and shelters to meet the crash and flame of the barrage, saw the leading tanks almost upon them, their appearance made the more grotesque and terrifying by the huge black bundles they carried on their cabs.

As these tanks swung left-handed and fired down into the trench, others, also surmounted by these appalling objects, appeared in multitudes behind them out of the mist. It is small wonder that the front Hindenburg Line, that fabulous excavation which was to be the bulwark of Germany, gave little trouble. The great fascines were loosed and rolled over the parapet to the trench floor; and down the whole line tanks were dipping and rearing up and clawing their way across into the almost unravaged country beyond.[21]

However, the German response was not long in coming. Pockets of resistance were encountered and the tank casualties began to mount:

> Shells from a single enemy gun were whizzing past us and falling among the infantry, who suffered several casualties. Then a machine-gun started; the rain of bullets on the right side of the tank was like the tapping of innumerable hammers. I had left the sponson door on my side open, so that I could see how the infantry were following my two main-body tanks. A side glance through the doorway gave me a sudden shock. There was a British soldier lying

face downward, dead, his inert body twisted. It seemed already slightly swollen. Any minute one of us might come to a similar glorious, but not particularly desirable, end.[22]

The leading tanks and infantry crossed the German line and cleared the enemy defenders as they went. It was then that the German batteries opened fire. A *leutnant* of 7. Feld-Batterie described what happened next:

> When the attack began, we suffered heavy artillery fire. The enemy knew our position well. Soon after 09.00 we got to know that the English were advancing to Flesquières with many tanks. The only usable gun was the one on the left. We drew it in the open, and we had to support a defective wheel with some beams. A little later the tank monsters came creeping to the ridge south of the village. Not one of us had ever seen such a beast before. We shot directly and disabled the leading tank with a few shells at a distance of about 950 metres. Every time, when a tank crept over the crest, the *Unteroffizier* shouted: '*Leutnant*, there's one coming... Let's give him it!' and he pointed the gun. Together with 2. Batterie Feld-Artillerie-Regiment 108 we put six tanks out of action, and no fewer than three of them were counted for us. At 11 o'clock the shooting-match was finished. We were still waiting, but we had only a few shells left.[23]

Feld-Batterie

The Battle of Cambrai 1917

The greatest setback for the tank attack was the destruction of 16 British tanks by a battery of 7.7cm. German field guns which had been trained in anti-tank work. This occured on the Flesquières Ridge.

Leutnant Richter of 9. Feld-Batterie commented:

> Retreating infantrymen gave us an account of crowds of tanks which they were not able to stop. An infantry *Leutnant*, wounded in the head, went into position near our guns. There were five riflemen with him with one machine gun but only three boxes of ammunition. And other infantrymen also stopped retreating near the guns, their last hope. They went back to the artillery positions because they would not surrender, and they were welcomed here as we had not enough infantry protection before. I ordered cease firing to save shells. With the help of the riflemen the guns were pulled in the open to be able to fire in each direction. Soon after that a tank appeared on the way out of the village. 'Distance ... 275 metres! ... Fire! Damn, too far. Fire! Very near it. Point a little to the right! ... Fire! ... Hit ... Hit! Oh Lord!' A column of fire was bursting out of the monster. Two of our men ran to the tank and when they returned they told of the half burned bodies of the crew.[24]

The village of Marcoing was the objective of 'A' and 'B' Battalions who advanced to the right and left respectively of the railway line that ran along the valley of Couillet Wood.

'A' Battalion comprised two companies. First Company advanced with No. 4 Section on the left, No. 1 Section on the right, and No.3 Section in the centre, with No. 2 Section in reserve. Second Company was set up with No. 7 Section on the left, No. 6 Section on the right, and No. 5 Section in the centre. No. 8 Section was held in reserve.

The rise which confronted them was known as 'Welsh Ridge' – christened some six months earlier by the 17th and 18th Battalions of the Welsh Regiment of 119th Brigade when it took the ground as part of the German retreat to the Hindenburg Line. These were 'bantam' battalions – so-called because the losses of the first years of the war and the decline in numbers of men volunteering meant that the height restriction of five feet three inches previously imposed on recruits was lowered to permit men of above five feet to enlist.

The first objective for 'A' Battalion on 20 November was the Blue Line. Their advance began at 6.10 a.m. when 18 tanks set off supported by 60th Infantry Brigade of the 20th (Light) Division. The first wave of the infantry was made up of the 12th King's Royal Rifle Corps on the left flank and the 6th Oxfordshire and Buckinghamshire Light Infantry on the right. Their orders were to follow no more than 75 metres behind the advancing tanks.

Once the first line of trenches was secure, the tanks then made for their second objective – the Brown Line. The second wave of tanks from No. 2 Section and No. 8 Section now advanced in support of the leading tanks, followed by the infantry of 12th Rifle Brigade and 6th King's Shropshire Light Infantry.

Between the two lines six tanks were hit and only 12 managed to reach the Brown Line. Most of the tanks were

Wrecked British tank

hit by one, or possibly two, batteries of German field guns or trench mortars as they advanced in the leading wave. These batteries were eventually overrun by the second wave of tanks and infantry.

The German trench mortars, known in German as *minenwerfer* (mine-thrower) were designed in 1908 and 1909. They were rifled mortars mounted on field carriages which fired a 25cm shell. Two other sizes were also produced – a medium mortar firing a 17cm shell and a light mortar which propelled a 7.58cm shell. First used against the French Army, their effectiveness was soon realised and the *minenwerfers* were produced in large numbers. The 7.58cm model was used as an anti-tank gun. It was a muzzleloader with a rifled barrel, with hydraulic cylinders on each side of the tube to absorb the recoil forces and spring recuperators to return the tube to the firing position. In 1916 a new model was introduced with a circular firing platform which permitted all-round firing.

An anti-tank mortar

During the advance on the Brown Line the infantry of 12th Rifle Brigade were held up by a German machine gun post and trench-mortar battery. Captain Fraser of 'A' Company asked for help from Richard Wain's tanks.

One by one, Richard's tank section was knocked out by fire from the trench mortar battery. His own tank was hit five times before it was stopped. A.2 was knocked out on the ridge between Villers-Plouich and Marcoing, near Good Old Man Farm. His crew were by now all dead or wounded and Richard Wain himself was badly wounded but he jumped out of the tank, accompanied by another member of the crew. A few minutes later he was dead.

The War Diary of Tank Corps Headquarters recorded the work of 'A' Battalion on 20 November:

> 'A' Battalion (less 1 Company) attacked in two waves, 18 Tanks in the first wave, and 6 in the second wave. Tanks led the assault throughout. Comparatively little opposition was encountered up to the first objective. In the attack on the second objective, hard fighting took place at various points, and many machine guns were knocked out. After the capture of the second objective, one company had orders to seize the crossings over the canal between Masnières and Marcoing, and this was successfully accomplished, the enemy being anticipated at the lock bridge.[25]

The War History of the 1st Tank Battalion stated:

> At 6 a.m. on the 20th the light of approaching dawn was heralded by the bursting of shells hurled from a thousand British guns which signalled the commencement of the Battle of Cambrai. As far as one could see lying in wait to test their powers as an offensive weapon correctly used, could be seen the Tanks at intervals of 200 yards screened from enemy view by the crest of the long ridge which ran parallel with the lines
>
> ...
>
> The greatly-discussed Hindenburg Line was easily crossed by means of the fascine, and what opposition was offered was quickly

overcome by the Tank gunners, except in the case of Captain Wain's Section of No. 1 Company who suffered the loss of all three cars from the direct fire of a field battery.[26]

III Corps of the Third Army attacked on the right. The attack was delivered from Gonnelieu to La Vacquerie by 130 tanks and two infantry divisions – the 12th and 20th. By just after 9 a.m. they had captured their first objective, the German main line of resistance. A mile ahead lay Lateau Wood. Here the defenders offered stiff resistance but, with the aid of the tanks, the wood was cleared of enemy troops and the second objective was taken. At around 10.30 a.m. 29th Division, in support, entered the front line between the 6th and 20th Divisions and seized the St Quentin Canal from Masnières to Marcoing.

Second Lieutenant Clarke of Richard Wain's section stated later in his report on the action of 20 November:

> I was commanding Tank A.3 A-MERRY-CAN. My direction was towards Goodman Farm, and on reaching this I found that the Infantry were not being held up here so I crossed the Hindenburg First Line over the fascine dropped by Tank A.1

Destroyed British tank

We then proceeded to our right, along a communication trench and succeeded in dispersing a Machine Gun Crew, killing the majority of them and wounding the others, and also succeeded in clearing part of the trench.

During this part of the operations one of my gunners (Pte. Coleman) was wounded by a bullet which penetrated into the Tank.

Afterwards we made for the Hindenburg Support Line, but on attempting to release my fascine it would not fall, the hook being too close to the cab. I used a Crow Bar but could not release the fascine from the hook.

After several attempts to release the fascine I then took a nose dive into the trench expecting this to move it, and after reversing as far as possible, I managed to make it drop.

This brought the fascine in front of the tracks, and the Tank failed to mount it in this position, in fact merely rolled it forward so causing the Tank to get bellied more each movement.

I immediately got out of the back door of the Tank to fix my unditching gear, but whilst doing this I got sniped by a bullet which caught me in my right arm.

Mr. Duncan's car was in rear, and I got in to tell my Section Commander (Capt. Wain) what had occurred, and that it would take me 15 minutes to get out.

Major Keating came along as I was going to unditch, and when he saw I was wounded he ordered me to hold out as a strongpoint in case of a counter-attack.[27]

In this report Clarke states that Corporal Stower became a casualty but this is an error, probably as the result of it being transcribed by a clerk.

The Commanding Officer of No. 1 Company 'A' Battalion, Major Tilly, wrote of No. 1 Section in his report of 25 November:

Tank No. 8078, A.1 ARMAGH II, was stuck on the Hindenburg Line with Auto Vac trouble, the Crew joining the Infantry with their Lewis Guns. The Tank Commander – Lt. R. T. Cronin and 5 of his crew were wounded.

Tank No. 2773, A.3 A-MERRY-CAN, 2/Lt. E. W. B. Clarke was

The Battle of Cambrai 1917

wounded while fitting his unditching gear on the Hindenburg Line. The Tank received a direct hit.[28]

On 25 November, Richard Wain's parents received the dreaded telegram from the War Office. It read:

Wain, 4 The Avenue, Llandaff.
Deeply regret to inform you Captain R. W. L. Wain, Tank Corps, was killed in action November twentieth. The Army Council expresses their sympathy.[29]

After the fighting on the first morning it appeared that victory was in sight. The British front line had advanced over 4,000 yards. But the advance had come at a price. Around 4,000 soldiers were casualties. Seventy-one tanks had broken down, forty-three had become ditched and were abandoned and sixty-five had been put out of action by German artillery fire. Despite these losses, church bells at home sounded and a great victory was celebrated. Over 4,000 Germans had been taken prisoner. It appeared that the tactics had been successful, and the Hindenburg Line had been breached.

On the right the 12th (Eastern) Division had advanced as far as Lateau Wood, the 20th (Light) Division had penetrated as far as Masnières, and in the centre the 6th Division had captured Ribécourt and Marcoing. West of Flesquières, the 62nd (2nd West Riding) Division were withing reach of Bourlon Wood and on the left the 36th Division had reached the Bapaume to Cambrai road.

There were, however, some worrying signs. The 51st (Highland) Division had been repulsed at Flesquières, though the Germans did abandon it that night. The losses in tanks affected the ability to surge forward the following day and the Germans were preparing their counter-attacks.

The following day Flesquières was occupied but the impetus had slowed. Fierce fighting continued around Bourlon and Anneux but German counter-attacks on the 21 and 22 November drove the British out of Mœuvres and Fontaine. On the morning of 23 November the British attacked the Germans in Bourlon Wood but made little progress.

On 27 November the 62nd Division, supported by thirty tanks, made a final attempt to take the wood but were repulsed and on 30 November the Germans began a major counter-attack across a thirteen-kilometre front. Only a British counter-attack by the Guards Division, supported by tanks, allowed the line to be held. On 3 December Haig ordered a partial withdrawal in the north salient and by 7 December the British gains were abandoned apart from a section of ground around Flesquières, Ribécourt and Havrincourt.

The advance at Cambrai was a failure in the long term

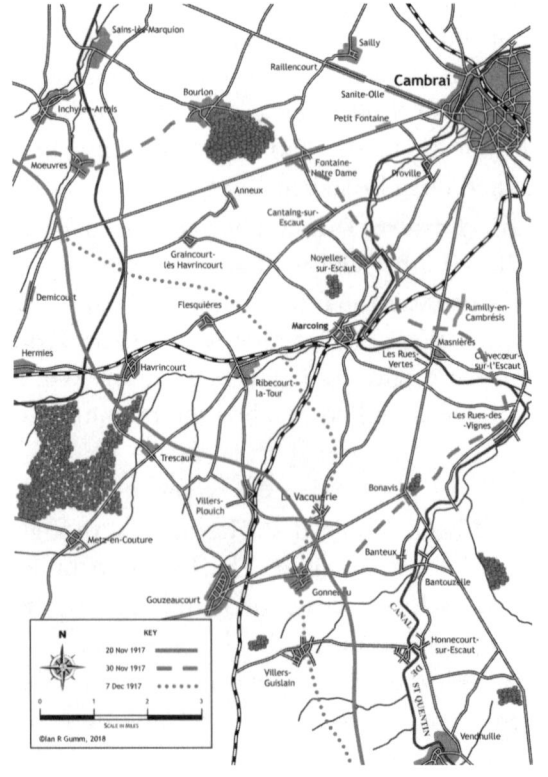

Map of British front line from 20 November to 7 December 1917

owing to the lack of adequate reserves available to be pushed forward to exploit the successes where they did happen. The German resistance grew in strength as the battle wore on and the counter-attack, when it occurred at the end of November, drove the British back, enabling the Germans to recover many of the abandoned tanks and to repair them for their own use.

A British tank captured by the Germans

CHAPTER 7

The German Perspective

OPPOSING THE 20TH (Light) Division and the supporting tanks was the German 90. Reserve Infantry Regiment, part of the German 54. Division, which had been raised in the Rostock/Wismar/Schwerin area of north Germany. Since November 1916 the issue of how best to deal with the British tanks had been seriously examined by this division, whose commander, *Generalleutnant* Oskar Freiherr von Watter, was himself an artilleryman; his younger brother had commanded the artillery of 27. Division in action against the first tank attacks at Flers in September 1916. As soon as 54. Division was withdrawn from the fighting at Verdun, von Watter senior met with his brother to discuss his experience.

Von Watter then called together the officers of 108. Field Artillery Regiment to determine the best method of dealing with enemy tanks. He ordered that the gun teams practise against moving targets, and, in an emergency, they were trained to gallop forward, unlimber their guns at close range and knock out the tanks by direct fire. As a result of this preparation, the artillery felt confident they could halt a tank advance, something they were able to demonstrate during the Nivelle Offensive in April 1917 when the divisional batteries had little difficulty in destroying the French tanks.

From 12 November onwards the weather became foggy, which affected air and ground reconnaissance. The British artillery was also quiet. Sensing something was imminent, von Watter ordered night-time trench raids to determine what the

The German Perspective

Oskar Freiherr von Watter

British were planning. The front-line trenches were found to be deserted and, when a body was found with Tank Corps badges on the overcoat, suspicion was aroused, compounded by the sight of coloured flags and bundles of brushwood. A significant raid on the night of 17/18 November resulted in the capture of six prisoners who told their captors that an attack was planned for 21 November.

From noon on 18 November, the 54. Division stood-to, ready for battle. The following day, 2. Battalion of the 27. Reserve Infantry Regiment was moved to Marcoing, with 3. Battalion and 3. Machine Gun Company moved to a position behind La Vacquerie; 1. Machine Gun Company was put into the front line at Havrincourt where the main assault was expected to occur. Extra ammunition and bombs were brought forward and armour-piercing bullets were issued – though it appears this final order was made too late for effective distribution before the battle began.

The day before the attack, 19 November, *Vizefeldwebel* Runkel of 90. Reserve Infantry Regiment had captured several British prisoners. These made clear statements to him that a British attack, involving tanks, was imminent. Von Watter was uncertain as to the date of the attack but he guessed it would be 20 November. In the front line of his 54. Division he had 90. R.I.R., 84. Infantry Regiment and a *Landwehr* regiment – the

131

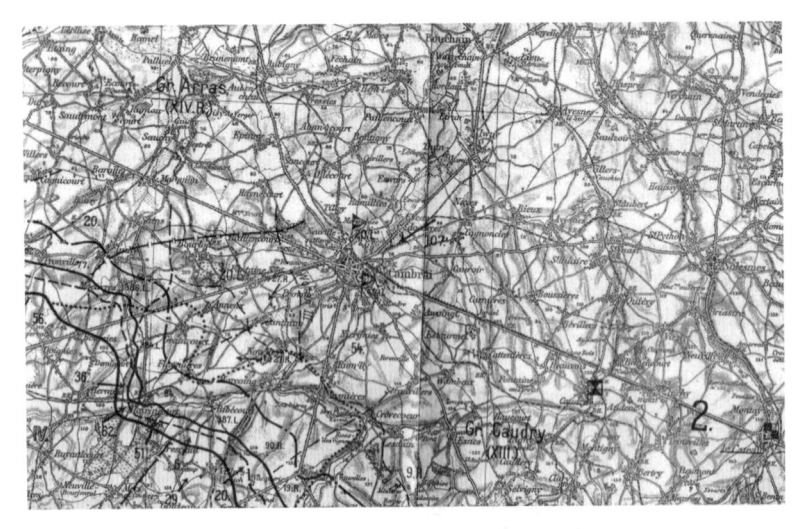

Map of the German positions on 20 November 1917

387th. In reserve he had 27. Reserve Infantry Regiment to use in any counter-attack that was required. They were situated near Novell.

The British thought that there were no supporting divisions available to reinforce the German front line at short notice but this was not the case. On 18 November, 107. Division arrived at Cambrai and was available to reinforce the left centre, south of Cambrai. Indeed, on 20 November it was sent forward to support the left of 54. Division around Rumilly. In addition, on 19 November, five batteries of 107. Division Artillery detrained at Cambrai and moved forward to reinforce 54. Division's front.

The 54. Division was formed in March 1915 by regiments from divisions which were at the time situated on the Western Front between the north of Noyon and the east of Soissons. The 90. Reserve Infantry Regiment was taken from 18. Reserve Division and was formed in the 9. Corps District of Schleswig-Holstein and Mecklenburg. This new division was sent from Guise to the area around Perthes in Champagne in the middle of April, remaining here until July 1915.

The German Perspective

In July it was moved to the Eastern Front and fought on the Narew River in Poland during July and August, and on the Niemen River, south-east of the city of Grodno on the Polish and Lithuanian border. In October 1915 it was brought back to France and went into the line on the left bank of the Oise River, where it spent the autumn and winter before being withdrawn in January 1916 and resting at La Fère until May. Here it was occupied in building defensive works in the Soissons-Craonne area.

It was transferred to Verdun in May, where it occupied Hill 304, and then in September crossed the River Meuse and advanced towards Fleury. On 24 October, French attacks drove it back with heavy losses north of Fort Douaumont and at the start of November it was relieved.

After receiving some reinforcements, it was sent back into the line north of Flirey en Haye on 5 November, where it overwintered. Relieved in mid-April 1917 and reinforcing the lines at Berry-au-Bac, it was attacked by the French on 4 May, suffering heavy losses, including 650 men being taken prisoner, before being withdrawn on 10 May.

On 25 July the soldiers of the 54. Division entrained at Machault for Charleville, where they rested until being sent to the Ypres Salient. They were in action from 5 to 19 August, suffering more losses during the British attack of 16 August. One company of 90. Reserve Infantry Regiment was reduced to just one officer and four men. After this fighting the morale of the division seems to have been weakened as frequent desertions were reported. At the end of the following month they were sent back into the line at Cambrai.

A German history of the war described what they next encountered:

> On 20 November at dawn, at about 7.15 a.m., a heavy English barrage erupted against the German positions at Havrincourt and the rest of the 2. Army's frontline. Immediately after that,

133

the first wave of British tanks arrived at the German outpost trenches in the attack zone of Havrincourt-Banteux under the protection of artificial as well as natural fog. Moving forward with approximately 40 metres between them, the tanks ripped wide gaps through the obstacles, proceeded along the trenches whilst firing, thus keeping the German troops down and neutralising them. Despite the unfortunate weather conditions which only allowed an altitude of approximately 50 metres, several flight squadrons accompanied the attack. Next came the Infantry under the mighty protective fire of the Artillery, tanks and planes. Shortly after that breach, batteries moved their positions forward. Artillery fire set the pace of the advancing tanks.

The weak garrison of the German outpost and the I. Position were not able to cope with the surprise attack of the British superior forces. The Germans did not have at their disposal sufficient means to fight the numerous tanks. The artillery sent barrage and annihilating fire into thick fog and smoke. They were, however, not able to provide any substantial relief. The heaviest brunt was borne by the 54. Infantry Division who were attacked by five British divisions, shortly followed by a sixth and a seventh who attacked the right flank of the 9. Reserve Division. The sheer number of tanks broke any resistance. The I. Position was lost. As the enemy approached towards the intermediate position, heavy fighting broke out at the copse of Le Pavé and at Flesquières where the remaining garrison already positioned there, and the only advancing reserve regiment, brought the British advance to a standstill. At Flesquières, 16 tanks were taken out by the fire of German field guns. However, on either side of this tenaciously held pocket of resistance, the attack against the II. Position surged forward by means of fresh waves of tanks. Soon, the German batteries noticed a lack of ammunition; the recently arrived artillery turned up without ammunition. The majority of batteries, especially the heavy gun batteries which were not horse-drawn, fell into the enemy's hands.

Despite the interruption of all means of communication, the German leadership realised very quickly that they were not just dealing with a localised approach but an attack on a large scale. However, they did not realise that until about midday. At 9.40 a.m., the 107. Infantry Division allocated two battalions of the frontline regiment and the last artillery detachment of the 54.

The German Perspective

Infantry Division, and a battalion of the 9. Reserve Division; 2. Regiment was ordered to advance on Fontaine-Notre-Dame and Cantaing and 3. Regiment, which had only just arrived, was to reach Cambrai. Three battalions and five batteries, which were ordered by the Army High Command as reinforcements from the squads Quentin and Oise, were barely able to reach the battlefield before dark. Reinforcements on the part of the army group were not expected until 21 November. In response to the news of an 'utterly surprising' British attack, they mobilised three divisions, artillery and aircraft of the 4. and 6. Army with prospect of three additional divisions from the Reserves of the Supreme Army Command.

Only from around midday did it become apparent, mainly through air intelligence, how extensive the British breach was. The 20. *Landwehr* (Reserve) Division was rolled out from the South to near Mœuvres. At Marcoing and Masnières the enemy had reached the wide and deep Schelde Canal, the crossings of which had fallen into their hands undamaged with the exception of the bridge in Masnières. In the afternoon, a weak British cavalry crossed the Schelde east of Masnières, and was only broken up by a fast approaching recruit depot south of Cambrai. Meanwhile, battalions of the 107. Infantry Division, who were advancing into unknown conditions, had reached the still largely incomplete II. Position at Anneux and Cantaing and had been able to recapture parts of Noyelles where cavalry had been reported to approach from. As a result, the British attack was brought to a standstill by weak German forces, although some local battles continued until nightfall. The Siegfried Line had been torn open 15 kilometres wide and up to 7 kilometres deep. Mœuvres, parts of Anneux, Flesquières and Noyelles, Rumilly, Crèvecoeur, Rue des Vignes and Banteux stayed in German hands. Additional British attacks at Bullecourt and south of Vendhuile took place without noteworthy success. Troops from the 20. *Landwehr* Division, 107. and 54. Divisions, as well as the 9. Reserve Division, all of which had been considerably weakened and were in disarray, built a still rather incomplete front around the breached area. Behind their right flank and middle, there were now only eight field batteries and three heavy batteries ready to engage; the left flank was slightly better equipped with artillery. During the night, Flesquières was vacated by our brave troops as ordered.[1]

135

Valour Beyond Measure

During the fighting on 20 November alone, 54. Division lost 2,789 men taken prisoner.

Leutnant Bibelje-Schwerin, Adjutant of 90. Reserve Infantry Regiment, wrote later:

> As we emerged into the trench we could see clearly off to our right individual tanks crossing the hills north-east of Marcoing and heading towards the low ground in the direction of Noyelles. In our regimental sector we could see them advancing towards us in line and some of them were already uncomfortably close. Altogether that day our ten-kilometre divisional sector was attacked by 350–400 tanks, which advanced deeply echeloned. The infantry held on well, tackling the dark monsters which sprayed machine gun and small calibre shells from their interiors with armour-piercing ammunition and bundles of hand grenades. Great fascines sat on top of the tanks, which could be released from within the tank if it had to negotiate a particularly wide trench. As a result, not even the relatively wide trenches of the *Siegfriedstellung* posed much of an obstacle and, even though they moved only slowly, these dreadful machines of war advanced surely and steadily.
>
> Now and then our artillery succeeded in scoring a direct hit. Even a 75mm shell could wreck a tank, or at least bring it to a halt and thus remove it from the battle. I personally counted a dozen

British tanks destroyed by German field guns

The German Perspective

burning tanks in front of our position, but what was this tiny number compared with the great mass which finally succeeded in capturing the second line of the First Position and was now bearing down on the *Zwischenstellung*? Some of our infantry, unable to hold off the enemy any longer, pulled back; others allowed the tanks to bypass them calmly, then brought down murderous fire on the British infantry which was following hard up behind the protective steel walls of the fire-spewing machines.

But some tanks halted at the edge of the trenches and brought down enfilading fire on our trench garrison. This fire from a flank drove the now helpless infantry down into the dugouts, into which the tanks poured fire or which were set on fire by the enemy infantry, which was equipped with incendiary grenades for the purpose.[2]

Major Buchholz, the commander of 227. Reserve Infantry Regiment, saw the remains of 90. R.I.R. later that morning:

> I trotted along the road. The weather was still foggy and damp and the visibility was poor. Rumilly was under heavy artillery fire, a large proportion of which was shrapnel, so I dismounted and followed the line of a shallow trench, only one foot deep, to the west of the road which led down to Masnières. I passed through two obstacle belts which had numerous wide gaps. I

German positions

had no idea that this was the so-called *'SII' Stellung*, the second *Siegfriedstellung*. I dropped down to the village and, having searched around, came across the regimental staff of 90. Reserve Infantry Regiment in the cellars of the factory buildings of a spinning mill. This was, in fact, only a rear headquarters. The sole officer manning it was the machine gun officer, who had just returned from home leave. The commander was forward in the command post. The telephone line to him had just been cut, probably because it had been captured by the British.

    The situation appeared grave. The British had attacked with a great many tanks that morning, apparently overrunning the entire position. I could obtain no more detailed information here, despite the reports and alarming information which had arrived. The British, supported by tanks and moving in great groups, were closing in on the houses of the villages of Masnières and Marcoing. Small groups of soldiers, the remnants of the 90th, were pulling back past us. We left the cellar and took up positions of observation. There we saw the British, complete with tanks, just forward of the village. I asked if the canal bank would make a suitable defensive position and, upon receiving a positive answer, I decided to head back to the regiment and to deploy it in that position.[3]

The 19. Reserve Infantry Regiment was positioned on the right flank of 90. R.I.R. *Unteroffizier* Moes of 6th Company gave this account of the morning of 20 November:

Drum fire came crashing down suddenly at 7.30 a.m. on 20 November. Everything was enveloped in smoke and dust. The artillery fire continued for forty-five minutes, then the cry was heard, 'Here they come!' I raced with some of my men to our allotted place in the trench and there we saw enemy infantry in several waves, being led by many tanks. We were fortunate; we were not in the direct line of the assault and were able, therefore, to fire into the British flank. This had no effect on the tanks, of course, and they brought down fire on us with their machine guns and heavy guns. It has a bad effect on the nerves when one of these monsters rolls slowly, but unstoppably, towards someone. This happened to us, too. Crawling slowly, getting closer and closer,

The German Perspective

spewing death and destruction, one came towards us, whilst above it circled low flying aircraft firing their machine guns. We shot one of them down and, joy of joys, suddenly the tank received a direct hit from an artillery shell and caught fire. We cheered with happiness and breathed a sigh of relief! The screams of the crew who were burned alive were truly terrible. One emerged engulfed in flames and ran around with his hands up, crying with pain, until he finally collapsed.[4]

Feldwebelleutnant Bierman 6th Company of the 19. R.I.R. told how he destroyed a tank and its crew:

The tanks could not be halted with small arms fire. I grabbed a grenade launcher and some ammunition. Fifty metres from a tank I set up the launcher and opened fire. Luck was with us. We could hear internal explosions coming from the tank as the ammunition caught fire. It was then a simple matter to adjust the aim of the launcher so that the rounds fell behind the tank and the crew was soon dealt with.[5]

The remaining tanks then headed north towards Marcoing. Reserve *Leutnant* Dieckmann of 7th Company 19. Reserve Infantry Regiment recalled:

A British tank bearing the marks of a catastrophic explosion

Our sector [east of Gonnelieu] had been under fire for half an hour when a man came running up, shouting, 'We are being attacked by tanks!' At that we noticed that tanks were tearing and flattening the wire obstacle as though it were composed of spiders' webs. Some of our men were angry when they realised that our S.m.K. [armour-piercing] ammunition and hand grenades were clattering uselessly against the armour. Making use of huge fascines they had brought with them, the tanks blocked off the trench in the centre of the company sector and then dismounted some of the crews who took over the trench, established a barricade behind the fascine and swept the ground with fire from a machine gun which was established there, thus rendering a counter-attack impossible.

It was impossible to hold the first trench of the Vacquerie *Stellung* [the entire outpost line running from La Vacquerie to Banteux] with the eight men who were still left. I gave orders, therefore, that, taking the machine gun with us, we were to pull back to the main company trenches in the Banteux *Stellung*. Because artillery fire made the communication trench impassable, we had to move across country. As we approached the position we lost one man to our own fire. In the dreadful, swirling smoke, he was mistaken for a British soldier and a machine gun opened up on him. In the trench I met up with [*Vize*] *Feldwebel* Lehmann, who had set up a machine gun and was bringing down flanking fire on the British who were storming forward through gaps in the barbed wire. He stood amidst piles of empty cartridge cases and was already on his second set of working parts in the gun. As soon as the tank crews realised how destructive the fire of this machine gun was, the weapon itself came under heavy fire.

However, the tank was knocked out with S.m.K. ammunition; a situation which permitted us to attempt to continue the battle. Two machine guns, operated by *Vizefeldwebel* Tennies and me personally, were set up in a sap where we had excellent fields of fire at the masses of British troops who were pushing through the gaps. However, we were soon spotted and brought under tank fire. One tank drove us out of the sap, back into the trench and then drove towards this section of trench. Through use of an explosive charge made up of twelve stick grenades bundled together, which was thrown forward of the trench against the approaching monster, the left-hand track was torn apart. It could advance no further, being able only to turn in circles. It brought down heavy

German soldiers with captured tanks

fire against us and we responded with more made up charges. Just as it was getting dark the petrol in the tank exploded and the crew baled out wreathed in flames. We shot them down swiftly. After that we searched the interior and rewarded ourselves by taking everything edible.[6]

The official German history of the Battle of Cambrai outlined the reaction to the advance of the tanks:

> At 9.30 a.m., the III. 27. Reserve Infantry Regiment had marched from Cambrai and had arrived at Flot-Ferme at 11 a.m. A wounded Reservist from the 90th informed the battalion commander that tanks and the English Infantry were already positioned a few hundred metres before Marcoing.[7]

A few hours later the situation was described thus:

> When the enemy approached the command post of the 90. Reserve Infantry Regiment at about midday, telephone communications were still in place. That was how the commander of the 227. Reserve Infantry Regiment, who had just arrived in the village, was informed of the situation. But some time went by before he was able to commit both his battalions, which were still in transit, to carry out a counter-attack.
>
> From their position in Masnières, the regimental staff of the 227. Reserve Infantry Regiment were able to watch the English Infantry and the tanks approach from the hills down to the village. The enemy became more and more visible. The machine gun officer of the 90. Reserve Infantry Regiment was busy trying to muster all of his regiment's forces who had evaded the enemy's clutches and capture. Only a small number of troops of the 90. Reserve Infantry Regiment managed to get to the canal and were promptly used to defend the crossings.[8]

Interestingly, it appears that the 227. Reserve Infantry Regiment in this sector had the usual trench mortars, not the adapted ones:

The German Perspective

The Commander of II. 227. Reserve Infantry Regiment, Captain of the Reserves Schilling, had used his remaining reserves to extend the front line and to protect his right flank from the attacking English tanks, but then had to lead almost his entire battalion to the extremely insufficient S.II. Position, with the permission of his Colonel. From this position, the 227. Reserve Infantry Regiment now used mortars to fire at the tanks. As they had not yet had any *Flachbahnlafetten* [a type of gun carriage that allowed high-angle firing as well as flat trajectory firing so that the mortar guns were used similarly to field artillery], they had to rely on high-angle fire only. The situation in the village became increasingly difficult for the I. Battalion, the sections of the II. Battalion who had stayed in Masnières, as well as the remnants of the 90. Reserve Infantry Regiment. At the rear, the sound of fierce infantry fire was heard. To the east, there was a large gap. Patrols attempted in vain to find a way through towards Crèvecoeur.[9]

Von Watter later summed up the German perspective on the events of 20 November. In the official history of 54. Infantry Division, he wrote:

> Once again, the group Caudry made the 54. Infantry Division available. However, the division was not put in their previous positions as the timing for the relief was rather inconvenient, but was instead, on 19 November, advancing with two battalions towards Marcoing, acting as support for the allegedly threatened Havrincourt and as reserve for the division. On the night of 19/20 November, the III. 27. Reserve Infantry Regiment returned from St. Quentin and was then, on the morning of 20 November, ordered to move from Cambrai to Marcoing.
> After the attack had started, Major Krebs and his 27. Reserve Infantry Regiment was ordered to march towards Flesquières in order to relieve Havrincourt from there. On the afternoon of 19 November, the previously mentioned five batteries of 213. Field Artillery Regiment arrived. Taking all that into consideration, it shows that the positioned troops were neither surprised nor blindsided.
> The artillery deployed saw a considerable increase mainly in heavy and long-range calibres. The enemy's artillery was, as proven

143

by the deployment of the seven attack divisions together with heavy response artillery and the positioned batteries, at least ten times superior to that of the 54. Infantry Division's artillery.

The enemy's deployment of reconnaissance and low-flying aircraft was intense and heavy. How many there were is not certain. As German aircraft had not been available until noon of 20 November, the enemy's low-flying planes were able to heavily attack the battling troops with machine gun fire

...

Many German critics of the tank battle of Cambrai refer to Haig's statement that it was only about accomplishing a 'local success'. Therefore, the decisive resistance of the 54. Infantry Division, along with their weak supporting troops on 20 November did not receive the attention it deserved when compared with the attacks and counter-attacks concentrating on Bourlon Wood carried out after 21 November.[10]

In his memoirs General Erich Ludendorff wrote of the Battle of Cambrai: 'We had won a complete victory over a considerable part of the British Army. It was a good ending to the extremely heavy fighting of 1917.'[11]

British tanks destroyed in Bourlon Wood

CHAPTER 8

The Victoria Cross Award

FOUNDED BY ROYAL Warrant on 29 January 1856, the Victoria Cross was originally intended as a decoration to be awarded solely to members of the Royal Navy and British Army who had distinguished themselves by performing some signal act of valour or devotion. Further Royal Warrants broadened the boundaries of the award but the requirement for conspicuous bravery remained. It was to be conferred by the Sovereign alone, on advice, and was to be awarded without regard to rank, long service, wounds or privilege. It was not until 1902 that King Edward VII approved the principle of awarding it posthumously. Six hundred and twenty-eight Victoria Crosses to 627 recipients were awarded during the Great War.

A self-evident factor of any award is that the act must be witnessed. Since the introduction of the Victoria Cross, countless acts of valour have undoubtedly taken place where the potential awardee was alone or where the witnesses perished before reporting what they saw. Such occasions would mean that the serviceman or woman's actions went unrecorded and therefore unrecognised.

Richard Wain's Victoria Cross was announced in the *London Gazette* in February 1918 and read:

> For most conspicuous bravery in command of a section of Tanks. During an attack the Tank in which he was, was disabled by a direct hit near an enemy strongpoint which was holding up the attack. Captain Wain and one man, both seriously wounded,

Richard Wain's medals and his memorial plaque

were the only survivors. Though bleeding profusely from his wounds, he refused the attention of stretcher-bearers, rushed from behind the Tank with a Lewis gun, and captured the strongpoint, taking about half the garrison prisoners. Although his wounds were very serious he picked up a rifle and continued to fire at the retiring enemy until he received a fatal wound in the head. It was due to the valour displayed by Captain Wain that the infantry were able to advance.[1]

More detail is added to this citation in the *Tank Corps Book of Honour* which was published in 1919:

> For most conspicuous gallantry in action near Marcoing on November 20, 1917, while in command of a section of tanks. During the attack, the tank in which he was became disabled by a direct hit near a German strongpoint in the Hindenburg Support Line, and at L.34.a.3.6, which was holding up the attack, Captain Wain and one man were the only survivors, and they were both seriously wounded. While the infantry were held up there, this officer, in spite of his wounds, rushed from behind the tank in front of the enemy strongpoint with a Lewis gun and captured the strongpoint, taking about half the garrison prisoners. Although his wounds were very serious, Captain Wain picked up a rifle and continued to fire at the retiring enemy until he received a fatal wound in the head. Though bleeding profusely from wounds, this gallant officer refused the attention of stretcher-bearers in order to carry on clearing the enemy out of the strongpoint. It was due to

The Victoria Cross Award

this most gallant act by this officer that the infantry were able to advance.[2]

Though there are similarities between these two descriptions, the exact circumstances surrounding Richard Wain's actions that morning are somewhat unclear. The official history of the war stated:

> The first objective was captured to time and the 6th King's Shropshire Light Infantry and the 12th Rifle Brigade, with six tanks, passed through to the attack of the second objective. Once more a gallant individual action enabled the advance to overcome a particularly stubborn resistance: a nest of five machine guns was rushed by a wounded tank commander who advanced firing a Lewis gun. Captain R. W. L. Wain's tank was hit and he and one other of the crew, both severely wounded, were the only survivors. He rushed the strongpoint single-handed, secured the surrender of half the garrison, and fired with a rifle upon the remainder as they withdrew. Fatally wounded in the head, he continued the fight until he collapsed.[3]

One of the witnesses to Richard Wain's actions were the infantry who were being supported by his tanks. The War Diary of the 12th King's Royal Rifle Corps stated that on 18 November final preparations took place in readiness for the attack. Bombs and small arms ammunition was issued and the following day the battalion paraded at 4.30 p.m. and marched via Gouzeaucourt to Station Quarry near Villers-Plouich where they remained until 2.15 a.m. when they took up their assembly positions in the rear of the tanks.

At 6.10 a.m. on 20 November the 12th King's Royal Rifle Corps attacked Farm Trench and captured it without much resistance. They then advanced up Welsh Ridge towards Good Old Man Farm. 'B' Company, under Captain Hoare, moved forward in support and crossed the first enemy trench, but when they reached a support trench they came under heavy fire and fierce hand-to-hand fighting began. Snipers and machine guns in the third line began to cause casualties, including Captain Hoare and the N.C.O.s. However, this war diary makes no mention of Richard Wain's actions:

> At 6.10 a.m. the Battalion attacked in accordance with Brigade orders. Farm Trench was carried with but little resistance. The enemy Trench Mortar barrage about Monument was however troublesome causing a few casualties. The Hindenburg Line was carried after some resistance in the second line – about the junction of the Hindenburg Support Line with the Marcoing Line. A centre of resistance caused us severe casualties. The reserve Company 'B' (Captain Hoare) had been ordered to take this point and carried its objective. In this Company 34 Other Ranks were left out of 3 Officers and 96 Other Ranks, after this operation, Captain Hoare being seriously wounded (he died of wounds in Hospital on 27.11.17). At night the Battalion front was extended in accordance with Brigade Orders.[4]

One other Victoria Cross was awarded that day. This was to Captain Hoare's orderly, Rifleman Albert Edward Shepherd, who was in the same sector as Richard Wain. Albert Shepherd's citation read:

> For most conspicuous bravery as a company runner. When his company was held up by a machine-gun at point-blank range, he volunteered to rush the gun, and although ordered not to, rushed forward and threw a Mills bomb, killing two gunners and capturing the gun. The company, on continuing its advance, came under heavy enfilade machine-gun fire. When the last officer and the last non-commissioned officer had become casualties, he took

Albert Shepherd

command of the company, ordered the men to lie down, and himself went back seventy yards under severe fire to obtain the help of a tank. He then returned to his company, and finally led them to their last objective. He showed throughout conspicuous determination and resource.[5]

The War Diary of the 12th Battalion of the Rifle Brigade describes the action as follows:

8-50 a.m. after halting just short of 1st objective, 'B' Company moved off to attack 2nd objective. 'D' Company on left met with practically no opposition, the Germans in this sector either ran away or surrendered.

'B' Company in the centre was somewhat hampered by machine gun fire from the right flank, but pushed on to final objective, while one platoon worked their way up the Hindenburg to get on the flank of the machine gun nest which was holding up the right company.

The right company had to fight their way almost from the start, as their tank went too far to the left, while the tanks of the King's Shropshire Light Infantry on their right had gone off down the La Vacquerie Valley, leaving a gap of at least 500 yards between tanks, until the KSLI could recover them.

With the help of covering fire from Lewis Guns and Rifle Bombers, with bombers working up the communications trench, the company got to within 200 yards of the Hindenburg Support where they were held up by a nest of 5 machine guns and a trench mortar.

At this stage Captain Fraser, commanding 'A' Company, managed to get hold of a stray tank which at once advanced on the nest [This was Richard Wain's tank]. He also sent a serjeant to explain the situation to 'B' Company and the supporting platoon of 'C' Company. A party was at once organised to work up and take the machine guns in the flank. The tank got within 50 yards of the nest when it received a direct hit from the trench mortar which killed 5 of the crew and seriously wounded the officer and remaining men. The officer, however, got out of the tank and rushed at the Germans with a Lewis Gun and, at the same time, 'B' Company rushed the position from a flank. The tank officer was killed in the melee, but the party of Germans who survived immediately surrendered. Only one of the machine guns was fit for use, and it was immediately turned on parties of the Germans who were running away.

'A' Company then reached the final objective without further difficulty, at the same time mopping up the ground on their right flank. This company took over 130 prisoners, a trench mortar and six machine guns during the advance.[6]

On 14 February 1918 Second Lieutenant R. H. Walpole of the 12th Rifle Brigade wrote to the Secretary at the War Office:

> Was T.Lt. (A/Capt.) R. W. L. Wain, late Tank Corps, killed in action on Nov. 20th, 1917. At about 12 midday, when leading with his Tank a Company ('A' Coy) of the 12th Rifle Brigade, at a point near a support trench of the Hindenburg Line, not far from Marcoing, on Cambrai front?[7]

A postscript to this letter added:

> If possible, can information required be sent to 2/Lt. Walpole at the above address. He was acting Officer Commanding the Company on the left on the occasion referred to.[8]

Walpole's letter was responded to, though it is unclear as to the purpose of his letter as the reply has not survived. On 20 February, Walpole wrote back to the Military Secretary, War Office, Whitehall:

> 2nd Lieut. Walpole thanks the Military Secretary for his letter of the 16th inst. And has acted upon his suggestion.[9]

This seems to have been the end of the communication. Robert Henry Walpole of 1 Eglinton Crescent, Edinburgh, survived the war and this correspondence may indicate that

The Victoria Cross Award

it was he who recommended Richard Wain for the Victoria Cross and, having seen the announcement in the *London Gazette* the previous day, was writing to confirm that it was the tank officer he had recommended for an award. Walpole was born in Auckland, New Zealand, in January 1892, the son of a clergyman. Thereafter, the family moved to New York and lived there until 1897 when they relocated to Durham and later to London. In 1910 his father became Bishop of Edinburgh. His brother Hugh was a famous novelist and Robert had graduated from Magdalene College, Cambridge, in 1914.

The war diary of the 6th Battalion, The King's Shropshire Light Infantry, is not helpful in establishing the exact circumstances, as it notes merely:

> 6.20 a.m. The Battalion attacked the German positions in accordance with attached operation orders. Zero 6.20 a.m. A Company attacked on the right, B Company centre, C Company left with D Company in Reserve. Numerous prisoners, guns and other war materiel was captured.[10]

However, Richard Wain's fellow Tank Corps officers did provide information on the circumstances that morning. Major Tilly wrote a letter to Harris and Florence Wain which stated the facts as they were known to him at the time, and is similar to the citation in exaggerating the number of casualties:

> Your son has been in my company since last Christmas [1916] and saw the whole of this year's [1917] fighting with it. He had already distinguished himself on several occasions, and always showed the very greatest gallantry. On November 20, after passing the Hindenburg Line, the tank in which he was in attacked a trench mortar battery and three machine-guns. It received five hits from trench mortar shells. The fifth shell stopped it and killed everyone except your son, who leapt from the car with a Lewis gun and engaged the three machine-guns and trench mortars in the open. He succeeded in putting them all out of action, but was afterwards killed by a sniper. He is buried on the Hindenburg Line by his

151

Tank, with Lieutenant [Duncan] whose commander he was, and the crew... In conclusion I will only say that you have the heartfelt sympathy of every officer and man in the company for the loss of so gallant a man. He was extremely popular with everyone in the battalion, and his loss is keenly felt both at work and play.[11]

The newspaper article which quoted this letter continued:

The award of the V.C. was not wholly unexpected, for following the Cambrai attack a Cardiff gunner in the Tank Corps said that he knew Capt. Wain well, and he was the bravest of the brave. He (the gunner) was wounded on November 30, and before he was removed he heard it whispered that Capt. Wain had been recommended for a high distinction. 'He certainly deserved it,' added the gunner, 'because all the men who were around him that day came back from the fight speaking in glowing terms of his gallantry.'[12]

Paying tribute to Richard Wain, it was stated in the same article that 'Taking a deep interest in mechanics and engineering, he qualified himself for work with the tanks.'[13]

In his official report, Major Tilly wrote of Richard's actions:

Preliminary Reconnaissance – This was carried out by Company R.C., Section Commanders and Company Commander. The time available was very short, but all approach roads were gone over, the Front Line and Starting Points were thoroughly reconnoitred. The approach march from Dessart Wood to Villers-Plouich was accomplished without difficulty.

The tanks began moving from Villers-Plouich at 7.20 a.m. on Y/Z night, the 19th inst., and were in position by 1 a.m., No.1 Section being on the right, No. 3 Section in the centre, and No. 4 Section on the left, No. 2 Section taking up a position in rear as Second Wave.

The march was necessarily done at an extremely slow pace. It had been previously arranged that a representative from each Infantry Platoon should meet the Tanks at the Surrey Cross Roads.

The Victoria Cross Award

Each Tank Commander had a slip of paper with the name of the Platoon Commander with whom he was operating.

On arrival at the Surrey Cross Roads, Platoon representatives went with the Tanks to their Starting Point. They then returned and led up the platoon.

At Zero we proceeded forward with the Tanks behind the Barrage. All went well, the Blue Line being taken at 7.20 a.m. The Hindenburg Line was crossed without difficulty. There was little Artillery Fire, except from Field Guns, but the Machine Gun Fire was extremely heavy.

Tank No. 2399, A.2. Abou-Ben-Adam II, Lieut. C. W. Duncan, M.C., was hit five times by a Trench Mortar beyond the Hindenburg Line. The 5th shot stopped the Tank, when Capt. R. W. L. Wain, Section Commander, jumped out of the Tank and engaged three Machine Guns with his Lewis Gun at a range of 50 yards, and put them out of action.

He was himself killed by a sniper from the rear. Lieut. C. W. Duncan and No. 40060, Pte. Browning, J. A., First Driver, were killed by the 5th shot from the Trench Mortar, and the remainder of the Crew were wounded.

I understand that Capt. R. W. L. Wain is being recommended for the V.C. by the Infantry with whom he was working.

Tank No. 8078, A.1. Armagh II, was stuck on the Hindenburg Line with Auto Vac trouble, the Crew joining the Infantry with their Lewis Guns. The Tank Commander – Lt. R. T. Cronin and 5 of his crew were wounded.

Abou-ben-Adam II knocked out

Tank No. 2773., A.3. A-Merry-Can, 2/Lt. E. W. B. Clarke was wounded while fitting his unditching gear on the Hindenburg Line. The Tank received a direct hit.

It is impossible to say how many Machine Guns, Trench Mortars, etc., were knocked out by No. 1. Company, but at a low estimate I should put it at 50 Machine Guns, 5 Trench Mortars, and a Battery of Field Guns, the latter of which were put out by No. 2 Section.

As far as could be seen, the enemy were running back from Marcoing in all directions, and if the Cavalry had been there ready to follow up, great losses would undoubtedly have been inflicted.[14]

The history of the 1st Battalion (as it later became known) of the Tank Corps stated:

Captain Wain's V.C. (Battle of Cambrai, 20th November 1917): At this time Captain Wain was travelling in the leading Tank commanded by Lieut. Duncan, and when it was hit and the Tank Commander killed, he jumped out with a Lewis gun and, though he was 200 yards in front of the infantry, he ran forward towards the enemy. This weapon he used with such effect that he succeeded in silencing two enemy machine guns and four trench mortars, thus enabling the infantry to advance. Captain Wain took not the slightest thought of his own safety and showed an example of initiative and a fine disregard of danger which were of the greatest value to the troops around him. Undoubtedly his action, which cost him his own life, saved our infantry many casualties as the guns which he put out of action were very strongly held and would have been difficult to dislodge. For this action the posthumous award of the V.C. was made to Captain Wain. This was the second V.C. given to the Tank Corps, and the members of the Battalion consider themselves highly honoured in having counted in their ranks, both recipients of this coveted decoration.[15]

A 1922 account of Wain's deed in *The Tank Corps Journal* stated:

The Victoria Cross Award

Captain Wain was a Section Commander in No. 1 Company, 1st Tank Battalion, and the first beams of light which heralded the approaching dawn of that memorable day saw him travelling in the leading tank of his section, and following closely behind the gigantic burst of shells, which, vomited from the mouths of thousands of British guns, signalled the commencement of the Battle of Cambrai. The advancing line of tanks at 200 yards interval found the enemy capable of putting up but a feeble resistance, and the initial success was almost complete. Dropping their fascines into the gaping trench of the formidable Hindenburg Line, most of the tanks of the 1st Tank Battalion made a comfortable crossing and found their way into Marcoing, where only the canal hindered their further progress.

Most of the tanks – but not all, for the three tanks of Captain Wain's section were all knocked out by direct fire from a field battery before they had made much progress, and the advancing infantry were, consequently, being held up. When the leading tank, in which Captain Wain was travelling, received its direct hit, the tank was put out of action, and its commander Lieut. Duncan, was killed. This disaster occurred near a strongpoint in the Hindenburg Support Line, the devastating fire from which prohibited any further advance. That one man single-handed should be able to remedy the situation, and turn what appeared a conclusive defeat into a decided victory, seemed utter madness. Wain, though mild in manner and unobtrusive in his intercourse with those who knew him, was imbued with the spirit of that genius who said: 'If it is difficult – it is done; if it is impossible – I will do it.'

Though seriously wounded and alone, save for one other survivor from his tank, his brain must have worked clearly and quickly to have grasped the precarious position in which he was placed. On vacating the destroyed machine, Wain seized a Lewis gun, and, though 200 yards ahead of our infantry, continued to advance towards the enemy, firing his gun, and succeeded in capturing the strongpoint, and putting two machine-guns and four trench mortars out of action. At this stage he must have been seriously hampered by his wounds, but he continued to fire upon the retreating enemy until he received a fatal wound in the head.

For a heroic deed such as this there is no tangible reward. His action not only affected the larger scheme of the battle but it also saved many lives among the infantry; for the machine-guns he put out of action were very strongly held, and would have been very costly to dislodge. It is, therefore, in the hearts of his comrades that Captain Wain may find a recompense; for truly his memory will live for ever, and be a source of noble inspiration to those who follow in his steps, to those who aspire to live, and maybe die, in the noblest calling of all – service to their fellow men.[16]

By 1919, Richard Wain's head wound was not described as being immediately fatal:

> Cambrai added a second V.C. to that of Captain Robertson. This was won by Captain Richard William Leslie Wain, commanding a section of Tanks of the 1st Battalion. Whilst leading an attack on a German strongpoint near Marcoing, he was checked by a direct hit on his Tank. Nearly all the crew were killed outright, and Captain Wain and one man, the only survivors, were both badly wounded. Our infantry were consequently definitely held up, and suffering from the concentrated machine-gun fire from the strongpoint. Though weakened by loss of blood, Captain Wain, by sheer will-power, pulled himself together, unshipped his Lewis gun, and, leaving the protection of his Tank, advanced alone against the enemy. Getting his gun into position he trained it on the strongpoint, opened a well-directed fire, and, single-handed, took the strongpoint, capturing as well about half the garrison.
> Most of the enemy were retiring, but continued to fire. Captain Wain was all but done in, and might have left the work of overcoming further resistance to others, but such was his sense of duty that he carried on, using a rifle he had picked up, until at length he was fatally wounded by a shot through the head. Even then he refused the help of stretcher-bearers until he had cleared every one of the enemy out of their strongpoint.[17]

These were the versions of Richard Wain's actions that held sway until the publication in 1967 of a book on the battle which led to a survivor from 'Abou-Ben-Adam II' giving his recollections of that morning, which may help in explaining why inaccuracies occurred in the contemporary accounts.

The Victoria Cross Award

Private Joseph Mossman described what happened in a letter he wrote to Bryan Cooper, the author of *The Ironclads at Cambrai*, in 1967:

> I have read your book with much interest and enjoyment. I was with Capt. Wain when he won his V.C. and I would like to give you a correct account of that action as all the books and articles I have read of this are incorrect. There were three survivors, myself being one. None of us returned to 'A' Battalion as we were wounded. Hence no report was given at that time to 'A' Battalion headquarters and as we were miles ahead of the infantry nobody witnessed the action.
>
> The following August (1918), whilst with 'J' Battalion, I called at 'A' Battalion headquarters which was near and I saw the C.O. and R.S.M., the only ones I knew. The C.O. kindly gave me a message I wrote and sent by our carrier pigeon whilst we were hung-up in a sunken road before the final action. He also told me that Roberts and myself had been recommended for the D.C.M. but we never saw the 'gongs'. The V.C. took precedence and it was well won.
>
> If you are in the West call and see me. I am retired.
>
> Action in which Capt. Wain won the V.C. (posthumously) at the Battle of Cambrai.
>
> Tank (Abu-ben-Ahmed II) 'A' Company 'A' Battalion
> Crew
> Lt. Duncan (Birmingham)
> Corp. Stower (Kent)
> Pte. Browning (driver) (Aberdeen)
> Pte. Mitchell (Lewis) (Cumberland)
> Pte. Mossman (6 pdr. gunner) (Aberdeen)
> Pte. Scott (6 pdr. gunner) [N. B. Scott was from Dundee] (Portsmouth)
> Pte. Roberts (Lewis) (Late Manchester Regiment)
> Capt. Wain – Company Commander who accompanied us on this occasion.
>
> Lt. Duncan was killed when helping our No. 2 tank which became ditched in the 2nd Hindenburg Line early in the action.

During the late morning we were held up by intense machine gun fire in front of Marcoing. Corp. Stower was wounded in the leg. Tank took shelter in sunken road whilst the situation was appraised. Fire came from a deep trench to our left. We attacked astride the trench with cannister shot and when turning to take the trench from the rear we were knocked out by a German field gun. (This gun which was manned by one German officer knocked out several tanks.)

Capt. Wain and Stower made a dash for the trench which was nearer their door. Roberts and self left by opposite door and were fired on by a German rifleman at point-blank range. Fortunately he was a poor shot and we made the trench. The only occupants were Capt. Wain, Stower, Roberts and self who were the only survivors. A German N.C.O. was calling to his men in the long grass but we persuaded him into the dug-out. Our only weapons were revolvers carried by Capt. Wain, Roberts and self. Capt. Wain got on the parados [the back of the trench] and threw German (tater-masher) bombs into the long grass but after a few minutes he was killed by an explosive bullet in the head and fell into the trench. Roberts and I turned round a German M.G. and fired it into the long grass until the belt ran out. We had no further trouble and some time later were joined by infantry of the Newfoundland Regt.[18] We made a report to an officer who later arrived. Some prisoners were taken from the dug-out. Stower, Roberts and self went back as wounded and did not again rejoin 'A' Battalion. Hence very sketchy reports have appeared in various books and articles on this small action during the Battle of Cambrai.

J. E. Mossman
(Pte. 76631)

Mossman was originally reported killed on 20 November but had been wounded and recovered. His letter is the first source that states that Lieutenant Duncan's death occurred before the trench mortar fire was received. In addition, how Mossman was aware of the origin of the field gun fire is unclear as other sources state the fire came from the German positions to the front of the tank.

The Victoria Cross Award

On 21 November 1968, Rifleman Walter Wilkinson wrote to the publisher of the same book:

> Dear Sir,
>
> Through the courtesy of a great friend of mine, who loaned me the book above mentioned, I have read some with great interest, careful consideration and admiration for the great work done by the tanks in the attack for Cambrai which unfortunately failed to succeed.
>
> I have read many accounts of the Battle and numerous incidents relating thereto and especially the one recorded by the author which appears on page 109 in the book. This is the incident which compels me to write this letter to you as the publishers of the book, and to draw your attention to the misleading, incomplete and definitely inaccurate account as given by the author.
>
> Before I give you the identity of the writer and the true and actual facts that took place during that memorable action, I will quote you the whole of the paragraph as it appears on the page above referred to and will also underline the words which are definitely incorrect.
>
>> The tanks of 1 and 'A' Battalions, after an easy start, were meanwhile suffering a considerable number of casualties from direct hits by German artillery. In attacking a building known as Good Old Man Fram near Marcoing, one of A Battalion's tanks, commanded by Captain R. W. L. Wain, was hit at point-blank range by mortar fire. Wain and another man were severely wounded, and the rest of the crew killed. Nevertheless, Wain picked up a Lewis Gun and rushed the stronghold single-handed, taking half the garrison prisoners, while the rest of the Germans retreated. Although bleeding profusely from wounds, he continued to fire at the retreating enemy until he was fatally wounded by a bullet in the head. For this action, which enabled the infantry to continue their advance, Wain was posthumously awarded the Victoria Cross – the second ever to be won for the Tank Corps, and the only one to be awarded to the Corps during the Cambrai battle.
>
> So much for the quotation. Now for the identity of the writer as he was on that memorable day 51 years ago yesterday, the 20th November 1917, and a full account of the above action.

159155 Rifleman W. Wilkinson, 12th Battalion, The Rifle Brigade, 'C' Company, 12th Platoon, 60th Brigade, 20th Division, B.E.F. France.

Place: Villers-Plouich. Zero hour 6.20 a.m.

The barrage opens, and we are ordered to advance. Everything went fairly well until we suddenly came under very heavy machine gun fire from a trench in Good Old Man Farm, and casualties soon began to thin out our line. Whilst we were making slow progress, a tank which came to our assistance, and which proved to be commanded by Captain R. W. L. Wain, received a direct hit from a trench mortar when it was roughly 50 yards or so from the German strongpost, which contained 5 machine guns and a trench mortar. I was in line with the tank, a few yards to its left, and I personally saw it hit. I can truthfully say that Capt. Wain did not immediately leave the tank, but did so some little time later: – in the meantime, there were only 2 other riflemen on my left and the three of us made for the left side of the trench. I must here explain that the trench itself was cut in two by a roadway, and as we got into this part of the trench, to our surprise the Germans had evacuated it. After a few seconds, I got on the old German firestep to have a peep over, and as I did so Gerry did the same and we both bolted down. Almost immediately German stick bombs came falling on the trench so we got out on the top and, as we had a few rifle grenades, we luckily dropped one dead in the trench: – as soon as we heard the explosion we rushed in the trench and on seeing us the enemy held up their hands and surrendered. There must have been about 20 or so of them: by now other riflemen began to come into the trench and it was to these men we handed over the prisoners.

It was perhaps about roughly 5 minutes after the prisoners had gone that I chanced to look back at the disabled tank. As I did so Capt. Wain, with his tunic torn away at the front, his chest covered in blood, and in a pretty bad way, jumped into the trench by my side and shouted, 'Give me a bloody rifle.' That is all he said. He got in front of me and I saw him snatch a rifle, put it to his shoulder, fire 2 rounds and was then himself shot dead in the head, and he dropped a lifeless corpse by my side. What I have just written, by the Grace of God I swear is the truth, the whole

The Victoria Cross Award

truth and nothing but the truth, as far as it relates to the action of which the author refers on page 109 of his book, and I say that Capt. Wain was not in a position at any time during that action to take any prisoners at all. In the first place, long before Capt. Wain entered the trench there were no Germans there to take. In the second place, taking into consideration the direct hit to the tank, the mess and debris inside, the whole crew wounded with 2 killed, and the consequent confusion, it is quite obvious that a certain amount of time must elapse before, not only a commander, but any person in that tank could possibly be in a position to carry on immediately.

If the author has not perused among his many 'sources' of information a book of my own which I have before me entitled *The History of the Twentieth (Light) Division* by Captain V. E. Inglefield, first published in 1921, I would like to quote the record which appears therein relating to the same incident as recorded by the author, but perhaps he would prefer to read the book himself.

Inglefield's account is as follows:

The 60th Brigade attacked the second objective with the 6th King's Shropshire Light Infantry and the 12th Rifle Brigade. The enemy gave little trouble except on the right of the Rifle Brigade, where 'A' Company found him defending his positions throughout with determination. A particularly difficult point to carry was a nest of five machine guns and a trench mortar in the Hindenburg Support Line. Capt. Fraser, commanding 'A' Company, obtained the assistance of a tank, which advanced straight on the post while a party of the Rifle Brigade worked round it. When the tank came within fifty yards of the enemy, a direct hit from the trench mortar killed two of the crew and severely wounded the rest. The tank section commander, Capt. R. W. L. Wain, got out and rushed at the enemy with a Lewis gun, while 'B' Company on the left turned the flank. In the fighting that ensued Capt. Wain was killed, but the post was taken, and the only gun of the five which could be used was turned on to those of the enemy who were able to get away. 'A' Company took over 130 prisoners, a trench mortar, and 6 machine guns during the day.[19]

161

Wilkinson continued:

After what I have written and drawn your attention to the facts, I would very much like to have your views on the matter, as I feel the author should have the article amended and put into its proper perspective so that people can know the truth concerning it.

There are quite a few reasons not only from my point of view, and not least of all what about the honour of my regiment, The Rifle Brigade, The Prince Consort's Own. How can the Tank Corps possibly be given the honour? Quite frankly the tank unfortunately did not do anything to assist us whatever in the circumstances.

I do not wish to bother you with any account of my four years' service in various battalions of the Rifle Brigade or of the many famous battles in which I am proud to have fought, but I, like thousands of others, fought for the truth, love the truth, and to live the truth.

If there are any survivors of the incident I have referred to, I would be glad if you know them and could put me in touch with them.

Yours faithfully,
W. Wilkinson
77 on 26/3/69

Walter Wilkinson served on the Western Front from 4 August 1915.

In the archives of the Tank Museum at Bovington there is a exchange of letters between the author Bryan Cooper and Colonel Hordern, then Curator of the Tank Museum, from January and February 1972 which may shed some light on this apparent contradiction.

Having received Mossman and Wilkinson's letters, Cooper wrote that he was:

in a quandary what to do about this. These two accounts of the action do not exactly tally with each other but they both seem to show that Captain Wain did not act as stated in the official citation. No doubt mistakes are made as to the actual events taking place in the heat of an action and I do not want to raise any controversy unnecessarily.[20]

Hordern responded:

I found the two accounts very interesting. There are inaccuracies in both of them, and they differ sharply in several cases, but they both agree in inferring that there was not all that much to justify a VC for Wain. Of the two, I feel more drawn to Wilkinson's; but I wonder how he and Mossman came to miss each other while Wain was being shot in the head and falling dead at the feet of both of them?

The process for the recommendation of a Victoria Cross was then discussed. This would have begun at Company Commander level and then risen through battalion, brigade, division, corps and Army Headquarters before arriving at the War Office. It would not have been made in the first instance without corroboration by witnesses to the event, and during its passage up through the system it would have been verified by each of the staff at the appropriate formation headquarters. Hordern summarised: 'Far from being rubber stamped, the system is, rightly, exhaustively thorough.'[21]

Hordern continued:

The conclusion I came to was that neither Mossman nor Wilkinson saw everything. A possible explanation may lie in Wilkinson's 'perhaps about roughly 5 minutes' between when he saw the tank hit and when he saw Wain... Mossman does not say he and Wain arrived in the trench simultaneously, and as they had baled out of opposite doors of the tank, they would have been out of sight of each other for an unspecified time. It was standard Tank Corps practice to take the Lewis guns when leaving a tank abandoned (why did not Mossman and the others do so?) and it is most likely that Wain, a Section Commander of experience, would not have forgotten the first item of bale-out drill. I assume that he did take a gun, and that when he had used up the 25-round drum on it, he would be looking round for something else to shoot with. Close ranges are mentioned in the citation and elsewhere, which is borne out by the map.

Speculating, one wonders if Mossman was motivated by a touch of pique at not getting the D.C.M. mentioned when he spoke to Commanding Officer 'A' (by then 1st) Battalion in August 1918; and Wilkinson at injured pride in his own unit? Both can justify their opinions by ignorance of the full story.

Whatever the facts were, I honestly do not believe that anyone can be awarded a VC without earning it. Mossman says that Wain's was 'well-won', so one wonders a little at his account.

Hordern concluded:

> Mossman does not account for Mitchell and Scott, who were apparently not killed in the tank, but only wounded as reported by their Regimental HQ. What happened to them, and where did they disappear to while the Wain performance was going on? Mossman does not mention them (and if not them, others – infantry – may also have been unobserved by Mossman).[22]

Mossman does make several other errors in his account:
- The tank was not named Abu-ben-Ahmed II; it was Abou-ben-Adam II.
- Richard Wain was not the Company Commander; that was Major J. C. Tilly. Wain was the Officer Commanding No. 1 Section.
- Lieutenant Duncan was not killed earlier; he was killed by the shot which knocked out the tank.
- The tank was not knocked out by a German field gun while turning. The Flesquières guns were 4,000 yards away and the tank was hidden by Couillet Wood and Flesquières Ridge. The German 76mm trench mortar was on a *Flachbahngestell* – a mounting which ensured a flat-trajectory to allow it to be used against tanks.
- The tank did not attack using cannister shot; it was case

shot according to Lt. Col. Lyons in his report on the battle.
- There were no infantry of the Newfoundland Regiment present. The Canadian Cavalry Brigade of 5 Cavalry Division did pass through the Couillet Valley on their way to Marcoing, but no infantry.
- Mossman was incorrect in stating that Scott was from Aberdeen; in fact, he was from Dundee.

Perhaps the passage of the years by its very nature had dimmed his memory of the events that morning somewhat.

In 1959, one historian wrote erroneously of the casualties inside A.2:

> On the right centre, with the 20th Division, the assault was led by the tanks of I and A Battalions. The first objective was gained with little difficulty, but progress then became slower on the right wing, where I Battalion was operating, and a considerable number of tanks were knocked out by direct hits from the German artillery. Even so, the second objective was gained well before midday, and on the left wing much earlier.
>
> Outstanding gallantry was here shown by Captain R. W. L. Wain of A Battalion. His tank was knocked out at point-blank range by a heavy mortar in attacking Good Old Man Farm, and all save two of the crew were killed, he himself being severely wounded. Yet he then got out and rushed the strongpoint single-handed, firing first with a Lewis gun and then with a rifle that he picked up. The defenders bolted or surrendered; but Wain himself was fatally wounded, by a bullet in the head, in the moment of triumph. He was awarded, after death, the V.C. – the second won for the Tank Corps.[23]

In December 1964 the comic *The Victor* portrayed Richard Wain's heroism, albeit that it said the deed took place on 22 November 1917. As a children's comic the errors are understandable.

Valour Beyond Measure

Images of *Victor* comic

The Victoria Cross Award

However, even modern accounts of the events repeat the same mistakes regarding the tank casualties and the manner of Richard Wain's death:

> Seven of the crew including Lt. Duncan were killed, the only survivors being one gearsman and Capt. Wain who were both severely wounded.[24]

In another book the author writes incorrectly:

> During the opening day of the Cambrai offensive, Wain's section was attacking the Hindenburg Support Line near Good Man's Farm when he spotted he spotted [sic] an enemy strongpoint that was holding up the advance of the infantry and made straight for it. While attacking the post his tank was knocked out by a shell, killing all the crew apart from Wain and one other man. Wain crawled to the sponson door and saw that the infantry were still held up, so he grabbed a Lewis gun from his crippled tank and ran outside, firing at the Germans as he ran towards them. Some of the Germans panicked and ran, but the Lewis gun ran out of ammunition and the Germans recovered. By now badly wounded, Wain picked up a rifle and continued his solo assault until he fell mortally wounded after being shot in the head. He was taken away to a dressing station by stretcher-bearers but died soon afterwards.[25]

His actions are also elaborated without basis in fact. This from a book published in 2017:

> Captain Fraser asked the tank called Abou-Ben-Adam II to silence five machine guns. Most of his crew were killed when it was knocked out by a trench mortar but the badly injured 20-year-old commander Captain Richard Wain grabbed a Lewis gun. He captured three machine guns only to be killed by a sniper as he shot at the retreating Germans. Wain's bravery meant the infantry could round up 130 prisoners before resuming their advance.[26]

167

By 1992 Wain's actions had even changed location: 'Just over the ridge, about half a mile away, Captain R. W. L. Wain was engaged in a desperate battle at the building called Good Old Man Farm; it ended with his death, charging alone with rifle and bayonet, and a posthumous VC.'[27]

Another modern account changes the circumstances of Richard's demise and exaggerates his undoubted bravery:

> Captain Richard William Leslie Wain of 1 Battalion, Tank Corps, his tank severely damaged by a direct hit, his crew killed or wounded and, despite being severely wounded himself, dismounted and took a Lewis gun, charged an enemy machine gun nest of five Maxim guns. He captured it and caused the remaining Germans to flee to the rear. Despite his serious injuries he picked up a rifle and shot at the fleeing enemy until he was again hit. Notwithstanding his desperate state, he stayed in action until he collapsed and died, but not before his tremendous bravery and resolute action allowed the infantry to take their objective. His body was not recovered and he is commemorated on the Cambrai Memorial at Louverval.[28]

It is indeed remarkable that the reports of Richard Wain's actions, of necessity witnessed at the time, were contradictory, and remain so even today. Over the intervening years his actions have been embellished and the circumstances altered, which is entirely unnecessary. His individual bravery should stand by itself, without hint of exaggeration. What this young man did was remarkable and it does not need added colour. Some errors were made initially and have been repeated over

Victoria Cross

the intervening years, but the number of casualties in tank A.1 would have been known shortly after the action finished, and thus the citation should have been accurate, which is curious. Nevertheless, the award of the Victoria Cross was much-merited and is lasting testament to the bravery of a young man on a day of indescribable horror under the most trying of circumstances.

CHAPTER 9

The Other Tank Corps V.C. Winners

RICHARD WAIN WAS one of only four Tank Corps men to be awarded the Victoria Cross during the Great War.

Captain Clement Robertson 1st Battalion Tank Corps was the first be awarded the V.C. His citation read:

> For conspicuous gallantry and devotion to duty in the Third Battle of Ypres.
> From September 30 to October 4 this officer worked without a break under heavy fire preparing a route for his tanks to go into action against Reutel. He finished late on the night of October 3, and at once led his tanks up to the starting point for the attack. He brought them safely up by 3 a.m. on October 4, and at 6 a.m. led them into action. The ground was very bad and heavily broken by shell fire and the road demolished for 500 yards. Captain Robertson, knowing the risk of the tanks missing the way, continued to lead them on foot. In addition to the heavy shell fire, an intense machine-gun and rifle fire was directed at the tanks. Although knowing that his action would almost inevitably cost him his life, Captain Robertson deliberately continued to lead the tanks when well ahead of our own infantry, guiding them carefully and patiently towards their objective. Just as they reached the road he was killed by a bullet through the head; but his objective had been reached, and the tanks in consequence were enabled to fight a very successful action.
> By his very gallant devotion, Captain Robertson deliberately sacrificed his life to make certain the success of his tanks.[1]

The Other Tank Corps V.C. Winners

Clement Robertson

Clement Robertson was the son of an officer in the Royal Artillery and was born in South Africa in 1890 while his father was serving there. Educated at Haileybury College, Hertfordshire, he graduated in Engineering from Trinity College, Dublin, in 1909. He subsequently worked in Egypt on a Nile irrigation project. When the war broke out he enlisted in the Royal Fusiliers and gained a commission in the Queen's (Royal West Surrey) Regiment in January 1915. He was attached to the Royal Engineers from June 1916 to February 1917 before joining the Heavy Branch of the Machine Gun Corps. At the Battle of Messines his tank was hit an enemy shell which killed his sergeant and wounded two of his crew. Nevertheless, he succeeded in returning his tank to base.

Lieutenant Cecil Harold Sewell 3rd (Light) Battalion Tank Corps won his V.C. the following year.

> When in command of a section of whippet (light) tanks in action in front of Frémicourt on the afternoon of August 29, 1918, this officer displayed the greatest gallantry and initiative in getting out of his own tank and crossing open ground under heavy shell and machine-gun fire to rescue the crew of another whippet of his section, which had side-slipped into a large shell-hole, overturned, and taken fire. The door of the tank having become jammed against the side of the shell-hole, Lieut. Sewell, by his own unaided efforts, dug away the entrance of the door and released the crew. In doing so he undoubtedly saved the lives of the officers and men inside the tank, as they could not have got out without his assistance.

After having extricated this crew, seeing one of his own crew lying wounded behind his tank, he again dashed across the open ground to his assistance. He was hit while doing so, but succeeded in reaching the tank, when a few minutes later he was again hit fatally, in the act of dressing his wounded driver.

During the whole of this period he was in full view and short range of enemy machine-guns and rifle pits, and throughout, by his prompt and heroic action, showed an utter disregard for his own personal safety.[2]

Cecil Sewell was born in Greenwich in 1895, one of nine children to a solicitor and his wife, and was educated at Dulwich College from 1907 to 1910. He gained his commission in the Queen's Own (Royal West Kent Regiment) after serving with the Royal Fusiliers. He was then attached to the Tank Corps.

Two of his brothers were killed during the war. Lieutenant Herbert Victor Sewell of the Royal Field Artillery was killed during the closing weeks of the Battle of the Somme in November 1916. He was a barrister-at-law. Lieutenant Harry Kemp Sewell, also of the Royal Field Artillery, was killed in August 1917. He was a solicitor and the Deputy Coroner for West Kent.

Lieutenant-Colonel Richard Annesley West, Commanding Officer of the 6th Battalion of the Tank Corps, was awarded his Victoria Cross:

For most conspicuous bravery and brilliant leadership on August 21 at Courcelles, and again for amazing self-sacrifice near Vaulx-Vraucourt on September 2, 1918.

Cecil Sewell

The Other Tank Corps V.C. Winners

On August 21, during the attack on Courcelles, the infantry having lost their bearings in the dense fog, this officer at once took charge of any men he could find. He reorganised them and led them on horseback through the village on to their objective in face of heavy machine-gun fire. He had two horses shot from under him during the morning. Throughout the whole action he displayed the most utter disregard of danger, and the capture of the village was in a great part due to his initiative and gallantry.

On September 2 it was intended that a battalion of light tanks under the command of this officer should exploit the initial infantry and heavy tank attack. He therefore rode forward on horseback to our front infantry line in order to keep in touch with the progress of the battle and to be in a position to launch his tanks at the right moment. He arrived at the front line when the enemy were in the process of delivering a local counter-attack. The infantry battalion had suffered heavy officer casualties, and its flanks were exposed. Realising that there was a danger of the battalion giving way, he at once rode out in front of them under extremely heavy machine-gun and rifle fire and rallied the men. In spite of the fact that the enemy were close upon him, he took charge of the situation and detailed N.C.O.'s to replace officer casualties. He then rode up and down in front of them in face of certain death, encouraging the men and calling to them, 'Stick it, men: show them fight, and for God's sake put up a good fight.' He fell riddled by machine-gun bullets.

The magnificent bravery of this very gallant officer at the critical moment inspired the infantry to redoubled efforts, and undoubtedly saved the situation. The hostile attack was defeated.[3]

Richard West

Richard West was from Cheltenham and was 40 years old. He had seen action in the South African War and served with the North Irish Horse. He was awarded the Distinguished Service Order at the start of 1918. The citation stated:

> On April 11, 1917, at Monchy-le-Preux, his squadron was sent forward to reinforce the right flank of the brigade under very heavy shell and machine-gun fire. By his excellent example, rapid grasp of the situation and skilful disposition of his squadron, he did much to avert an impending German counter-attack. He had shown great ability in command of a squadron since July 1915.[4]

He was awarded the Military Cross in November 1918:

> During the advance on Aug 8 at Guillencourt, in command of a company of light tanks, he displayed magnificent leadership and personal bravery. He was able to point out many targets to his tanks that they could not otherwise have seen. During the day he had two horses shot under him, while he and his orderly between them killed five of the enemy and took seven of them prisoners. On the 10th he rendered great service to the cavalry by personally reconnoitering the ground in front of Le Quesnoy, and later in the day, under very heavy machine-gun fire, rallied and organised the crews of tanks that had been ditched, withdrawing them after dark.[5]

The same month he was awarded a bar to his Distinguished Service Order:

> For conspicuous gallantry near Courcelles on August 21, 1918. In consequence of this action being fought in a thick mist, this officer decided to accompany the attack to assist in maintaining direction and cohesion. This he did mounted until his horse was shot under him, then on foot until the final objective was reached. During the advance, in addition to directing his tanks, he rallied and led forward small bodies of infantry lost in the mist, showing throughout a fine example of leadership and a total disregard of personal safety, and materially contributed to the success of the

operation. Major West was in command of the battalion most of the time, his commanding officer having been killed early in the action.[6]

Clement Robertson's Victoria Cross award was announced on 18 December 1917, Richard West and Cecil Sewell's awards were announced the following year, on the same day, 30 October 1918. None of the recipients survived the action for which they were awarded their Victoria Crosses and each act of exceptional courage took place outside their tanks.

Four V.C. winners

CHAPTER 10

The Crew of Abou-Ben-Adam II

IN ADDITION TO Richard Wain, they were eight other members of the crew of 'Abou-Ben-Adam II' that morning: the Tank Commander and driver, two six-pounder gunners, two Lewis gunners and two brakesmen/loaders. The names of seven of them are known, thanks to Joseph Mossman's later account.

The Tank Commander

Lieutenant Christopher William Duncan, M.C., was born in Hampstead, London, in February 1897 to George James Duncan and his wife Jane Frances. He had four brothers and sisters: George Harold Douglas was born in 1876, Winifred in 1877, Katherine Primrose in 1890, and John Francis in 1892. His father was a barrister at Lincoln's Inn in London. In 1911 the family was living at 4 Queen's Road, Ramsgate in Kent, but by the start of the Great War they had moved to 53 Windsor Road, Ealing.

Duncan had volunteered for the 14th (2nd Reserve) County of London Regiment (otherwise known as the London Scottish), a Territorial Battalion, at the age of 18 on 9 January 1915. At the time he was student at St Lawrence College, Ramsgate.

On 14 July 1915, at the Military Hospital, Fort George, St

Peter Port on Guernsey, he was examined and passed fit for appointment to a commission in the 4th Battalion of the North Staffordshire Regiment, which commenced on 8 September 1915.

Christopher Duncan was awarded the Military Cross earlier in 1917 for his service at the Battle of Messines, when he was a second lieutenant. The citation for his M.C. read:

> When his section commander was wounded on June 7, 1917, near Wytschaete, he took command of the section of tanks and led them on foot throughout the day, showing fine judgement. He kept three tanks in action driving and fighting for thirty-six consecutive hours, showing a complete disregard for his personal safety. Two counter-attacks were broken by his three tanks in the neighbourhood of Joye Farm, where the line had not been consolidated.[1]

On 25 November 1917 the Duncan family received a telegram similar to the one that arrived the same day at the Wain household in Cardiff:

> Mrs. Duncan, 53 Windsor Road, Ealing W.
> Deeply regret to inform you Lt. C. W. Duncan Tank Corps was killed in action November twentieth. The Army Council express their sympathy.[2]

A local newspaper reported:

> The mother of the late Lieut. C. W. Duncan who formerly lived in Queen's-road, has received a letter from the Major commanding the Tank Corps to which her son was attached. It concerns the great gallantry of the late officer who won the Military Cross at the Battle of Wytschaete. 'He was not only one of the bravest, but a fine leader of men as well,' says the writer. 'He was marked down for speedy promotion... The whole company feel for you at the loss of so gallant a son.'[3]

His father had died just a few weeks earlier on 21 October, leaving his mother as his legitimate heir. A report of his death was carried in the same newspaper:

> Barrister's Death – The death occurred at Ealing on Sunday of Mr. G. J. Duncan, barrister-at-law, formerly of 4 Queen's Road, Ramsgate. Mr. Duncan was for many years Rector's warden of Holy Trinity, Ramsgate, and an active worker in many good causes. He had a large practice at the Chancery bar. The funeral took place on Thursday at Richmond.[4]

His widowed mother died on 26 February 1929 and left her estate to her daughter, Katherine Primrose.

Christopher Duncan's body was buried with Richard Wain's and John Browning's, but the grave was lost and he is commemorated on the Cambrai Memorial at Louverval.

His brother John was serving as Captain and Adjutant to the 10th Battalion of the Cameronians (Scottish Rifles) when he was killed on 25 September 1915 during the Battle of Loos. His body was never recovered and he is commemorated on the Loos Memorial. He had been mentioned in dispatches.

A report of John's death appeared on 9 October that year:

> A Fatal Attempt – Conveying the sad news to the relatives, a brother officer of Captain Duncan states that the attack in which they took part was launched in the early morning, several

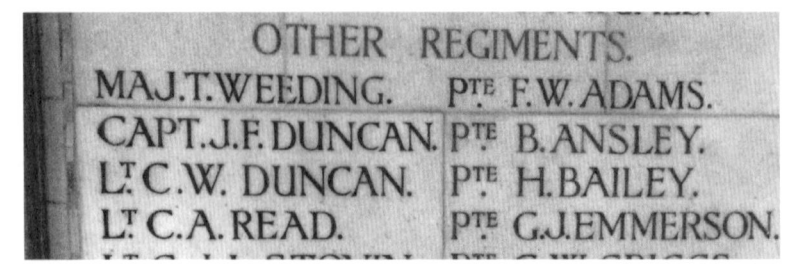

Christopher Duncan's name on the war memorial in Holy Trinity Church, Ramsgate

German trenches being captured. Under heavy fire the troops dug themselves in and repelled many fierce counter-attacks. Captain Duncan, who had a splendid hold over his men, was walking up and down behind the line encouraging them.

When the shelling and rifle fire recommenced at day-break, the officers and men became subjected to severe machine-gun fire on the left, but not a man wavered. Failing to get a message through to Brigade Headquarters requesting support, Captain and Adjutant Duncan finally decided to make the attempt himself.

'He had not gone more than twenty yards,' says his comrade, 'when he was shot through the leg, an artery being severed. He died in a few moments without a word... All our confidence had rested in him.'

Captain Duncan's elder half-brother, N. C. Duncan, was formerly in the Worcester Regiment and served in the South African War, receiving the King's medal and five clasps. For service in West Africa he gained the medal and clasp. He is now a District Commissioner in South Africa, and has recently been on service in the Cameroons.

A younger brother of Captain J. F. Duncan, C. W. Duncan, has recently been gazetted to a commission in the Special Reserve of Officers and attached to the 4th North Staffordshire Regiment.

Mr. Duncan on Wednesday received a telegram from their Majesties the King and Queen, who expressed their regret at the loss sustained by his parents and the Army at the death of Captain J. F. Duncan and added their deep sympathy with the relatives.[5]

The First Driver

Joseph William Stower was born in America in 1882. In 1907 he married Ellen Saunders in Birmingham. The 1911 Census states he was a hardware merchant and a naturalised British subject. At this time the family was living at 60 South Road, Handsworth, Birmingham. By 1915 they were living at 32 Lansdowne Road, Handsworth. He and Ellen remained in this house for the rest of their lives and he died there on 26 December 1950, leaving £12,747 to her. His business was by now situated at 55 Constitution Hill, Birmingham. Ellen died in 1968. They had five children: Joseph John Stower married

Edna N. Berry in 1936 and died in 1977; Aileen Lillian Stower died in 2001, aged 92, apparently unmarried; Leonard was born in 1911, Edana in 1913, and Elizabeth Kathleen May a year later in 1914.

Joseph had served four years with the 5th Warwick Volunteers by the time he enlisted in the 18th Battalion of the Motor Machine Gun Section in May 1915, leaving Ellen in charge of the business and their five children. He was promoted to acting bombardier in June 1915, based on his previous military service, and to acting corporal in September the following year, before being appointed corporal and transferred to the Tank Corps in November 1916.

In August 1918 he was promoted to acting serjeant before being discharged on 20 February 1919, and received a pension for chronic bronchitis, aggravated by his military service. He had been wounded on 20 November 1917 at Cambrai, and again on 21 August 1918. Joseph Stower was described in his service papers as: 'Very intelligent. A good N.C.O. with good knowledge of guns and driving.'[6]

The Six-Pounder Gunners

Joseph Ewart Mossman from Cumberland operated one of the tank's six-pounder guns. His father was the Reverend George C. Mossman, the Minister of Knowe Presbyterian Church in

George and Kitty Mossman on their wedding day

Bewcastle, Cumbria from 1881 to 1910. At the end of August 1894 George married Catherine (Kitty) Goodfellow.

George Mossman died in 1910. He had been educated at Edinburgh University and The New College, Edinburgh. An accomplished linguist and scholar, he had written a best-selling book of his travels entitled *Three Hundred Miles in Norway*. His death meant that Kitty was charged with raising their four children on her own.

Joseph Mossman was born in Bewcastle in 1895 and was working as a chemist's assistant and living at Fernleigh, Tree Road, Brampton, Carlisle, when he enlisted in the Royal Army Medical Corps in Carlisle in October 1915. He passed a Class of Instruction in February 1916 as an Unqualified Dispenser and was posted to 10 General Hospital in France in March 1916, sailing across the English Channel aboard the SS *Queen Alexandra*.

From here he joined the Field Ambulance in August 1916 before being attached to the Heavy Branch of the Machine Gun Corps on Christmas Day 1916. The reason for this was 'benefit of the public service and employment at trade'.[7] Two days

SS *Queen Alexandra*

later he transferred as a gunner. He underwent a six-pounder training course in May 1917 and was wounded in action on 20 November 1917, receiving a gunshot wound to the right arm. He was evacuated to the General Hospital in Rouen before being posted again in December 1917. He was appointed Tank Mechanic 2nd Class in January 1918 and was wounded once more on 21 August 1918; this time by a shell fragment hitting his shoulder. He returned to duty the following month before being transferred to the Reserve in January 1919.

The other six-pounder gunner was Private William Wallace Scott, the son of James and Isabella Scott of 9 Tannadice Street, Dundee. James Scott was a jute and flax stower and William was one of six children. The family later lived at 60 Lilybank Road, Dundee.

Born in Dundee in 1895, William had previously served with the 18th Battalion of the Motor Machine Gun Service, which consisted of motorcycle/sidecar combinations carrying Vickers machine guns. Formed in 1914, it was incorporated into the Machine Gun Corps in October 1915. He also served in the Royal Field Artillery as a gunner and this knowledge and experience would have made him an excellent choice as a six-pounder gunner.[8]

William Scott survived the Battle of Cambrai but was killed in action the following year at the Battle of Amiens on 8 August, aged 23. His body was not recovered and he is commemorated on the Vis-en-Artois Memorial. His father James died not long afterwards.

The *1st Tank Corps War Diary* stated of the attack that day in 1918:

> Owing to the French having been held up, the British were subjected to a heavy enfilade fire from the villages of Beaucourt and Le Quesnel and 9 out of the 11 tanks belonging to 'A' Company received direct hits from a field battery firing over open sights from Le Quesnel. The majority caught fire and were burnt out, and very severe casualties resulted, three out of the four Section

The Crew of Abou-Ben-Adam II

Commanders being killed and the remaining one wounded and captured. These gallant Officers lost their lives while engaged in directing their Sections.[9]

The Lewis Gunners

Private Robert James William Mitchell operated one of the Lewis Guns fitted to the rear of the tank's sponsons. Originally from Aberdeen, he had also served with the 18th Battalion of the Motor Machine Gun Service, and was also a gunner in the Royal Field Artillery. Given these facts and that his service number was 200033 and William Scott's was 200026, they may have been close friends who enlisted together.

German Field Gun

Knocked-out British tanks

The Lewis gunner on the opposite side of the tank was Private Thomas Kendal Roberts from Portsmouth. He had enlisted in the Hampshire Regiment before transferring to the Tank Corps. The son of the late William Roberts and his wife Sophia, he was one of four sons, and was born in 1892. His father had been a labourer and boilermaker, while Thomas worked as a labour boy in the dockyard. The family lived at 13 Arnaud Street, Buckland, Portsmouth.

The Brakesmen

Private John Alfred Browning was 20 when he died on 20 November 1917. He was the son of William James Browning, a woodworking machinist, and Violet Browning. John had a sister, Alice Leah, who was three years younger than him. In 1911 the family resided at 5 Belgrave Place, Foots Cray, Sidcup, Kent, but later moved to 5 Church Road in the same town. John was born in Sidcup and enlisted in the Machine Gun Corps at Bexleyheath in Kent.

The other brakesman's identity is unknown.

John Alfred Browning

CHAPTER 11

The Other Officers of 'A' Battalion

EACH SECTION OF 'A' Battalion was commanded by an officer, usually a captain, and each tank by an officer or a non-commissioned officer. Living and working in such close proximity, it is inevitable that each of these officers would have known Richard Wain, inasmuch as they would have shared accommodation, attended the same briefings and training, and gone on leave with him. He played a part in each of their lives.

1st Company
This company was commanded by Major Justice Crosland Tilly. Born in Bedford in 1888, he was commissioned into the Leicestershire Regiment in 1907 and served in East Africa before joining the Tank Corps. Post-war he became the Chief Instructor at Bovington Camp. When the Second World War broke out he served as the General Officer Commanding 2nd Armoured Division from May 1940 before being killed in an accident in the Western Desert theatre in January 1941. He was awarded the Distinguished Service Order in 1918, and the Military Cross in January 1918, a bar in July 1918, was wounded three times and mentioned in dispatches.

The citation for his second Military Cross stated:

Justice Tilly

For most conspicuous gallantry and devotion to duty during the operations of March 22–27, 1918, when 2nd in command of a battalion. While left in command of the battalion at various intervals, he displayed great initiative and determination in organising tanks for action, and in leading them to their starting points. Also, on March 2, when in actual command of Lewis gun teams on foot during a rearguard action on the Bray-Corbie road, he showed great skill in handling the various groups. It was very largely due to his skill that the infantry were able to withdraw successfully to various positions. He has throughout set a wonderful example.[1]

No. 1 Section

Commanded by Captain Richard Wain, there were three tanks in this section:

A.1 ARMAGH II, commanded by Lieutenant Richard Thomas Cronin, became stuck in a German trench and Cronin was wounded. Attached to the Tank Corps from the Connaught Rangers, he had been born in Newry, Ireland, in 1898.

A.2 ABOU-BEN-ADAM II was destroyed. Lieutenant Christopher William Duncan M.C. was killed.

A.3 A-MERRY-CAN received a direct hit. Second Lieutenant Emil Clement Beatson Clark was wounded. Born in Ticehurst, Sussex, in 1897, he was the son of a glass manufacturer. He died in 1977.

The Other Officers of 'A' Battalion

No. 2 Section

This section was commanded by Captain Maurice James Miskin, who was killed in action on 17 October 1918, aged 27, by which time he had risen to the rank of major. A graduate of Oxford, he was a master at Oundle School in Northamptonshire from September 1914 until Christmas that year, when he joined the 9th North Staffordshire Regiment. He had served on the Western Front as a second lieutenant from 29 July 1915, before being transferred to the Tank Corps in January 1917. Miskin was awarded the Military Cross for his service at Cambrai, the citation stating:

> For conspicuous gallantry and devotion to duty in an attack. Though he had mechanical trouble with his three tanks he successfully overcame it, and was the first to arrive at the objective. He secured the crossings of a canal, and went forward to reconnoitre on foot. He gave valuable information to the infantry commanders, and was instrumental in getting a battalion across the canal. He set a splendid example of courage and initiative.[2]

Miskin was buried in Honnechy British Cemetery. His parents lived at 20 St Oswald's Road in York.

A.6 AJAX was one of the first tanks to reach Marcoing. Second Lieutenant Arthur Henry Dawkes was from Leamington in Warwickshire and had enlisted in the Royal Warwickshire Regiment. Commissioned in 1916

Maurice Miskin

into the Royal Welsh Fusiliers, he had served on the Western Front since March 1915. He was later promoted to the rank of captain and in November 1918 was awarded the Military Cross.

> For most conspicuous gallantry and devotion to duty in the operations near Beaucourt-en-Santerre on 8 August 1918. He commanded a section of tanks, and by skillful handling his tanks reached their final objective. At all times of the day he exposed himself to heavy fire regardless of his own personal safety, and on reaching his objective collected information of the utmost value, causing the dispersion of an enemy concentration. During the action Captain Dawkes showed great initiative and coolness, and was responsible for the great success of his section in the battle.[3]

After the war ended Dawkes became an accountant. He also served as an Air Raid Precaution warden during the London Blitz of the Second World War.

A.7 ARABIA also reached Marcoing. Second Lieutenant Sydney Taylor lived at West Mill House, Dorchester in Dorset and was the son of a traction engine proprietor. Born in Broadmayne in Dorset in 1897, he survived the war and later worked as an engineer. He and his wife Constance emigrated to Toronto, Canada, in 1925 but returned in 1927.

A.10 ANTIGONE broke down after leaving Marcoing. Born in 1889, Second Lieutenant Reginald Wybert Liles had worked for his father's firm and lived at York Place, Newport, Monmouthshire. A pre-war Regular as a serjeant with the Army Service Corps, Base Horse Transport Depot, he served on the Western Front from September 1914. He was commissioned into the East Kent Regiment in September 1916, before being attached to the Tank Corps, and later rose to the rank of captain.

He was awarded the Military Cross in 1917:

The Other Officers of 'A' Battalion

For conspicuous gallantry and devotion to duty. On September 23, 1917, in Inverness Copse, while returning from his objective, the tank which was immediately in front of him received a direct hit, killing and wounding all the crew. This officer immediately ran to it, and although the six-pounder ammunition was exploding, he entered the tank and dragged out the wounded, had them carried to his own tank, and took them to the dressing station.

On September 26, 1917, he remained in the open during several heavy barrages in the neighbourhood of Glencorse Wood encouraging the tank crews. Previous to this he assisted his section commander to tape the route and afterwards lead up the tanks to the starting point under very heavy shell fire.

This officer interviewed his commanding officer on September 25 to get permission to accompany a section of tanks that were to be put into action on September 26, as he stated he knew the country and considered it most difficult. All the crews report that he was of great assistance and walked from tank to tank showing a total disregard for his personal safety. There was a very heavy hostile barrage at the time.[4]

On 30 June 1918, Liles married Yvonne Claire Pruvost, a French woman, in Humerœuille, France. He died in Newport in 1922.

Reginald Liles with his parents

Reginald and Yvonne Liles

No. 3 Section

Captain Thomas Wilson Pearson was wounded while commanding this section. He had joined the East Yorkshire Regiment and served in Egypt as a second lieutenant from December 1915 before transferring to the Tank Corps and being promoted to captain. Pearson survived the war and lived at Willow Cottage, Westgate, North Cave Brough in East Yorkshire.

A.11 ANGOSTURA II developed mechanical trouble during the advance and Second Lieutenant Harold Godsalve Shouler was wounded. Born in Hammersmith, London, in 1892, he was a pre-war Territorial in the Middlesex Regiment before being commissioned into the Liverpool Regiment in October 1915. After the war he emigrated to New Zealand, where he died in 1944 while serving as a sergeant in the New Zealand army.

A.12 ANDROMEDA caught fire in a sunken road near Marcoing. Its commander was Lieutenant John S. Hall who had enlisted in the 9th (Glasgow) Battalion of the Highland Light Infantry in 1908. After serving with this Territorial unit, he was called up in August 1914. Promoted to sergeant in 1915, he was commissioned as a second lieutenant in the

Harold Shouler in later life   John Hall

The Other Officers of 'A' Battalion

Motor Machine Gun Service in November 1916. In May 1917 he rose to the rank of full lieutenant and transferred to the Tank Corps in July 1917. As the result of wounds sustained on 20 November, he lost his hearing in one ear. Hall later rose to the rank of captain and was mentioned in dispatches in the *London Gazette* on 10 July 1919.

A.13 ALLAH also suffered mechanical problems after becoming ditched. Second Lieutenant Frederick Bertram Keogh was twice awarded the Military Cross. The citation for his first Military Cross read:

> For conspicuous gallantry and devotion to duty. When his tank was broken down, he kept in action for twenty-four hours, working all his guns and giving great assistance to the infantry in repelling two counter-attacks at a critical time. When the situation was safe, he withdrew, handing over his guns to the infantry. He had been for several hours without infantry support.[5]

A year later he was awarded the Military Cross for the second time, by which time he had been promoted to captain:

> For conspicuous gallantry and devotion to duty. He was in charge of eight Tanks to cover the withdrawal of the infantry brigade, and made repeated attacks on the advancing enemy, and so prevented him from enveloping the left flank of the brigade, which was totally unprotected. Later, a group of Lewis gun teams from the Tank battalion was cut off, when he ordered two of his Tanks to go to their relief, himself accompanying and directing the operation. For many hours he displayed the utmost gallantry and coolness.[6]

Born in Ireland in 1881, after leaving school Keogh worked for the National Bank in Dublin. He was commissioned in October 1915 into the 4th Battalion of the Connaught Rangers and served on the Western Front from Christmas Day 1916. He was killed in action on 8 August 1918, the first day of the Battle of Amiens, alongside his Orderly, Gunner Henry Smith, while serving as a Section Commander. The *1st Battalion War Diary* described what occurred:

> Nine out of the eleven Tanks belonging to A Company received direct hits from a field battery firing over open sights from Le Quesnel. The majority caught fire and were burnt out, and very severe casualties resulted, three out of the four Section Commanders being killed and the remaining one wounded and captured. These gallant officers lost their lives while engaged in directing their Sections.[7]

Keogh was buried in Bouchoir New British Cemetery; Smith lies just a few graves away.

No. 4 Section

The commander of this section was Captain Richard Hampden Hobart Dorman, who attended Marlborough College before enlisting in the Royal Munster Fusiliers. Born in Armagh, Ireland, in 1897, he served in the Royal Tank Regiment during the Second World War.

A.17 ACHILLES II was hit by a smoke shell which started an internal fire but it did reach Marcoing. Lieutenant John Carolan Brown, from a prominent business family in Dundalk, was later a captain in the Connaught Rangers, attached to the Tank Corps. He was killed in action on 8 August 1918, aged 34, during the Battle of Amiens when his tank was hit by shells from a German field battery at Le Quesnoy; he was buried in Beaucourt British Cemetery.

Earlier that year he had been awarded the Military Cross:

> For conspicuous gallantry and devotion to duty while in command of a section of tanks. He led his tanks forward and successfully engaged enemy tanks. He accompanied his tanks on foot under heavy machine-gun fire and enemy barrage. He showed fine courage and determination. He had previously done good work.[8]

The Other Officers of 'A' Battalion

The action for which he was awarded his Military Cross was the first occasion in history when two enemy tanks had engaged each other. The incident took place on 24 April 1918 when a Mark IV tank in his section, commanded by Second Lieutenant Frank Mitchell, engaged a German A7V tank commanded by *Leutnant* Wilhelm Biltz – formerly a university professor.

A.16 ARGUS II was commanded by Second Lieutenant Thomas Sheen Oulton who was wounded at duty. He and Serjeant McClumpha and First Driver Leonard Brokenshaw were all wounded by machine gun bullet splashes. Oulton was born and brought up on a farm at Tilstone Fearnall in Lancashire. After serving with the 11th Hussars, he transferred to the Machine Gun Corps and was commissioned into the Tank Corps in March 1917. After the war he returned home to work as a farmer but by 1923 had put the farm up for sale and bought Brassey Green Hall in Tiverton, Cheshire.

A.20 AIRS & GRACES, under the command of Lieutenant Francis Guy Monckton, reached Marcoing without difficulty at 10.50 a.m. before rallying at Marcoing Copse at 2.50 p.m. Monckton was born in Boxley, Kent, in 1891. His father was a partner in a law firm in Maidstone. Francis Monckton was educated at Malvern College, where he joined the Officer

John Carolan Brown

Francis Monckton in later life

Training Corps. Returning to Maidstone, he studied law and enlisted in the Kent Cyclists Battalion as a second lieutenant. He transferred to the Army Service Corps in 1914 and was gazetted lieutenant in October that year. After the war he joined the family firm and later lived at Overstrand Mansions, Battersea Park, in London.

2nd Company

This company was led by Major Patrick William Keating, a career soldier who had been commissioned into the Connaught Rangers in April 1913. He rose to the rank of captain in the 1st Battalion of the Royal Irish Rifles before transferring to the Machine Gun Corps and being promoted to acting major in January 1917. He later served in north Russia.

No. 5 Section

This section was commanded by Captain Eric Dean Blackburn who was wounded at duty. A South African by birth, he was commissioned into the Motor Machine Gun Service in October 1915. For his gallantry at Cambrai he was awarded the Military Cross:

For conspicuous gallantry and devotion to duty. He personally led his section of tanks on foot under heavy shell fire and intense machine-gun fire, and it was entirely due to his complete disregard for danger that they reached their forward position of deployment. He showed the utmost skill in directing over

Patrick William Keating

The Other Officers of 'A' Battalion

extremely difficult ground, and set a fine example of courage and coolness to his section.[9]

In 1918 he was awarded the Distinguished Service Order. The citation read:

> For conspicuous gallantry and devotion to duty when in command of a company of tanks in a counter-attack. He personally led the tanks on foot under heavy machine-gun fire. Again, hearing that the enemy were advancing on a village, he rushed a Lewis gun party up on a lorry, riding forward to reconnoitre, and denied the village to the enemy, on whom he inflicted heavy casualties and took about 20 prisoners. He was responsible for rallying the infantry in the vicinity, and throughout the whole action showed the greatest determination and total disregard for his own safety.[10]

After the war Blackburn became a farmer in Rhodesia.

A.22 AULDREEKIE II was commanded by Lieutenant Lionel Christopher Flanegan, who lost his life on 20 November 1917. He was born in January 1896 at Notting Hill in London. In 1901 the family were living at St Giles, Northamptonshire, but by 1911 they had moved to Great Clacton in Essex.

A local newspaper carried an account of his death:

> Lieutenant Lionel Christopher Flanegan, of the Tank Corps, son of Dr. and Mrs. Flanegan of Wellesley Road, Clacton, was killed in action on November 20. Deceased, who was 21 years of age, left school shortly after war was declared, and passed through the Royal Military College, Sandhurst. He received a commission in the Essex Regiment, and, after seeing service at the Front, transferred to the Tank Corps. It was on the first day of the last great push by the Third Army in Flanders that he met his death.[11]

The subsequent action report was completed by Lance Corporal T. Murdoch who wrote:

195

Tank A.22 AULDREEKIE II moved to Starting Point from whence we started at Zero plus 60 minutes and preceded the 2nd wave of Infantry.

After crossing the Hindenburg Line we came into action with enemy Infantry and Machine Guns, and shortly after about 40 Germans stood up in a trench and surrendered. Soon after this my Officer Lieut. Flanegan was killed by a bullet through a loop-hole. I then put him down out of the car and carried on forward towards Marcoing. On going down the sunken road towards Marcoing we ran into a battery of Field Guns which had knocked out 3 of Number 3 Company's Tanks. We fired at this Battery and succeeded in making the gunners of one gun run away from their gun. However the other gun got in 4 direct hits on my Tank and put it out of action. Shortly after this all the gunners of the Battery having been killed, the Infantry came through. I was then ordered by Major Clough, 2nd in command No. 2 Company, who came up then to stand by, which I did. On the 21st I received orders to go back with my guns to Villers-Plouich.[12]

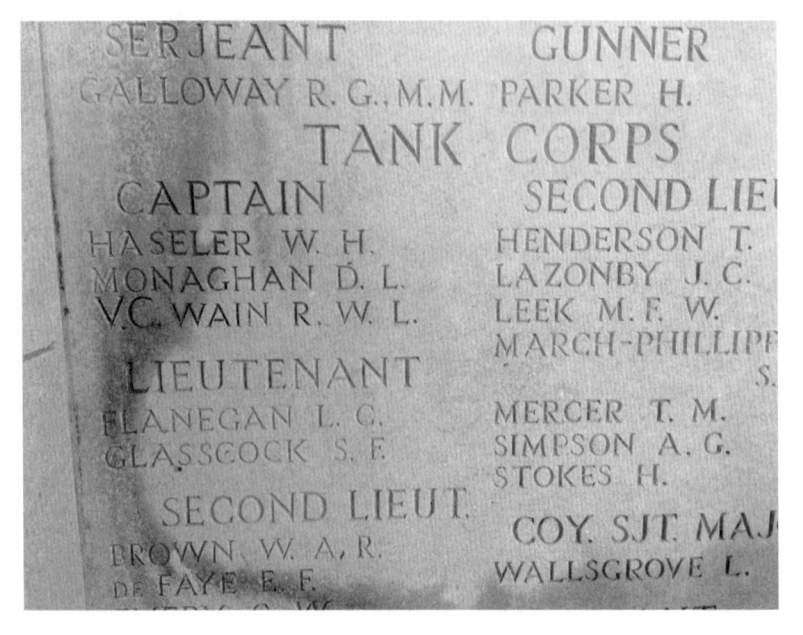

Lionel Flanegan's name just below Richard Wain's

The Other Officers of 'A' Battalion

Lionel Flanegan's body could not be identified later and he is commemorated on the Cambrai Memorial, Louverval, just below Richard Wain's name.

A.23 AVIATIK was hit several times and returned to Villers-Plouich. Second Lieutenant Benjamin Frank John Bradbeer had served in France from April 1917. He later rose to the rank of captain, was mentioned in dispatches and was awarded the Military Cross in 1918:

> For conspicuous gallantry and devotion to duty as company reconnaissance officer. He led the Tanks until the moment they came into action, and rendered invaluable service to his company commander throughout the day.[13]

Bradbeer was from Lowestoft in Suffolk and was educated at Framlingham College in the same county. After the war he was the Chief Assistant Engineer for Surrey County Council. He joined the Territorial branch of the Royal Artillery during the Second World War.

A.25 ARETHUSA was hit several times and was forced to return to Villers-Plouich. Second Lieutenant Edward Francis de Faye was the commander and, although he survived the day, he was killed in action on 1 December 1917.

The third son of Francis and Phoebe de Faye of La Rocque, Jersey, in the Channel Islands, he was born in 1892. After leaving Victoria College at 16, he was a Great Western Railway clerk at Jersey Station before working at the Jersey branch of the London City and Midland Bank. He was a singer of some merit and performed at various concerts on the island.

In July 1915 he enlisted in the Ambulance Corps of the Motor Transport Section and served in France from September 1915, later working as a mechanic in the Army Service Corps. Commissioned into the Machine Gun Corps in January 1917, both he and his driver were killed when their tank received a direct hit as it was returning from action in Gauche

Wood, Gouzeaucourt. He is commemorated on the Cambrai Memorial.

His senior officer wrote of him:

> I never had a better officer, an example to all, always cool and determined under fire, a general favourite, the life and soul of our mess. We shall miss him terribly.[14]

A.24 ARISTOTLE II was commanded by the Section Commander, Captain Blackburn. He and the driver were uninjured when their tank was hit by a shell from a field gun at close range but the rest of the crew were all badly wounded; Lieutenant John Richard Rodgers was killed. The action report stated:

> On night of 20/21st [sic] Tanks moved up into position at Starting Point, this was accomplished according to Schedule. At Zero minus 10 minutes, the Tanks moved off followed by the Infantry. I was leading my Section in Lieut. Rodgers's tank A.24. Direction was very hard to keep, but I hit Farm Trench at the right spot and proceeded down the communication trench. At the Hindenburg Line I swung right instead of left owing to intense machine Gun Fire coming from the right. When we had silenced these Machine Guns I headed along the Hindenburg Line, and leaving my other two Tanks to clear up these lines I went straight for the Canal Crossings at Marcoing.
>
> When well into the German Lines we saw a party of about 30 Germans go into what

Edward de Faye

The Other Officers of 'A' Battalion

looked like a trench and dug-out so we headed for these. When about 15 yards from the dug-out we received direct hits from a Field Gun at close range, and the Tank caught fire. We were forced to evacuate it, and took shelter in a shallow trench, all the crew being badly wounded, with the exception of myself and the 1st Driver, who were both slightly wounded. Lieut. Rodgers was killed in the open about 40 yards from the Tank. We had to be quiet for about half an hour until the Infantry came up and the Germans retired.[15]

John Richard Rodgers was born John Lay in St Pancras, London, in 1895. He was also known as John Willcock. Later adopted by Beaumont and Matilda Rodgers of Emsworth, Hampshire, he was educated at Westbrook House School in Emsworth and was subsequently employed as a printing compositor. He then trained as a journalist before enlisting as a private in the Inns of Court Officer Training Corps in London in June 1915. He was commissioned into the Hampshire Regiment in October of that year. On Christmas Eve 1915 Matilda Rodgers, by now a widow, was knocked down by a motor car. John attended her bedside but she died of her injuries and shock a few days later. John is remembered on the Cambrai Memorial to the Missing.

No. 6 Section

Captain Frank Murray Maxwell Hallowell Carew was the section commander. He served in France and Flanders in the Machine Gun Corps from July 1915 until transferring to the Tank Corps, where he was later promoted to major. He was awarded the Military Cross for his work on the first day of the Third Battle of Ypres:

> For conspicuous gallantry and devotion to duty during the operations on July 31, 1917. He personally led his section of tanks on foot to its objective in the vicinity of Westhoek, although they were being subjected the whole time to very heavy shelling and

199

intense machine-gun fire. This officer showed great coolness and courage, going from tank to tank and helping them out of difficulties. It was entirely due to his total disregard for personal danger when leading his tanks that they were enabled to reach the infantry when they were held up on the Westhoek Ridge. Before the action he carried out several good reconnaissances under heavy shell fire.[16]

Lieutenant Kenneth Wootton described his actions thus: 'Captain Carew, our section commander, dashed madly about to try and get our tank up to an impossible speed. He imagined a tank could behave like a new motor car.'[17]

Born in Ferryside, Carmarthenshire, in 1866, Carew led a very colourful life. He was divorced by his wife Edith in 1892 who described him as a man 'of loose pursuits, who favoured the companionship of prizefighters, frequenters of racecourses and loose ladies who indulged in the midnight amusements of dancing saloons'.[18] In 1921 he was shot in the arm in Dublin by an I.R.A. man while serving as an Auxiliary. He survived the shooting and was awarded the M.B.E. in 1923.

A.27 ABERDONIA II was commanded by Captain James Percy Thompson who was commissioned into the 5th Northumberland Fusiliers before joining the Tank Corps. He had served on the Western Front since April 1916. Wounded in action, he was mentioned in the *London Gazette* on 20 March 1919. He lived at Lydford Road, Willesden Green, in London.

The report of the action stated:

Frank Carew

The Other Officers of 'A' Battalion

When the Aberdonia II reached R.4.a. the first opposition was met, the right Lewis Gun and the foremost Lewis Gun came into action and fired at a party of 30 to 40 Germans at a range of 400 yards: this party was completely disposed of as none surrendered in time.

The Aberdonia II then advanced and knocked out 2 Machine Guns which were firing on the Tank. The Lewis Guns now onwards fired several times at small parties of retreating enemy.

The Aberdonia II was now at L.34.c. and came within range of a Field Battery. The Aberdonia II passed the Adventuress II which had just been hit and got 50 yards nearer the enemy battery firing its Lewis Guns at the Crew of the Battery as far as observation permitted. The Tank then received a direct hit on the inside of the Left Idler Sprocket which badly bent the nose of the Tank and smashed the Track, which however held together by one pin. Captain Thompson was very badly wounded: Gunner Smith the driver was blinded but attempted to continue driving: Smith had to stop driving but in spite of being blinded, and hit around the eyes he changed over to the brakesman's seat and eventually had to be pulled down by one of the crew.[19]

A.28 ADVENTURESS became entangled in the German barbed wire. Second Lieutenant Thomas James Shaw was the commander. He was awarded the Military Cross twice. His first citation read:

> For conspicuous gallantry and devotion to duty. In the attack on Marcoing on November 20, 1917, he displayed great skill and determination in getting his tank to its objective. On the way he silenced many enemy machine-guns. Later, in attacking an enemy field battery, his tank received two direct hits. On December 1, 1917, he commanded a tank in a composite section. His tank successfully attacked Gauche Wood and put several enemy machine-guns out of action. He then, unsupported by either infantry or other tanks, proceeded to Villers-Guislan. The enemy were concentrated here, apparently massing for a counter-attack. Although under very heavy shell and machine-gun fire, he brought a destructive fire from his 6-pndr. guns to bear on the enemy, inflicting very severe casualties. As no support was forthcoming,

201

he returned to fetch reinforcements. None were available, so his section commander ordered him to 'stand by'. This officer's example was a splendid inspiration to all ranks in a most difficult situation.[20]

He won his second Military Cross:

For great devotion to duty in the operations in the vicinity of Beaucourt-en-Santerre on August 8 and 9, 1918, when in command of a tank. He did great damage to the enemy and destroyed many machine-gun posts which were holding up our advance, and greatly assisted the infantry in consolidating their line by the skilful manoeuvring of his tank. During action he was under most intense machine-gun fire and his tank was riddled. By his skill and courage he emerged from action with his crew and tank complete. His coolness under fire was an example to all.[21]

After the war Shaw studied at Seale-Hayne Agricultural College, near Newton Abbot in Devon.

A.29 APOLLYON II received a direct hit and was stopped. The tank was commanded by Second Lieutenant Kenneth Edwin Wootton. In his later account of the day he wrote:

We moved forward over fairly even ground at about 4 miles per hour. The noise inside was absolutely deafening; the eight-cylinder engine was going at full speed, both six-pounder guns were firing as rapidly as possible and I was emptying drum after drum from the machine-gun. Any order I gave to Fagg – the driver – who was close beside me, had to be shouted in his ear and any order to the NCO – Sergeant Harkness – was given in a similar manner. Everything else had to be done by signs.

After driving over such impossible ground as we had been doing in Belgium, where even a few yards might cause endless difficulties and delays and often completely hold you up, this ground on Welsh Ridge seemed almost like an ordinary field and was, in fact, actually so in most places, except for trenches, gun-pits and so on with shell holes fairly widely distributed and almost entirely absent over quite long stretches.

The Other Officers of 'A' Battalion

> The periscope usually used was one that you pushed through a hole in the roof of the cab over your head. Owing to the fascine on top, this was not possible. I now and again lifted the flap on my side and very cautiously peered out to see if anything was in front of us. As the light was by now improving, things gradually became more or less distinct through the morning haze. So I crossed no man's land, dividing the time between firing off the Lewis gun, peering out the flap and shouting to Fagg.[22]

When Wootton reached the German front-line trench he drove along the parapet as ordered, machine-gunning the occupants. Once the trench was cleared he ordered the driver to halt the tank.

> Telling the Serjeant to keep the tank there till I returned, I cautiously opened the door of the left sponson… and peered out. Then, drawing my revolver, I jumped down from the doorway, ran round the back of the tank and leaped down into the trench. There was no one to be seen in the trench, so I turned to the right and quickly but cautiously made my way down the trench and, after passing one or two traverses, came upon a few of the Infantry that had made the attack with us; they were extremely cheerful and said they had got into the trenches very easily and did not think they had had any men either killed or wounded.
> On rounding a bend, I found myself facing a large man about to lunge at me with his bayonet and I, pointing my revolver at him; we stood like this for a second and then realised we were friends instead of enemies, we both exclaimed something like 'all right – British', in a very relieved tone. He said he had heard me coming and thought I was a Jerry. I was wearing no hat which made matters worse, quite against the regulations, but I couldn't stand shrapnel helmets. We wore no hat inside a tank and I had omitted to put one on.[23]

Wootton returned to his tank and ordered it forward.

> We had to cross one very deep and wide trench and made ready to lower the fascine into it but the driver had spotted a small flag

stuck into the top of this trench and had driven for it. We found it was marking the spot where a tank had already dropped its fascine and so we rode out over that one and kept ours in its position. We resumed our position in line with the others and, after assuring myself that we were now well up, by looking through the portholes on the left and right, I once more pushed a Lewis gun through the ball-mounting in front of me.

I fired at anything I could see that looked like a target, any rise in the ground, trench, bush, anything that might shelter someone, and I dropped most of the empty drums out of the flap in front. By now the inside of the tank was terribly hot, caused by the engine chiefly and the air was heavy and close and caught your throat when you breathed; this, owing to the back-blast of the two guns and the ejector of the machine-gun and the noise was appalling. The driver had the worst of it, as the Lewis gun ejected its empty cartridge cases a few inches from his left ear. Poor Fagg was worried by this a great deal, as I could see by his expression every time I put on a fresh drum.[24]

Wootton then spotted an enemy battery.

I saw one gun, with a few men by it, not far away from us and turned the machine-gun on them. My six-pounder gunner on the right side had also seen it. I remember seeing the burst of his shell a short distance behind them... Evidently my machine-gun and the six-pounder were too much for them, as they bolted off almost at once without apparently any of them being hit... I should say the six-pounder was the thing that terrified them most, as it was firing at a point-blank range, just suitable for it. Johns was the gunner on that side. He was a deadly shot – having put a shell into the opening of a pill-box at Ypres – and was probably dead on target. So that gun was captured. It was annoying not to be able to actually get it ourselves, but we couldn't stop, so had to leave it for others.

Soon after we came almost face to face with at least four more guns, also in the open. All pointing in our direction. I remember noticing that some of the guns were unmanned, but one, at any rate, was still working. Whether I had time to fire at it I do not remember but they fired at me, just point-blank and the shell struck us in front just where I was sitting and, bursting as it hit, blew a hole in the armour-plating by my left knee.

The first thing that made me realise we had been hit was 'coming to', finding myself lying back over my seat with my head nearly on the floor and my left foot caught in something so that I couldn't move it. With the help of Fagg, I got into a sitting position and freed my foot, which was caught under the brake lever. I felt no pain of any sort, being dazed and numb all over, with a tremendous sort of singing noise in both ears and some blood running into my left eye, which I wiped with my hand now and then. I slid back off the seat and sank to the floor, having no use in my legs or arms, but still feeling nothing.[25]

Six of his crew were also wounded.[26]

Kenneth Wootton was subsequently awarded the Military Cross for his actions. The citation stated:

For conspicuous gallantry and devotion to duty in the operations near Marcoing on November 20, 1917. His tank was the leading tank of his section, and he skilfully guided it along its exact route, putting many enemy machine-guns out of action on the way. It was due to his exceptional skill and determination that the infantry working with his section were enabled to obtain their objective with very few casualties. Later he attacked an enemy field gun at very close range. He was finally very badly wounded and his tank put out of action by receiving a direct hit from an enemy field battery which he was engaging.[27]

Kenneth Wootton

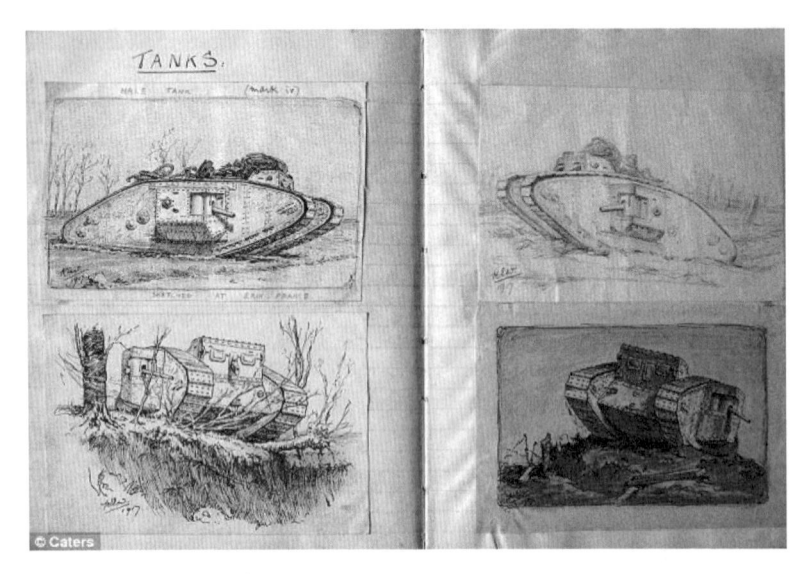

Wootton's drawings of tanks

The son of a professor of Chemistry at the London College of Pharmacy, Kenneth Wootton was born in 1885 and studied at the Royal Academy of Art between 1905 and 1910. He was then employed as an art teacher by the London County Council until he gained a commission in the London Regiment in 1915, and served in France from December 1916 before transferring to the Tank Corps. After being wounded at Cambrai, he spent time recovering in a hospital at Rouen. He married in April 1918 and after the war ended he and his wife settled in Coventry, where he taught at Bablake School and continued to draw and paint.

A.30 ARGYLLE was disabled on 20 November but was repaired two days afterwards. Second Lieutenant Philip Hardy was serving as a serjeant with the 9th Battalion of the Canadian Infantry when he applied for a commission in the Tank Corps, which he received on 30 January 1917. Born in Croydon, Surrey, he had emigrated to Canada with his parents before the war began. He worked as an architect and pre-war had served for four years in the 1st Battalion of the

Hertford Regiment before re-enlisting in July 1915. After the war he lived in De Lisle Road, Bournemouth.

No. 7 Section

This section was commanded by Captain James Gerald Fitzmaurice, who was wounded at duty. Born in 1893, he served with the Royal Munster Fusiliers before being attached to the Tank Corps. He was twice mentioned in dispatches and in January 1919 was awarded the Military Cross. He remained in the Tank Corps post-war and was killed at Dunkirk on 21 May 1940 while commanding the 4th Royal Tank Regiment as Lieutenant-Colonel when the tank he was in was hit by a shell from a German field gun. The night before he died he had insisted a subaltern take the remaining bed in their billets while he slept on the floor. James Fitzmaurice was buried in Dunkirk Town Cemetery.

A.31 ARIADNE was commanded by Second Lieutenant James Shutt Riley. Born in Accrington on Boxing Day 1887, in 1908 he travelled to Constantinople as the representative of Messrs. F. Steiner and Co., Calico Printers, returning to England just before war began. Riley enlisted in the Royal Field Artillery in October 1915 and was commissioned into the Tank Corps in February 1917. He was promoted to captain in August 1918 and was killed just a few days later near Chilly on 10 August. A fellow officer wrote:

James Fitzmaurice

on in command of a section of Tanks. His body
it of the line of attack; he had evidently led his
ince of anyone else when he was killed. He was
of mine, and was exceedingly popular with
s loss is keenly felt.[28]

Another officer wrote: 'He was always good nature and cheerfulness personified, and I cannot say how much we miss him in the company.'[29]

A.32 ANNE II received six hits and was destroyed. It was commanded by Serjeant Leonard Cory Lose. Lose, an insurance official from Plymouth who had served as a Territorial in the Devonshire Regiment for four years, had enlisted in the Machine Gun Corps in February 1916. Two months later he was promoted to lance corporal and by August 1916 was a serjeant. Awarded the Military Medal, he was rejected for a commission in July 1918.

A.33 ACE II was commanded by Second Lieutenant John Dennis Goulty MacFadyen. The son of a church minister, he was from Letchworth and was educated at Highgate and Rossall schools, obtaining an open scholarship in History at Magdalen College, Cambridge, before enlisting in the Tank Corps. He served on the Western Front from April 1917 until he was killed during the Battle of Amiens on 8 August 1918, aged 20. John MacFadyen was buried in Hourges Orchard Cemetery, Domart-sur-la-Luce.

Awarded the Military Cross for his work during the Battle of Amiens, the citation read:

> For conspicuous gallantry and devotion to duty. On his own initiative he made four separate attacks on the advancing enemy, inflicting on them on each occasion very heavy losses. Though subjected to a very heavy bombardment at close range, during which period his Tank was on two occasions hit by shells, he nevertheless succeeded in keeping it running, and rendered invaluable assistance to the infantry with whom he was co-operating. His courage and dash were most marked.[30]

The Other Officers of 'A' Battalion

A.34 ALBATROSS was commanded by Second Lieutenant Guy Vickers Trehane Dingle who was born in Malvern in 1898, the son of a wine and spirit merchant from Australia. He was awarded the Military Cross in 1918:

> For great gallantry and devotion to duty in the operations near Beaucourt-en-Santerre on August 8, 1918, when in command of a tank. He showed great skill and courage in dealing with enemy machine-gun posts, which were holding up and inflicting severe casualties on the infantry. When he reached his objective he patrolled in front of the infantry for five hours and ran the greatest risks in manoeuvering his tank to take hostile fire. On August 9, 1918, he was again in action, and although wounded he continued to fight his tank until it caught fire and he was compelled to evacuate it. Throughout the operations he showed most splendid courage and devotion to duty.[31]

Dingle was commissioned into the Wiltshire Regiment in January 1917 and seconded to Tank Corps. Promoted to lieutenant in July 1918, he was also mentioned in dispatches and remained in the Army post-war. He reached the rank of captain in May 1920 and retired in June 1922. When the Second World War broke out he rejoined the Army but tragedy was to follow. In December 1939 it was reported in a newspaper:

> Inquest on shot Army officer. A verdict that he died from a gunshot wound, self-inflicted during a sudden impulse brought on by mental depression, was returned by the Wiltshire county coroner at an inquest held on Lieut. Guy Vickers Trehane Dingle, a 42-year-old Army officer, whose dead body with a wound in his head was discovered by his batman in the early hours of Wednesday morning. Deceased's batman told the coroner that he had known Dingle to be depressed. He was on the Regular Army Reserve of Officers and rejoined in June last. He had been acting as messing officer, and his duties in this respect seemed 'to worry him quite a bit'. A revolver was found underneath the body. Dr Seggers said deceased had a wound in the forehead and another in the roof of his mouth.[32]

NO. 8 SECTION was charged with wire pulling and was commanded by Captain James Percy Thomson of the Northumberland Fusiliers, attached to the Tank Corps. He was wounded in the head and evacuated to a hospital in London for treatment. Born in 1888 in East Cowick, Yorkshire, he survived the war but his older brother Samuel was killed at Ploegsteert in April 1918.

A.36 was burnt out. The commander was Lieutenant William Patrick Burns who served with the East Lancashire Regiment before transferring to the Tank Corps. Later promoted to captain, he was awarded the Military Cross in June 1919. He was born in Salford, Lancashire, and worked as a clerk in the family drapery business before enlisting. Burns served in France and Flanders from December 1916 and was also mentioned in dispatches.

A.37 was also burnt out. It was commanded by Second Lieutenant George Herbert Dudley who had only arrived in France in September. He was born in Dudley, Staffordshire, in 1881 and was a schoolmaster in Meersbrook, Sheffield, before enlisting.

A.38 Unknown

A.39 suffered mechanical trouble. The commander, Second Lieutenant George R. Pettigrew, was born in Glasgow in 1896 and had served in the 16th Royal Scots before being commissioned into the Tank Corps in May 1917.

3rd Company

Major Michael Lawrence Lakin commanded this company. The son of Sir Michael Henry Lakin, he was a career soldier who joined the Army in 1900 and fought in the Boer War. Promoted to captain in 1908, he retired in 1911 but on the outbreak of war rejoined his old regiment, the 11th (Prince Albert's Own) Hussars. Twice mentioned in dispatches, he was awarded the Distinguished Service Order in 1915 for distinguished service in the field. Transferred to the Machine

The Other Officers of 'A' Battalion

Michael Lakin

Gun Corps in January 1917, in 1918 he won the Military Cross:

For conspicuous gallantry and devotion to duty in operations, whilst commanding a company of tanks. He led his company across most difficult country, and successfully held up the enemy for ten hours. Later, when fighting on foot a rearguard action with Lewis guns, he remained behind the infantry, who had retired, for eight hours, inflicting severe losses on the enemy. Throughout he displayed an absolute disregard of danger, and his splendid example greatly encouraged all ranks with him.[33]

Lakin survived the war and resigned his commission in November 1920. In 1918 he bought Horetown House, a country mansion in Wexford, Ireland. Tragically, his wife died in a hunting accident in 1930, and his son, Captain Gerald Lakin, died of his wounds in North Africa in 1943. The Lakins were descendants of Henry VII.

No. 9 Section

This section was commanded by Captain George H. Ingham who was awarded the Military Cross:

> For conspicuous gallantry and devotion to duty in the operations near Nine Wood and Noyelles on November 20–21, 1917. On November 20, 1917, Captain Ingham was in the leading tank of his section, and led the attack on Nine Wood and Noyelles. His tanks

211

put many enemy machine-guns out of action and inflicted very heavy casualties, thus enabling the infantry with whom he was working to gain their objectives with very few losses and in good time. It was entirely due to his brilliant and gallant leadership that, whenever the advance of the infantry was held up, a tank appeared and cleared the situation. Particularly was this the case with a machine-gun on the outskirts of Noyelles which was holding up our advance. A tank appeared from behind the machine-gun and with two shots from its 6-pndrs. put the gun out of action. On November 21, 1917, this officer's section again went into action and rendered excellent service to our infantry and inflicted heavy casualties on the enemy. On both days Captain Ingham led his section with great gallantry and skill, and brought all his tanks successfully out of action.[34]

Ingham was promoted to the rank of major before the end of the war and later lived at Caerau Crescent, Newport, Monmouthshire. He was employed as an electrical engineer by Newport Borough Council.

A.41 AUTOGOPHASTA was commanded by Second Lieutenant John Edgar Jones who lived at 25 Romilly Road, Barry, not many miles from where Richard Wain was born, and they would undoubtedly have shared many memories of the local area. Jones was awarded the Military Cross in 1918:

> For most conspicuous bravery and devotion to duty during operations with the French on Hangard Wood on April 28, 1918. On April 27 this officer made a very thorough reconnaissance, under very heavy shell fire, of the area in which he was to operate. On April 28 he took his tank into action against the enemy machine-gun strongpoints in the western edge of Hangard Wood, which were harassing the infantry, and successfully dealt with these, inflicting very heavy casualties on the enemy. This gallant officer was severely wounded shortly after going into action, but, with great courage and perseverance, he continued to fight his tank until his task was accomplished. He set a splendid example to his crew throughout the operations.[35]

The Other Officers of 'A' Battalion

A.42 ATLANTIC This tank was commanded by Second Lieutenant Ernest John Urquhart, from Fife, who had served as a private in the Army Service Corps in France and Flanders from July 1915 until he was commissioned into the Machine Gun Corps in April 1917. His tank reached Marcoing after having been in action for nine hours. The following day he advanced through Marcoing towards the German trenches outside Rumilly. In his later report Urquhart noted that several armour-piercing bullets entered the tank, silencing five of his Lewis guns and forcing him to withdraw, but not before he had accounted for several German machine guns and a good number of infantry.[36]

A.44 AHMED II Lieutenant Arthur Ellerson Paxton-Hall, its commander, was born in 1894 in Essex. He served on the Western Front with the Essex Regiment and the Tank Corps from July 1916, and after the war lived at Carisbrooke Road, Walthamstow. His tank reached Marcoing on 20 November and went into action the following day with A.42. He wrote in his later report:

> The enemy second line was crossed and though the Tank was under very intense fire, the gunners continued at their guns till the ammunition was exhausted. Soon afterwards another four of the crew (his first driver having been hit earlier in the attack) fell victims to armour-piercing bullets, and were too badly wounded to be of use as gunners. We then turned and made for the Rallying Point Marcoing Station, and reached there about 3.30 p.m. All the crew were wounded, five so seriously as to render their admittance to hospital imperative. It is difficult to make distinctions as regards bravery and devotion to duty shewn by every member of the crew, for all acted with great promptitude under all circumstances, including the extinction of a fire.[37]

A.45 ASTICA was commanded by Second Lieutenant George Matthews who had served as a private in the 4th Hussars in France and Flanders from 17 October 1915 until

213

he was commissioned into the Welsh Regiment on 11 October 1916. He transferred to the Tank Corps and rose to the rank of captain. Matthews lived at North Side, Wandsworth Common, London.

He was awarded the Military Cross for his service at Cambrai. His citation read:

> For conspicuous gallantry and devotion to duty in the operations near Noyelles on November 20, 1917. Five of the members of his crew had been wounded when his tank caught fire, and although surrounded by the enemy and under very heavy fire he, with the help only of his N.C.O., kept the gun going and inflicted heavy losses on the enemy. On four other occasions his tank caught fire during the action. When all his Lewis guns were put out of action he continued to fight with his 6-pndrs. until all the ammunition had been expended. He then, with the aid of his N.C.O. and first driver, successfully brought his tank out of action. Throughout the whole of the operation he set a fine example to his crew.[38]

He was later awarded a bar to his Military Cross:

> For conspicuous gallantry and devotion to duty in the operations on August 8, 1918, near Beaucourt-en-Santerre. He commanded a section of tanks and led them towards their objective under very heavy machine-gun fire. He co-operated successfully with other crews, and to a very great extent was responsible for the splendid work done by his section. Throughout the day he set a very fine example to all ranks by his coolness and bravery under fire.[39]

No. 10 Section

This section was led by Captain Cecil Oliver Rich, who was wounded. After serving as a private in the 28th London Regiment on the Western Front from 11 August 1915, he was commissioned into the Wiltshire Regiment in September 1916, before transferring to the Tank Corps.

The Other Officers of 'A' Battalion

Cecil Rich

He was awarded the Military Cross for the second time for his work at Cambrai. The citation stated:

> For conspicuous gallantry and devotion to duty in the operations near Marcoing on November 20, 1917. This officer led his section into action with great skill and coolness. After advancing about 2,000 yards, a masked field battery opened fire on the tanks at about 100 yards range. In spite of the fact that one tank was almost immediately put out of action and he himself very seriously wounded, Captain Rich carried on and effectively silenced the battery, thus enabling the infantry to continue their advance. This officer set a splendid example to all ranks of his section and paid no regard to his own personal safety.[40]

Rich had previously won the Military Cross while serving with the Wiltshire Regiment:

> For conspicuous gallantry and devotion to duty. He continually carried out daring patrols of the enemy's wire, and the success of a raiding party was largely due to his information.[41]

Born in Crowthorne, Berkshire, in 1891, he was later the Headmaster of Kingswood College, Grahamstown, Eastern Cape, South Africa.

A.46 ARTIMUS II was commanded by Second Lieutenant James Timmis who had served as a private with the Royal Army Medical Corps in France and Flanders from July 1915 until he was commissioned into the Machine Gun Corps in April 1917. His tank led the way on the morning of 20 November and attacked an enemy field battery at about 200 yards range, destroying one of the guns. It was then hit twice by German shells and caught fire, the crew evacuating the tank.

A.47 AMAZON Its commander, Second Lieutenant Harold Rushforth, had arrived in France on 9 August 1917. His tank developed engine trouble and broke down.

Harold Rushforth had served as a Tank Commander at the Third Battle of Ypres and was later promoted to lieutenant. He was with Captain Clement Robertson on 3 October 1917, the last night before the tanks went into action, putting down the white tape for the tanks to follow. Robertson was to win a posthumous Victoria Cross for his actions the following day.

Rushforth lived in Grimsby and was a steam trawler owner's clerk before enlisting in the Lincolnshire Regiment in December 1915. After a period of Home Service, he was commissioned into the Machine Gun Corps at the end of January 1917. He was wounded at Cambrai on November 23 and suffered from shell-shock which ended his military service at the age of 20. He once told his grandson a story that at Cambrai their tank destroyed a German tank after which the German officer attacked the tank, firing his revolver until he was shot and killed. 'The bravest thing I ever saw,' he said.[42] His brother Benjamin was killed in action in August 1918.

A.48 ABDULLAH The commander, Second Lieutenant Charles Ralph Campbell, was wounded. He served in the 2nd Life Guards before transferring to the Tank Corps. His tank received two direct hits and was set on fire, forcing him and his crew to evacuate.

The Other Officers of 'A' Battalion

More correctly known as Sir Charles Ralph Campbell of Auchinbreck, 12th Baronet, he was born in 1881 and in 1915 married Nancy Chapman from Canterbury, New Zealand. They lived in Christchurch, New Zealand, post-war. He had inherited the title after his older brother was killed in 1915.

A.50 AUTOWIN II Second Lieutenant John Charles Turvey was also wounded. Born in 1895, he resided in Ilford, Essex, before joining the Royal Navy. As an able seaman he transferred to the Tank Corps and by the end of the war had risen to the rank of captain. His tank was hit three times, damaging the right sponson and gun and stopping the engine. The crew evacuated safely.

John Charles Turvey

No. 11 Section

The commander was Captain David Taunton Raikes, who reported after the battle:

> On the morning of the 21st the Infantry holding the line asked me for my three Tanks to help them in the attack on the line of trenches running from Flot Farm to Rumilly at 11 o'clock... They did not finally move up until 12.30 p.m. and, as soon as they came into view, they came under heavy Machine Gun fire. Having got up to the trenches, they found that the enemy had concentrated a very large number of machine guns during the night and the effect of their fire on the Tanks was so great that out of the two Tanks 2/Lt. Wright's ANGELINA II and 2/Lt. Johnston's ADSUM II I had 7 Lewis Guns put out of action, both the Officers and 10 men wounded and one Tank with nearly 100 holes through it, with Armour-Piercing Bullets.[43]

217

Raikes served with the South Wales Borderers but was seconded to 'A' Battalion of the Tank Corps. He was awarded the Distinguished Service Order in 1918:

> For conspicuous gallantry in action at Marcoing on November 20 and 21, while in command of a section of tanks. During the afternoon of November 20 this officer controlled the movement of his section of tanks under heavy machine-gun fire with absolute disregard for his personal safety. He got out of his tank at least a dozen times to give instructions to the tank commanders, in spite of the fact that his tank was on most occasions subjected to machine-gun fire and the intervening space between the tanks was entirely devoid of cover and in full view of the enemy. Again, on November 21, under similar conditions, he directed his own section of tanks and also nine others who were in need of confirmation as to the situation. Throughout the two days' fighting, he never rested as long as his services could be of any use, and his utter disregard for danger and his great cheerfulness throughout set a fine example to all ranks.[44]

He had previously been awarded the Military Cross and was to win it again in 1918. His first citation for his work at the Third Battle of Ypres stated:

> For conspicuous gallantry and devotion to duty during the operations on July 31, 1917. He personally led his tanks to their objective near Surbiton Villa under heavy shell and machine gun fire. When progress became otherwise impossible, he got into a tank, which soon afterwards received a direct hit, which killed the tank commander and wounded most of the crew. He then went forward, on foot, with the remaining tanks and directed them towards enemy machine-gun emplacements and silenced the guns. When three of his four tanks were placed out of action, he organised a party and salved all the Lewis guns, again under very heavy fire.[45]

The citation for his second Military Cross read:

The Other Officers of 'A' Battalion

David Raikes

During the advance beyond Villers-Bretonneux on August 8, this officer displayed quite exceptional courage, initiative, and devotion to duty. He closely followed his company on foot, horseback, and bicycle, as he found the means, redirecting his tanks as the situation demanded. On August 10, near Fouquescourt, he displayed the same high soldierly qualities in superintending the operations. Throughout the operations from August 8 to 15 this officer has been continually reconnoitring and doing good work in the front area with an utter disregard to danger, and frequently under very heavy machine-gun and shell fire. His example to all has been quite exceptional, and his initiative and untiring energy have rivalled any in my recollection.[46]

Born in London in 1897, Raikes was an amateur rower and rowing coach.

A. 52 ARTFUL ALICE II Second Lieutenant Cyril James Charles was born in Bosham, Sussex, in 1891, and was employed as a junior draughtsman at the Vulcan Works in Paisley before enlisting in the 17th Royal Fusiliers. He was promoted to serjeant before being commissioned into the Tank Corps in June 1917. Mentioned in dispatches, he had served on the Western Front since November 1915. After the war ended he was promoted to lieutenant and served in the Tank Workshops Training Battalion at Bovington Camp.

A.53 ANGELINA II Its commander, Second Lieutenant Alfred Wright, was promoted through the ranks of the Machine

Gun Corps to a commission in the Tank Corps on 27 June 1917. He lived in Tunstall, Stoke-on-Trent, and was a winch worker in a local colliery before enlisting. In his report Wright wrote: 'Four of the Crew and myself were wounded by splinters through 6-Pdr. Slits and loopholes.'[47]

A.54 ADSUM II Second Lieutenant William Johnston stated: 'Six of the Crew and myself were wounded by Armour-Piercing Bullets, which came through the side and sponsons.'[48] Johnston, from Portrush in County Antrim, had served in France and Flanders since the second week of August 1917. He rose to the rank of captain and survived the war.

A.55 AGGRESSIVE II was commanded by Second Lieutenant John Kenneth Lipscomb who was captured by the Germans, and survived his period of captivity to return to his home in Swanley, Kent. He was mentioned in dispatches in December 1917 and was released by the Germans on 18 December 1918. His tank had received a direct hit from an artillery shell which badly wounded him, shattering his right arm and inflicting severe wounds to his right side and face. His serjeant and two other crewmen assisted him back towards the British lines but he collapsed when 150 yards away. The men went to get a stretcher to carry him the rest of the way but when they returned the Germans had advanced, meaning he could not be recovered. He was initially reported as missing, presumed dead.

John Lipscomb survived the war and in his later years he was a resident at Holy Cross Priory in East Sussex where he gained praise for his work as a gardener – an occupation which perhaps gave him some solace after the terrible suffering he had experienced during the Great War.

No. 12 Section

Commanded by Captain Eric Charles Heaton Shillaker, it did not attack on 20 November. Shillaker was born in 1894 in Islington, London, and studied at Cambridge University before

The Other Officers of 'A' Battalion

being commissioned into the 1/5th West Yorkshire Regiment in July 1915. In 1938 he was the Managing Director of General Motors U.K. before re-enlisting in the Army and serving during the Second World War. Shillaker was awarded the Military Cross in 1916:

> For conspicuous gallantry and determination. He volunteered for a dangerous reconnaissance, and on reaching the enemy parapet was wounded in two places by bullets and received about ten shrapnel wounds. He hid for a time in a shell hole, and then coolly completed his reconnaissance alone, bringing back a valuable report.[49]

Shillaker had taken over command of the section on the death in action of Captain Clement Robertson V.C. the previous month. Several of the officers in this section had served alongside Robertson during his V.C. action. Within three minutes of the start of the attack on 4 October, A.60 was hit. Second Lieutenant Hunnikin and his crew attempted to repair the damage, which included a crack in the fuel line, but Robertson pushed on with his remaining tanks.

Lieutenant Foxwell, in command of tank A.58, reported later: 'Captain Robertson guided me along the path through Polygon Wood until I could clearly see the fortified road towards De Reutel.'[50] After disposing of several German machine gun posts, his tank was hit and disabled. The crew evacuated and made their way back on foot.

Tank A.59, commanded by Second Lieutenant Ehrhardt, also knocked out several enemy machine gun nests but eventually the tank became stuck and the crew was forced to evacuate. Nevertheless, Ehrhardt and his men continued to fight alongside the infantry for two further hours.

A.56 AMAZON II Its commander, Second Lieutenant Alexander Grove, had served as a private in the Yorkshire Regiment before being commissioned into the Machine Gun Corps on 23 November 1916. He was born in Chesham in

Alexander Grove

Buckinghamshire in 1891 and trained as a school teacher at St Peter's College, Peterborough. After enlisting in the Princess of Wales's Own (Yorkshire Regiment), he was commissioned into the Heavy Branch of the Machine Gun Corps in November 1916. He spent three months in hospital following this and was operated on twice for appendicitis, marrying the nurse who cared for him in August 1917, before taking part in the Battle of Cambrai.

He wrote in his diary:

> Monday, 19 November 1917 – Cleaning up all day – made things a bit like business – at 6.0 moved off on approach march to Beaucamp – ditched for 20 mins. – slept on and off until 4 – went to see Brigade Commander. Waited until 9 a.m.
>
> Tuesday 20 November – Attacked at dawn – barrage at 6.20 – tanks advanced splendidly – saw the whole show – attached to 86 Brigade Staff for wireless – saw Ribécourt attacked and taken – moved on to Marcoing on 4th speed and erected installation. Slept in Amazon. Marcoing taken and cavalry through Noyelles.
>
> Wednesday, 21 November – Magnificent success – Lipscombe and Wain killed – Turvey, Rich, Campbell wounded – many of the men killed and wounded. Saw Urquhart and Jones – looked 'done up'. Moved my 'bus after dismantling my wireless Near one with a 5.9. Bed 11.0.
>
> Thursday, 22 November – Much easier day today – greased up and filled up again ready for action – warned to 'stand by'

The Other Officers of 'A' Battalion

– Germans holding line east and west of Noyelles – cavalry do dismounted duty – 9th Lancers and 19th Hussars came up. Bed 11.0.[51]

A.58 ALBION II was commanded by Lieutenant Victor Henry Glandfield Foxwell, who was born in Clapham, London, in 1897. A former student of Eastbourne College, he was commissioned into the Essex Regiment in January 1916 and served on the Western Front from August that year. Attached to the Heavy Branch of the Machine Gun Corps in December 1916, he commanded his tank at the Third Ypres on 4 October 1917 and remained in the Army after the war ended.

A.59 AMBROSIA II Second Lieutenant John Albert Ehrhardt represents all too clearly one of those absurdities of war. He was born in Ludwigshafen, Germany, in 1898, the son of a research chemist and an English mother. Educated at his uncle's English School in Heidelberg, when he was 12 the family moved to Merseyside where his father continued his work as a research chemist. John and his three brothers all attended King Edward's School in Birmingham.

When the war began the family was in Germany visiting relatives and just managed to return to England. Dr Ehrhardt was not allowed to return and was put under house arrest in Germany, owing to his knowledge of the German chemical industry, but with the assistance of the

John Ehrhardt

223

American Consul he fled to Switzerland. John and his eldest brother William enlisted in the British Army. William was commissioned into the 1st Birmingham Pals Battalion in October 1914, and in April 1916 he was seriously wounded by a German sniper. He had a series of operations but eventually contracted septicaemia and died.

John was superb sportsman. At school he captained his house shooting team, won his rugby colours, and was an excellent swimmer and gymnast. In 1916 he left to go to London University but soon afterwards enlisted in the Army and was commissioned into the Tank Corps. He served as a Reconnaissance Officer during the Battle of Cambrai.

On 26 March 1918 he was fighting on foot near Bray when he was wounded in the thigh. He continued to operate his Lewis gun until he was shot through the lung and killed. Captain F. S. Hunnikin wrote: 'I cannot do justice to Jack unless I tell you of his generous and brave conduct out here. You may rest assured that he has been very instrumental in ridding this world of very many of the enemy.'[52]

The *1st Battalion War History* stated:

> On the 26th the enemy broke through at Maricourt and Bray and all available spare crews were immediately organised into Lewis gun posts, and took up positions behind the Bois de Tailles. The enemy then attacked heavily, and for four hours were held in check by the gun teams, who succeeded in inflicting heavy casualties on the attacking infantry. During this attack the gun teams were absolutely without support of any kind. A very fine example was set by one gun team consisting of Captain F. S. Hunnikin, Lieutenant J. A. Ehrhardt, and Serjeant Scott, who continued to fire their gun till it burst, succeeding in putting 400 rounds into the enemy at point-blank range. Lieutenant Ehrhardt was unfortunately killed, and the other two made an escape which was nothing short of miraculous, being as they were hemmed in on three sides by the enemy.[53]

The Other Officers of 'A' Battalion

John Ehrhardt was 20 years old and is commemorated on the Pozières Memorial as his body was never identified.

A.60 ATALANTA II Second Lieutenant Francis Sidney Hunnikin, born in London in 1889, was a rifleman in the 12th London Regiment when the war began and landed in France on Christmas Day 1914. He rose to the rank of serjeant before being commissioned into the Tank Corps in April 1917.

Hunnikin was awarded the Military Cross for his actions at the Bois de Tailles in 1918. His citation stated:

> For most conspicuous gallantry and devotion to duty on March 26, 1918, at the Bois-de-Tailles. When his company was fighting a rearguard action, covering the withdrawal of the infantry from Bray, it became partially surrounded, and running short of ammunition Captain Hunnikin at once volunteered to cover the withdrawal of the remainder of the company with two Lewis guns and crews. He continued using his Lewis guns and inflicting very severe casualties on the enemy, who had worked up very close to within 50 to 60 yards.
>
> When the withdrawal of the company was complete, Captain Hunnikin remained where he was, inflicting severe losses on the enemy until his ammunition was expended, except for two drums. He was by then completely surrounded, but succeeded in cutting his way out with the two remaining drums. Throughout the day this gallant officer showed the utmost coolness, courage, and determination, and was a splendid example to all ranks.[54]

In November 1957 a sad postscript to his life appeared in a newspaper:

> A couple were found shot dead in their bedroom in Weighton Road, Harrow Weald, Middlesex, yesterday. They were Mrs. Elsie May Hunnikin, aged 65, and Francis Sidney Hunnikin, aged 68, a lawnmower engineer. A service revolver was found near Mr. Hunnikin. His wife had been ill recently.[55]

Officers of No. 12 Section at Marcoing 1917: from left to right 2nd Lt. Hunnikin, Cpt. Shillaker, Lt. Foxwell, 2nd Lt. Ehrhardt and 2nd Lt. Grove

Besides John Browning in Richard Wain's tank, nine other ranks of 'A' Battalion were killed on the same day. All bar one are commemorated on the Cambrai Memorial.

Private Cyril Sheldon Allen was born in Normanby, Lincolnshire. He was the third son of Mr Ernest S. Allen, the Head Gardener to Sir Berkeley Sheffield of Normanby Park. Before enlisting, Cyril worked as a partner in the family drapery business. He had been alongside Captain Clement Robertson when he won his Victoria Cross on 4 October 1917, and had himself been awarded the D.C.M., the citation reading:

> For conspicuous gallantry and devotion to duty. He twice marked out routes under heavy enemy barrages, though on the first occasion he was blown up and badly shaken. Later he accompanied the tanks into action on foot, showing magnificent courage and contempt of danger.[56]

The Other Officers of 'A' Battalion

Cyril Sheldon Allen

A local newspaper reported:

At the beginning of 1915 Sid underwent a special course of training and in May went to France, taking part in the first advance of the Tanks. Since then he has had many thrilling experiences. Early in October his conspicuous bravery won him the D.C.M. As in civilian life, he has been popular in the Army and congratulations have poured in on him from the G.O.C. to his fellow 'Tankites'.

The captain, who was his section commander, said he was proud to think that Sid had volunteered and accomplished such good work for another section, and while he is naturally elated at the honour he has won, our hero is full of grief at the loss he has just sustained through the death of his commander. They had been together all the time and had led the Tanks in the face of hordes of Boches, and on the last occasion had reached all their objectives when the commander was mortally wounded and died in Sid's arms.

He is expecting shortly to have a leave. While at Scunthorpe he was a prominent player in the old Thursday football team, and the hero of many a hard-fought game.[57]

Gunner Edward Bourne died of his wounds on 20 November and was buried at Rocquigny-Equancourt Road British Cemetery, Manancourt. The son of a carter, he was born in Howden-le-Wear, Durham, in 1897, and had served with the Durham Light Infantry before transferring to the Tank Corps.

Private Harold Percy Chitty was born in Clapham in Surrey

in 1889, the grandson of Lord Justice Chitty. Before enlisting he had worked as a designer of wallpaper for Wallpaper Manufacturers Limited of 107 Great Portland Square, Fitzrovia, London. He lived with his parents at 44 Crescent Lane, Clapham Park, and had enlisted in the 21st Battalion of the London Regiment as a Teritorial in February 1909. He served until February 1913 and attended all the summer camps during those years. When war broke out he joined the Royal Field Artillery before transferring to the Tank Corps. A local newspaper carried an account of his death:

> Tank Driver Killed in Action – Gunner Harold Percy Chitty, of the Motor Machine Gun Corps (Tank Section), who was killed in action on November 20th, was the second son of Mr. Arthur Chitty, of Marion Cottage, Raleigh-drive, Esher, and grandson of the late Mr. Thompson Chitty, barrister-at-law, of the Middle Temple. Deceased, who was 28 years of age, and had been recommended for a commission, was a first driver of the Tanks, in which he, with his brother, had been serving for the past 15 months. It is a pathetic circumstance that he met his death the morning following the night on which his brother returned to the Tanks after 14 days home on leave.[58]

Private Victor Joseph Edward Craddock was 20 years of age. Born in Wolverhampton, he was the youngest son of Frederick and Mary Craddock. Frederick was a merchant's metal buyer. Victor enlisted as a gunner in the Royal Field Artillery before transferring to the Tank Corps. The family lived at 10 Oaklands Road, Wolverhampton.

Private William Davidson was 21 and had been born in Skerton, Lancashire. Before the war commenced he lived at Bath Street in Lancaster and had been educated at Christ Church School prior to being employed at Lune Mills. A member of the Centenary Pleasant Sunday Afternoon Brotherhood, he attended the Church of Christ Sunday school. He had formerly served with The Seaforth Highlanders and was a tank gunner.

The Other Officers of 'A' Battalion

Private George David Hunt was born in Blandford, Dorset, in 1891. His father was a baker and grocer, and after leaving school he worked as a baker in his father's business. His personal effects were left to his sister, Ethel Smaldon. His elder brother Ernest had been killed at Passchendaele in August.

Private Thomas Edward Scholey was the third son of William John Scholey, a farmer and butcher, and his wife Florence. Born in Beal in Yorkshire in June 1897, Thomas was educated at the local Council School and at the King's School in Pontefract. He enlisted in the Mechanical Transport section of the Army Service Corps at Knottingley, Yorkshire, in October 1916, and later volunteered for the Tank Corps. He worked one of his tank's six-pounder guns.

Corporal Arthur John Squire was born in Lynton in Devon in 1896, the son of a grocer and shopkeeper. After leaving school he began working at Parr's Bank at Weston-super-Mare, before joining the Army. By 1917 he had been promoted to the rank of corporal.

Private William Walker, aged 23, was born in Brechin, Forfar. His father was an overseer in a flax mill. He had formerly

William Davidson

Thomas Scholey

The family grave

served in the Machine Gun Corps before being transferred to the Tank Corps. His brother John served with the Black Watch and survived the war. John played professional football for Brechin City and Forfar Athletic.

In addition, two men wounded on 20 November died later that month of their wounds:

> Gunner Edmund Ellis Yarrow died on 21 November, aged 31, and was buried in Tincourt New British Cemetery. The eldest son of James and Margaret Ellis Yarrow, he was born in South Shields and after leaving school he worked as a gas stoker. He joined the Tank Corps after serving with the 18th Northumberland Fusiliers and left his effects to his sister Mary.

Corporal Hubert Gower George died on 28 November and was buried in St Sever Cemetery Extension, Rouen. The son of William and Elizabeth George of Port Eynon, Swansea, he and his wife Mary lived at 9 Morgan Street, Hafod, Swansea. He was 33.

CHAPTER 12

The Aftermath

ACCORDING TO INFORMATION in his service papers, Richard was buried in a cemetery, map reference 1.20000 sheet 57.c. N.E. 13737. Square L 34.a.0.3.[1]

The nomenclature 'cemetery' is probably overstated as its general usage appears to cover simply a place of burial for more than one casualty. Buried at the same spot were Lieutenant Christopher Duncan and Private John Browning. All three were buried some distance from their tank for the reason explored earlier – that the wrecked tank would have been a target for enemy artillery and by moving the bodies some distance away it was hoped that the graves would remain undisturbed. Duncan and Browning's bodies would have been recovered from the tank, Richard Wain's from the trench in which he fell.

After the armistice the battlefields of the Western Front were cleared of most of the detritus of war by Army salvage teams. Ammunition, discarded equipment and abandoned tanks were retrieved to be recycled or scrapped. Identified burial sites were visited by the Imperial War Graves Commission teams who exhumed many of the dead and moved them to larger cemeteries in a process known as 'concentration'. Those who could not be identified were listed as 'missing'. The missing of the Battle of Cambrai are commemorated on a special memorial at Louverval.

Richard Wain, Christopher Duncan and John Browning's

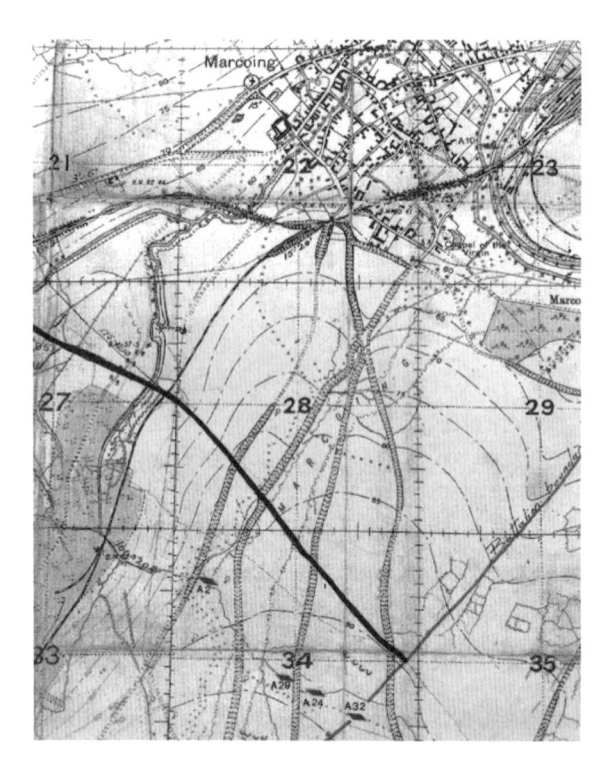

Map showing the location of Square 34 relative to Marcoing

bodies were never identified. There appears to be no record of their original burials having been exhumed, so they may still lie where they were buried in November 1917. The ground was fought over subsequently and the Germans advanced over the area in 1918 so the bodies may have been disturbed by artillery shelling.

When Richard Wain died his parents were living in Llandaff. They placed a notice of their son's death in the newspaper the following week: 'WAIN, Killed in action. 20th November 1917. Captain Richard William Leslie Wain, Tank Corps, the dearly-loved only son of Mr and Mrs Harris Wain, The Avenue, Llandaff, aged twenty.'[2]

The effects that were forwarded to Richard's parents on 19 December were: a rule, two protractors, one pair of dividers in a case, a prism compass and case, a leather card and stamp

The Aftermath

case, four Manchester Regiment badges, four Machine Gun Corps collar badges, a receipt and a leather case.

A copy of his will could not be found so it was determined that he had died intestate. The next few months saw an exchange of correspondence between his father and the War Office regarding the value of the gratuity due. Harris Wain also asked for compensation for the kit his son possessed:

> I hear from Messrs. Cox & Co., that you have allowed £3-3-0 compensation for lost kit. If this is for the tunic destroyed on the 22nd September I am satisfied.
>
> With regard to the articles destroyed on the 20th November 1917, namely Fur Lined Trench Coat, Sam Brown and Revolver, I have made enquiries and now quote reply from A Battalion Tank Corps Head Quarters: 'The articles you mention were taken into action. The coat he wore all the night previous as it was rather cold. I am afraid they were all destroyed in the Tank, as it is a general practice to take off extra kit.'
>
> The Tank was hit five times by Trench Mortar Shells and the fifth stopped it, killing or wounding all inside. I have seen an Officer of the Rifle Brigade[3] who searched the Tank afterwards and he informed me everything was destroyed.

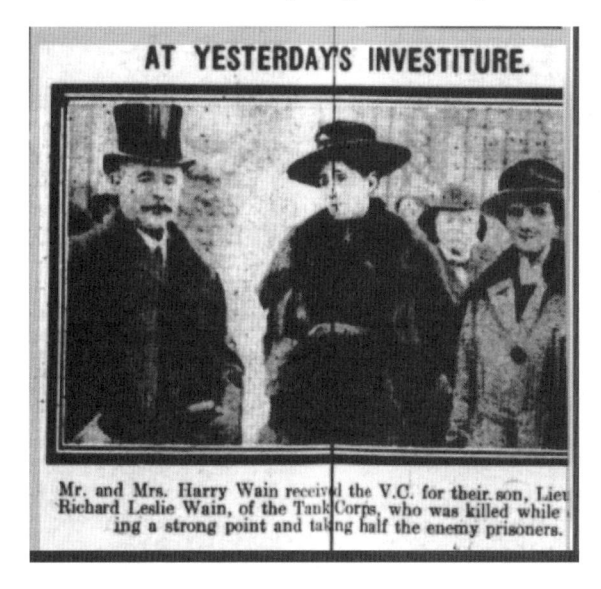

Richard Wain's parents receiving his Victoria Cross

Under these circumstances I ask for further compensation for destroyed kit.[4]

It was pointed out to him that compensation was only paid if an officer needed to re-equip himself; it was not payable to the relatives of a deceased officer.

Richard's Victoria Cross was the second to be won by a soldier serving with the Tank Corps and the only one awarded to the Tank Corps at Cambrai. Harris and Florence Wain travelled to Buckingham Palace to receive their son's Victoria Cross on 20 April 1918 from King George V.

The *Western Mail* reported:

> During the investiture by the King at Buckingham Palace on Saturday, Mr Harris Wain, The Avenue, Llandaff, father of Capt. Richard Wain, of the Tank Corps, received the V.C. bestowed on his son for leaving his disabled tank, while seriously wounded, with a Lewis gun, capturing a strong enemy point, inflicting heavy casualties, and capturing prisoners on November 20 near Marcoing. He was ultimately killed. Commenting on this magnificent feat, his Majesty said: 'A fine piece of work your son did. I only wish I could have handed the cross to him.' Mrs Harris Wain was also at the Palace.[5]

On 29 November, Lieutenant-Colonel Lyon submitted his report on the performance of his tanks at what was already being called 'The Battle of Cambrai'. In it he wrote:

Nos. 1 and 2 Companies	
No. of Tanks to reach 1st Objective	24
No. of Tanks to reach 2nd Objective	12
No. of Tanks to reach final objective Marcoing	8
No. knocked out before Blue Line	Nil
No. knocked out between Blue and Brown Lines	6
No. knocked out after Brown Line	3 and 1 Burnt out

The Aftermath

Total Casualties for the whole of the operation were:-

	Officers	Other Ranks
Killed	4	5
Missing believed killed	1	3
Wounded	17	60
Accidentally wounded	1	
Wounded at duty	4	25

Lewis Guns
These were satisfactory but very vulnerable. A number of Guns were destroyed by hostile fire.

6 Pounders
Very satisfactory. It is suggested that in future case shot be issued. This type of ammunition would give the gunners a much better chance of knocking out the crews of the enemy's Field Guns, and thus minimise direct hits on Tanks from this type of gun.

Fascines
These were very useful and undoubtedly helped the Tanks to cross wide trenches which would otherwise have been a very serious obstacle. The hooks for holding the fascine are not strong enough, and are not considered satisfactory by the majority of Tank Commanders. In some cases they were found to be too near the cab.

Direction
Tanks experienced no difficulty in maintaining direction as the landmarks were well defined.

Observation
The present means of observation from Tanks is extremely poor, and it is suggested that some better method than the prisms and periscopes at present in use be devised. Tank Commanders state that it is almost impossible to pick up the position of a Machine Gun until the Tank is almost on top of it, and that even Field Batteries are almost invisible at a greater distance than 100 yards.

Wire
Wire was mostly strong and thick, but the Tanks in all cases made a pathway that the Infantry were easily able to get through.

Supply Tanks
Sledges are not a satisfactory method of getting supplies forward, as the friction caused through moving over a hard, rough surface is too great to allow a full load to be carried, and caused the towing gear to break. Should sledges be used in future operations a standardised method of loading and lashing should be devised and taught to the Crews.

Armour Piercing
Several of the Tanks were pierced by armour piercing bullets, and in one case a Tank of No. 3 Company had the whole of one side simply riddled.[6]

When the war was over the Tank Corps formed a special salvage detachment whose role it was to comb the battlefields of the Western Front for the wrecks of tanks, blowing them up and recovering the scrap metal, or burying them where they lay if this was not possible. This work continued for many months and it is likely that it was during this period that Richard Wain's tank A.2 'Abou-Ben-Adam II' was buried where it was knocked out. In 2018 roadworks were carried out at the site and parts of the tank were recovered.

The remains of Tank A.2

CHAPTER 13

The Memorials

RICHARD WAIN IS commemorated on a number of memorials, both in the United Kingdom and in France.

St Bees School War Memorial was unveiled on 30 June 1921 in a ceremony conducted by the Bishop of Carlisle. There are 183 names listed on the school memorial, and its three Victoria Cross winners are listed on a separate memorial in the St Bees School Chapel Memorial.

(Richard Wain is also commemorated on the war memorial at a school in Liverpool but this is a different Richard Wain, though the two are sometimes confused.)

Llandaff War Memorial, Cathedral Green, Llandaff was erected in 1924. It consists of three standing bronze figures on three separate granite plinths, two soldiers with a female figure in the centre, and was designed by the famous sculptor Sir William Goscombe John RA. The plinths were designed by J. P. Grant. It was unveiled by the Earl of Plymouth, who said of the fallen:

> They are heroes all, but I cannot mention them all by name. I would, however, like to mention a single one, because I think it is symbolical of what all did. That one is Captain Richard William Leslie Wain, V.C., of the 10th Tank Corps, who was killed in action in November 1917. May this noble monument remain standing through the centuries that are to come ever to be a reminder to those who pass by it of the brave men whose names are inscribed thereon and who, though departed, are not forgotten by a country that bears them honour.[1]

Richard's name is also carved on the Llandaff Cathedral School Memorial. The school also named one of its pupil houses after him.

He is also remembered on a brass plaque inside Llandaff Cathedral.

The Penarth War Memorial in Alexandra Park, Penarth, was also designed by Goscombe John and was unveiled on 11 November 1924. It includes the names of 307 casualties of the Great War, including Richard Wain, though his name and that of the town's other Victoria Cross winner of the Great War, Serjeant Samuel Pearse, were added sometime later.

The Cambrai Memorial to the Missing at Louverval, France, stands on an elevated terrace in Louverval Military Cemetery and commemorates those who died at the Battle of Cambrai in November and December 1917, listing the names of those who have no known grave. There are several Victoria Cross holders listed amongst its 7,117 names, of whom Richard Wain is one. It was designed by Harold Chalton Bradshaw and was sculpted by Charles Sargeant Jagger. It was unveiled on 4 August 1930, at the same hour on the same day as the memorials at Le Touret, Vis-en-Artois and Pozières in France.

St Bees School Chapel Memorial

Florence Wain laying a wreath at the Llandaff Memorial in memory of her son

The Memorials

Richard's name on the Llandaff Memorial

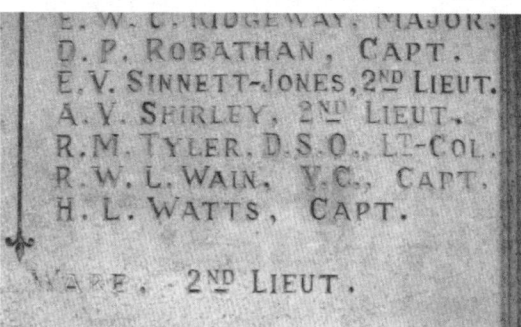

Richard's name on the Llandaff Cathedral School Memorial

A Wain House badge

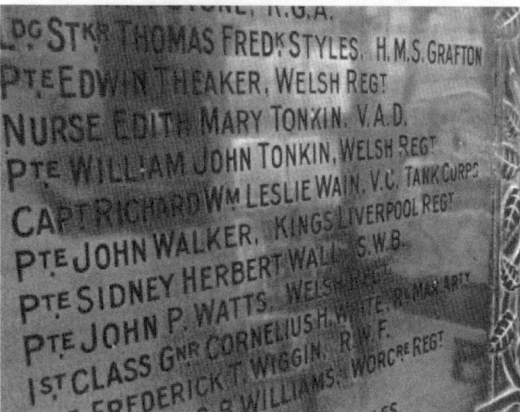

Richard Wain's name on the Llandaff Cathedral Memorial

Richard's name on the Penarth Town Memorial

Florence Wain with Welsh V.C. winners in 1928

The unveiling ceremony at the Cambrai Memorial, Louverval

The Memorials

The plaque outside Penarth Town Council offices, West House, Penarth, was unveiled in April 2008. It also commemorates the name of Serjeant Samuel Pearse of Penarth who won his V.C. in Russia in 1919. Unfortunately, Richard's year of birth is incorrect, as is the naming of his regiment as the 'Royal Tank Corps'.

The national Victoria Cross memorial stone in the Garden of Remembrance, Alexandra Gardens, Penarth, was sourced by the author. It was dedicated in a moving ceremony on 9 November 2018 and relatives of Richard Wain were present to pay their respects.

Richard Wain's name on the Cambrai Memorial

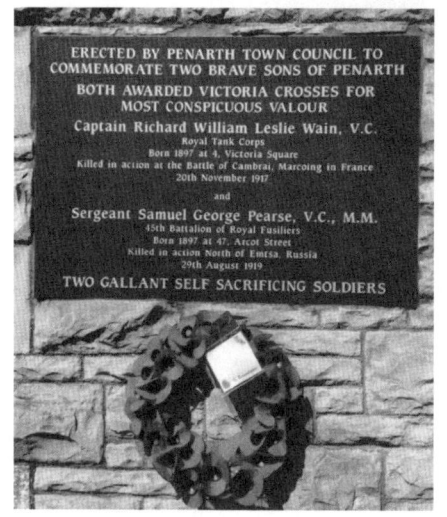

The plaque outside the Penarth Town Council offices

The family grave in St John's Churchyard, Sully, also commemorates Richard Wain. His parents Harris and Florence were buried together and an inscription on the grave recalls their son.

The Royal Tank Regiment headquarters has named a road after him – Wain Road at Bovington Camp, Dorset.

As part of the redevelopment which took place at Penarth Heights in 2014, one of the roads in the area was named after him too – Wain Close.

In addition, Richard is commemorated by the University Officer Training Corps building, Tŷ Richard Wain V.C. at Maindy Barracks, Whitchurch Road, Cardiff.

His sister Elsie inherited Richard's medals and when she

Richard Wain's memorial stone unveiled in 2018

The family grave in Sully

The Memorials

passed away in 1962 she left his Victoria Cross to St Bees School. It has since been returned to the family and, in 2017, to commemorate the centenary of his death, it was placed on display at the Tank Museum at Bovington.

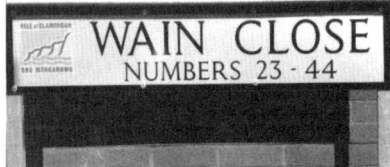

Bovington Camp

Penarth

Display at the Tank Museum, Bovington

243

Epilogue

AFTER THE WAR had ended, towns which had raised significant sums of money towards the war effort were given decommissioned tanks for public display. In June 1919 the National War Savings Association donated such a tank to Penarth. Sited in Alexandra Park, where it survived for many years as a symbol of the town's sacrifice during the Great War, it was finally sold to a firm of scrap merchants in 1937 – just two years before another world war broke out.

Harris Wain passed away on 8 May 1925; the following month his widow Florence sold the family home at Woodside, 4 The Avenue, Llandaff. She died on 11 August 1938. Given their family connection with Sully, and the fact that they are buried together in the grounds of their local parish church in the village, Harris and Florence would have visited nearby

The donated tank in Windsor Terrace, Penarth

Epilogue

Penarth regularly in the post-war years. One may wonder how they would have felt to see the tank which had been donated to the town sitting near the town's war memorial – such poignant symbols of the death of their only son.

They would have reflected on the tragic set of circumstances that combined to take Richard away from them on foreign soil. The grief they would have felt not knowing where his body lay in that quiet earth would have been unimaginable. There was no grave for them to visit but they did possess the precious memories of him that stayed with them for the rest of their lives.

Truly, the pity of war.

Richard Wain

Endnotes

Chapter 1: The Wain Family
1. *South Wales Daily News*, 16 August 1875.
2. *Western Mail*, 16 March 1882.
3. *South Wales Daily News*, date unknown.
4. Ibid.
5. Ibid.
6. *Bristol Mercury Guide Book*, 1884.
7. See Hicks, Dr J., *The Welsh at Passchendaele*, Y Lolfa, Talybont, 2017, p. 267.
8. *South Wales Daily News*, 26 May 1884.
9. *Western Mail*, 30 May 1885.
10. *Barry Dock News*, 16 October 1891.
11. *South Wales Echo*, 15 October 1891.
12. *South Wales Echo*, 20 October 1891.
13. *Western Daily Press*, 4 January 1892.
14. *South Wales Echo*, 29 March 1892.
15. *South Wales Echo*, 31 March 1892.
16. *Western Mail*, 31 July 1893.
17. Ibid.
18. *South Wales Star*, 15 June 1894.

Chapter 2: The Junior Officer
1. John Fox Russell and William Leefe Robinson were the others.
2. *Barry Dock News*, 18 September 1914.
3. *The Scotsman*, 27 August 1914.

Chapter 3: The Somme 1916
1. In Hartley, J., *17th Manchesters*, Reveille Press, Brighton, 2012, p. 37.

Endnotes

2. Hartley, op. cit, pp. 38–39.
3. Hartley, op. cit., p. 40.
4. *17th Manchester Regiment War Diary*, WO 95/2339/2.
5. Ibid.
6. Ibid.
7. Richard Wain's Service Record, WO_339_36624.
8. Aldous, J. W., *St. Bees School, Cumberland. The Roll of Honour & The Record of Old St. Beghians Who Served their King & Country in the Great War 1914–1919*, 1921. p. 31.
9. Author's collection.
10. Author's collection.
11. *Whitehaven News*, July 1916.
12. In Tait, J. and Fletcher, D., *Tracing Your Tank Ancestors*, Pen and Sword, Barnsley, 2011, p. 27.
13. Henriques in Fletcher, D., *British Mark I Tank 1916*, Osprey, Oxford, 2004, p. 17.
14. Williams-Ellis, C. *The Tank Corps*, G. H. Doran, New York, 1919, p. 52.
15. Serjeant Harry Emans in Pullen, R., *Beyond the Green Fields*, Tucann Books, Lincoln, 2008, p. 21.
16. *London Gazette*, 11 May 1917.
17. *The Tank Corps Honours and Awards 1916–1919*, Midland Medals, Birmingham, 1982, p. 165.
18. *Bristol Grammar School Chronicle*, December 1916.

Chapter 4: Messines 1917

1. In Williams-Ellis, op. cit., p. 78.
2. In Williams-Ellis op, cit., p. 79.
3. WO-95-109-7.
4. Courtesy of the Tank Museum, Bovington Camp.
5. Courtesy of Feriel Small and Stuart Middleton.
6. Corporal C. H. Clements was later awarded the Military Medal for his actions. His citation read: 'This N.C.O., when Pte. Bryant was wounded in No Man's Land, near Joye, on June 7, 1917, volunteered to leave the tank and dress his wound. He remained with him in a shell-hole for five hours until stretcher-bearers were obtained. During all the time he was under heavy fire from our own and enemy machine-guns. Prior to this he had been twelve hours directing his

247

tank and doing exceptionally hard work, particularly when his tank was ditched. Throughout, under most exhausting conditions, he set an excellent example of keenness and hard work to his men.' *The Tank Corps Honours and Awards*, op. cit. p. 174.
7. Private Charles McCoy from Connaught Road in Liverpool. He was 22 years of age. His body could not be identified later and he is remembered on the Menin Gate Memorial to the Missing.
8. Foster Evans Brash from Edinburgh, later a colour sergeant in the Royal Scots, was awarded the Military Medal. His citation stated: 'When his tank was ditched near Joye Farm on June 7, 1917, he went to and fro under heavy fire for ammunition, and dressed a wounded man and assisted to carry him to safety in the Oosttaverne Line. He also displayed great courage and coolness under very trying and dangerous circumstances.' *Tank Corps Honours and Awards*, op. cit. p. 174.
9. Small and Middleton op. cit.
10. WO-95-92-3.
11. WO-95-109-7.

Chapter 5: Third Ypres – Passchendaele 1917

1. Hickey, Captain D. E., *Rolling Into Action*, Naval and Military Press, Uckfield, 2007, p. 59.
2. WO-95-109-7.
3. WO-95-109-4.
4. Ibid.
5. Ibid.
6. Ibid.
7. WO-95-92-3.
8. WO-95-109-4.
9. Ibid.
10. Ibid.
11. Ibid.
12. In Sheldon, J. *The German Army at Passchendaele*, Pen and Sword, Barnsley, 2007, p. 152.
13. Wain Service Record, op. cit.
14. WO-95-109-7.

Endnotes

Chapter 6: The Battle of Cambrai 1917

1. Becke, Major A. F. *Gun Fire No. 47*, undated.
2. Ibid.
3. WO-95-109_4_031.
4. WO-95-109-4_033.
5. WO-95-109-7.
6. Hickey, op. cit., pp. 97–98.
7. In Cooper, B., *The Ironclads of Cambrai*, Cassell, London, 1967, p. 86.
8. Cooper, op. cit., p. 47.
9. Lee, A. G., *No Parachute: A Fighter Pilot in World War I*, The Adventurers' Club, London, 1969, pp. 161–162.
10. Lee, op. cit., p. 162.
11. *London Gazette*, 9 January 1917.
12. *Flight*, 13 December 1917, p. 1318.
13. Cooper, op. cit., p. 101.
14. Hickey, op. cit., pp. 101–102.
15. Bion, W. R., *The Long Week-End*, Karnac Books, London, 1982, pp. 161–162.
16. Bion, op. cit., p. 48.
17. Unknown. http://www.scarboroughsmaritimeheritage.org.uk/article.php?article=591.html
18. Cooper, op. cit., pp. 101–102.
19. 'Some Reminiscences of Cambrai and the German March Offensive', Brown, G., Tank Museum, E2007.591.
20. War Diary Headquarters Tanks Corps, WO-95-92-3_034.
21. Browne, D. G., *The Tank in Action*, Leonaur, 2009, pp. 282–283.
22. Hickey, op. cit., pp. 102–103.
23. In Gibot, J-L. and Gorczynski, P., *Following the Tanks*, 1999, p. 73.
24. Ibid.
25. WO-95-92-3.
26. WO-95-109-7.
27. WO-95-109-4.
28. Ibid.
29. Wain Service Record, op. cit.

Chapter 7: The German Perspective

1. *Der Weltkrieg 1914–1918*, Berlin, 1942, pp. 128–131.
2. In Sheldon, J., *The German Army at Cambrai*, Pen and Sword, Barnsley, 2009, pp. 84–87.
3. Giese, Leutnant d. Res. Franz, *Geschichte des Reserve-Infanterie-Regiments Nr. 227 im Weltkrieg 1914–1918*, Berlin 1931, pp. 412–413.
4. Schwenke, Oberstleutnant a.D. Alexander, *Geschichte des Reserve-Infanterie-Regiments Nr. 19 im Weltkrieg 1914–1918*, Oldenburg, 1926, p. 289.
5. Schwenke, op. cit., p. 291.
6. Schwenke, op. cit., p. 290–291.
7. Strutz, Dr. G., *Die Tankschlacht bei Cambrai*, Didenburg, Berlin, 1929, p. 58.
8. Strutz, op. cit., p. 60.
9. Strutz, op. cit., pp. 61–62.
10. Von Watter, General O. F., *Dem Gedenken eines großen Soldaten von den alten Kameraden der 54. Infanterie-Division des Weltkrieges*, Berlag Broschef, Hamburg, undated, pp. 134–135.
11. Ludendorff, General E., *My War Memories, 1914–1918*, Naval and Military Press, Uckfield, 2005, p. 497.

Chapter 8: The Victoria Cross Award

1. *London Gazette*, 13 February 1918.
2. *The Tank Corps Honours and Awards*, op. cit., pp. 1–2.
3. Miles, Captain W., *Military Operations, France and Belgium 1917, Volume 3*, The Naval and Military Press, Uckfield, undated, p. 54.
4. WO 95/2120/1.
5. *London Gazette*, 13 February 1918.
6. WO-95-2121-5_4.
7. Wain, Service Record, op. cit.
8. Ibid.
9. Ibid.
10. WO-95-2122-1_2.
11. *Western Mail*, 14 February 1918.
12. Ibid.
13. Ibid.

Endnotes

14. WO-95-109-4_077.
15. Courtesy of the Tank Museum, Bovington.
16. *The Tank Corps Journal, Cambrai Anniversary Issue*, 1922.
17. Wilson, G. M. (ed.), *Fighting Tanks*, Seeley, Service and Co. Ltd., London, 1929, pp. 78–79.
18. The *Newfoundland Regiment War Diary* makes no specific mention of this, stating only: 'Artillery formation was kept until we reached the Blue Line when Companies opened out into attack formation as here we began to come under the enemy's sniping and machine gun fire and to have our first casualties. The advance of our army was preceded by tanks whose purpose was to trample down the wire and deal with any machine guns that opposed. Our advance was continued to the canal and the bridge captured after severe opposition and ground gained on the further side.' Author's collection.
19. Inglefield, Captain V. E., *The History of the Twentieth (Light) Division*, Nisbet and Co., London, 1921, p. 185.
20. E2006.2470, Tank Museum Archives.
21. Ibid.
22. Ibid.
23. Hart, Liddell B. H., *The Tanks*, Cassell, London, 1958, pp. 140–141.
24. Pullen, R., *The Landships of Lincoln*, Tucann Books, Lincoln, 2007, p. 101.
25. John, S., *The Welsh at War. Through Mud to Victory*, Pen and Sword, Barnsley, 2018, p. 83.
26. Rawson, A., *The Cambrai Campaign*, Pen and Sword, Barnsley, 2017, p. 58.
27. Smithers, A. J., *Cambrai The First Great Tank Battle 1917*, Leo Cooper, London, 1992, p. 113.
28. Horsfall, J. and Cave, N., *Cambrai, The Right Hook*, Pen and Sword, 1999, p.48.

Chapter 9: The Other Tank Corps V.C. Winners

1. *The Tank Corps Honours and Awards*, op. cit., p. 1.
2. *The Tank Corps Honours and Awards*, op. cit., p. 2.
3. *The Tank Corps Honours and Awards*, op cit., p. 3.
4. *London Gazette*, 1 January 1918.
5. *London Gazette*, 7 November 1918.
6. *Tank Corps Honours and Awards*, op. cit., p. 116.

Chapter 10: The Crew of Abou-Ben-Adam II

1. *London Gazette*, 16 August 1917.
2. C. W. Duncan Service Record, WO_339_39727.
3. *Thanet Advertiser*, 9 February 1918.
4. *Thanet Advertiser*, 27 October 1917.
5. *Thanet Advertiser*, 9 October 1915.
6. Author's collection.
7. Author's collection.
8. The previous month William Scott had inserted a poignant notice in *Dundee People's Journal* in memory of his close friend Private George McGregor who had died of his wounds on 13 September 1917. William wrote: 'What happy days we once enjoyed,/How sweet their memory still;/One of the best that God could lend./A loving chum and a faithful friend.'
9. WO-95-109-7.

Chapter 11: The Other Officers of 'A' Battalion

1. *The Tank Corps Honours and Awards*, op. cit., p. 54.
2. *London Gazette*, 18 July 1919.
3. *The Tank Corps Honours and Awards*, op. cit., p. 104.
4. Ibid., p. 30.
5. *London Gazette*, 16 August 1917.
6. *London Gazette*, 26 July 1918.
7. WO-95-109-7_090.
8. *London Gazette*, 16 September 1918.
9. *London Gazette*, 9 January 1918.
10. *London Gazette*, 26 July 1918.
11. *Chelmsford Chronicle*, 7 December 1917.
12. WO-95-109-4.
13. *London Gazette*, 7 November 1918.
14. *Victoria College Book of Remembrance*.
15. WO-95-109-4.
16. *London Gazette*, 8 January 1918.
17. *Daily Mail*, 14 September 2010.
18. National Archives, J77/458/3951.
19. WO-95-109-4.
20. *Edinburgh Gazette*, 22 July 1918.

Endnotes

21   *The Tank Corps Honours and Awards*, op. cit., p. 103.
22   Unsigned account of action of A29 'Apollyon' on 20 November 1917 in N. M. Dillon papers (no ref) by Lieutenant Kenneth Wootton, Tank Museum, Bovington.
23   Ibid.
24   Ibid.
25   Ibid.
26   George Fagg received a compound fracture of the fourth finger on his left hand, which later required amputation. Before being conscripted in 1916, he was employed as a sub-postmaster in Smeeth, Kent.

John Frederick Harkness was wounded on 20 November, having also been wounded the previous July. He was gassed in April 1918 and was hospitalised for six months. A solicitor's clerk from Hitchin in Hertfordshire, he had enlisted in 1915.

Frank Johns from Ystrad Mynach was an electrician before the war. He received gunshot wounds to the right thigh and arm but survived the war.
27   *London Gazette*, 16 July 1918.
28   De Ruvigny, *The Roll of Honour*, Volume 4, Uckfield, 2009, p. 169.
29   Ibid.
30   *London Gazette*, 26 July 1918.
31   *London Gazette*, 7 November 1918.
32   http://www.auction-net.co.uk/viewAuction.php?id=2691 (note 46).
33   *London Gazette*, 26 July 1918.
34   *Edinburgh Gazette*, 26 August 1918.
35   *London Gazette*, 13 September 1918.
36   WO-95-109-4.
37   Ibid.
38   *London Gazette*, 16 July 1918.
39   *The Tank Corps Honours and Awards*, op. cit., p. 103.
40   *London Gazette*, 18 July 1918.
41   *London Gazette*, 28 March 1917.
42   Courtesy of Jonathan Rands.
43   WO-95-109-4.
44   *London Gazette*, 18 July 1918.
45   *London Gazette*, 9 January 1918.
46   *London Gazette*, 11 January 1919.

[47] WO-95-109-4.
[48] WO-95-109-4.
[49] *Edinburgh Gazette*, 28 August 1916.
[50] Courtesy of Filip Debergh.
[51] Alexander Grove's diary, courtesy of Simon Toon.
[52] King Edward's School Roll of Honour.
[53] WO-95-109-7_77.
[54] *The Tank Corps Honours and Awards*, op. cit., pp. 59–60.
[55] *Western Mail*, 6 November 1957.
[56] *London Gazette*, 6 February 1918.
[57] *Hull Daily Mail*, 3 November 1917.
[58] *Surrey Advertiser*, 10 December 1917.

Chapter 12: The Aftermath

[1] Wain, Service Record, op. cit.
[2] *Western Mail*, 27 November 1917.
[3] This officer may have been Second Lieutenant Walpole.
[4] Wain, Service Record, op. cit.
[5] *Western Mail*, 22 April 1918.
[6] WO-95-109-4_039.

Chapter 13: The Memorials

[1] *Western Mail*, 13 October 1924.

Appendix

Shortly before he passed away in 1968, Joseph Mossman left the following account of his service during the Great War. I am indebted to his grandson Keith Nisbet for permitting it to be published for the first time.

I JOINED THE Royal Army Medical Corps in 1915 about a year after the commencement of the war. I was not allowed to join up until I had done three years of my apprenticeship as a pharmacist.

I was sent to the R.A.M.C. Barracks Aldershot and did my training there, mostly 'square bashing' (drill) and classes on First Aid and stretcher bearing. It was not a very happy time for me as the life was rough and totally different to anything I had imagined or been used to. However, I had several leaves back to Carlisle during this period.

In March 1916 I was put on draft for France and one morning found myself marching behind a military band playing 'You'd be far better off in a Home'. How appropriate! We entrained for Southampton and next day sailed for Rouen via La Havre, the first time I had been abroad. I enjoyed the sail up the Seine and on arrival at Rouen we were marched about four miles to the racecourse and to No. 9 General Hospital. I was detailed as assistant dispenser to Sergeant Tait [or Tart] MPS who was in charge of the dispensary, a fairly large wooden building. The hospital was under canvas, huge marquees for the most part. I enjoyed my work and play here and spent a lot of my off-time rowing on the Seine and finding delightful little cafés on the islands which dotted the

Seine above Rouen. I also had plenty of time to explore the town and went to the top of the cathedral spire which was a hair-raising experience.

In July [1916] I was posted to No. 76 Field Ambulance as dispenser. I was sorry to leave Jock Tait [or Tart] my canny Scotch boss and move up the line behind the Somme battlefield where I heard my first guns firing in anger and saw the Very Lights and tracer bullets in the night sky. Rather disturbing and frightening. Soon I was moved up the line and was posted to a forward First Aid post; my job as dispenser was finished pro-tem and I found I was only needed as such when the F.A. was on rest.

This was my first experience of being under fire. Shell and mortar fire with occasional machine-gun fire to liven things up. Our First Aid post was at the ruins of a village, Ovillers in front of Albert, and my weeks there allowed me to settle down to continuous shellfire (ours and theirs). It was a desolate spot but we had the advantage of being able to sleep in a deep German dugout in comparative safety but the slaughter that was going on just in front of us was disturbing to say the least and we had hundreds of British Tommies and the odd wounded German prisoner through our post during the few weeks I was there. We came out on rest and had a thirty-five-kilometre march from headquarters back to the line. Here I set up my dispensary for about three weeks whilst new replacements came to the F.A.

In November 1916 we moved to Pont-de-Nieppe which was across the river bridge from Armentières (of 'Mademoiselles' fame) and back up the line to waterlogged trenches and rat-infested dugouts. It was about now that I got fed up with the R.A.M.C. I wasn't cut out to attend wounded soldiers and have rows at headquarters with a disgusting regular Q.M.S. who had appeared from England.

I applied for a transfer to the Heavy Branch Machine Gun Corps and my pal said, who went with me, 'It sounded a long

Appendix

way back'. I arrived at Bermicourt near St Pol (Saint-Pol-sur-Ternoise) after Christmas 1916 and found I'd joined what was to become the Tank Corps.

We were a ragtag lot drawn from every regiment in the British Army but I was to learn what real soldiering meant. I was introduced to all sorts of weapons, rifle, Lewis Gun, Hotchkiss Gun and 6-pdr naval gun. I took a great interest in this and quickly became proficient in their use. The winter of 1916/17 was one of the coldest ever experienced in northern France. We were billeted in farm outbuildings, barns etc. and being a new unit our food was woefully scarce and poor and we had to supplement what little we had as rations with egg and chips (oeufs & pomme de terre frites) from the local villagers who made a fortune out of us. At this time I had two friends, Jim Roberts, a carpenter by trade, and Tom Oakley who was an officer's batman. Roberts did odd jobs in his spare time for the local farmers and occasionally got himself invited out for a meal. I usually was included. Oakley was given the job of batman to Lord Rodney (Scots Greys) who came as Battalion Adjutant. He had his own caravan in which he lived and did not mix with the Battalion officers. He was all that was wrong with the old regular army. He was never seen again after 'A' Battalion went into action. Rodney spent all his spare time wining and dining at the bases. He had his car chauffeur and came home the worse for wear most nights. He used to take the morning parade, each day turned out in the most immaculate cavalry uniform by my pal Oakley. Oakley always had pockets full of francs; these were obtained when he put the Noble Lord (dead drunk) to bed each night. Consequently Roberts, Oakley and myself had 'bags of dough' to spend in the local estaminet on rum & cognac during the bitter winter. It was due to the Noble Lord that one of my company, for some slight misdemeanour, was tied to a wagon wheel for punishment, this was the first and last time I saw this barbaric punishment, it was done away with shortly afterwards, but it had the effect on me to make me hate all the class distinction, snobbery and so-called superiority that was rampant amongst the regular army officers of the old army. I have never got over the distaste when one considers that Lord Rodney was a creature of charity; £3,000 per annum were given to him in gratitude for what his ancestor Admiral Rodney had done a hundred years before. I was pleased to read after the war that Lord Rodney had his £3,000 pension taken from him. He wasn't fit to lick the boots of the officers and men of 'A' Battalion Tank Corps and he was only one of many regular officers who got 'cushy' jobs on the staff and did no fighting whatsoever and that included many of the generals. Shades of Montgomery and his staff in World War II. How different!

I have digressed to mention all this as it had a profound effect on my attitude to the ordinary Tommy who was a volunteer like myself and no doubt explains my preference even now to the 'spit and sawdust' rather than the saloon bar.

After three months of intensive training we had our new tanks. I was one of the crew of Tank A, sect A, Comp A, 'A' Battalion. My tank commander was Lieutenant Duncan who was to be killed in the Battle of Cambrai. We did a small action in support at Vimy Ridge and then left Bermicourt for the Ypres Salient. Our tanks were taken up beyond Ypres among the 18-pdr batteries at a place named 'China Walk' (don't ask me, I don't know). We were stationed under canvas some ten miles behind the front at Mont Des Cats. It was a wet but pleasant summer among the hop fields of Flanders, broken by guard duty at China Walk to service the tanks. Incidentally all tanks were given a name, usually the choice of the Tank Commander. Mine was Abul-ben-Amhed. On one occasion when doing guard duty up the line, we were cleaning out machine guns sitting outside the tank when a salvo of Whizzy Bangs landed right among the crew. Fortunately I had just gone in the tank for more guns and escaped but we lost five men killed and wounded and had to have a replacement crew. In September

Appendix

we went into action in the Battle of Passchendaele; most of our tanks were bogged down and took no part but we managed to reach our objective and return to China Walk – no sleep for two nights then back to base camp to sleep it off.

In October we again went into action at Inverness Copse, still on Passchendaele Ridge. We gained our objective but had the tank knocked out by artillery fire. Lt. Duncan, Roberts and myself were unhurt and Roberts and myself trudged back to China Walk three miles under shrapnel fire. We eventually got back to base camp and slept the clock round (again no sleep for two nights previous). I was awakened the following afternoon and told I was first on the list to leave (I had been eighth the previous day). I got a lift to Poperinge, had a snack in Tubby Clayton's Toc H and next day was back in Blighty. My first leave home from France after nine months. I came back in the uniform I had been wearing when in action but we were 'deloused' before entrainment at Poperinge. I must have looked a scarecrow but was soon in 'civvies' that I'd almost grown out of. Ten glorious days of leave and back to the Battalion, now waiting behind the Somme and preparing for the great tank battle of Cambrai. My crew was Lt. Duncan, driver Browning, Roberts – gearman, self – 6-pdr runner starboard side, Corp Stower, Mitchell, Scott, port side. I should mention that the 6-pounder gun was a shortened naval gun with telescopic sights and when properly calibrated a joy to fire. Very accurate and deadly to 1,000 yards. We were allowed to use our own judgment and pick out targets. A gunnery school had been opened at Merlimont-Plage, a few miles south of Paris-Plage and there I spent ten days cruising round the sand-dunes and firing at targets with live ammunition, this was a welcome break in the usual training routine and was as good as a holiday. It was soon time to move the tanks up to Havrincourt Wood in the Cambrai sector. The attack was to be made across the Hindenburg Line. This line was where the Germans withdrew after the Somme battle. It was a formidable obstacle, three lines of trenches too wide and deep to permit a tank to cross. However, large bundles of sticks – named fascines – were compacted and each weighed two tons. These were placed on the cabin (forward) on the tank and could be released and rolled into the trench. The tank then went across the trench on the fascine. Over 300 tanks took part in the Battle of Cambrai and the ground was dry and hard with rolling countryside rather like Cambridgeshire. We left our rail head after disembarking the tanks and made for a coppice near the village of Villers-Plouich, about one mile from our front line and about two miles from the Hindenburg Line. This was all done at night and the tanks were safely camouflaged before morning as this was a surprise attack. We spent two days servicing the tanks and guns and on the night of the 19th/20th November we moved the tanks along tapes that had been previously laid into position for zero hour 6 a.m. on the 20th. This was a long and tedious job as the tanks moved very slowly so that the enemy was not alerted.

Our crew was the usual one except that Capt Wain, the Comp Cdr, rode in the first tank No. 1 Section. At 5.55 hours the artillery opened up with an intense barrage and at 6.00 hours we were off across no-man's-land. Our tanks went through the immense wire entanglements and crushed them flat. The supporting infantry had no trouble in following. We crossed the first line. The Germans were taken completely by surprise and hundreds of prisoners were taken by the infantry. At the second line we had to wait as No. 2 tank had got stuck. Lieut. Duncan got out of the tank to help and unfortunately got killed: after clearing No. 2 tank we followed across and very soon had followed No. 3 tank across the third line and we were in open country. We rolled along at top speed, 5 m.p.h., and I was able to pick out several targets for my 6-pdr gun. We were eventually halted by intense machine-gun fire from the front and took shelter in a sunken road while a reconnaissance was made. The fire came from a trench about 200 yards long and we made a frontal attack crossing the trench and using

Appendix

our 'grapeshot' shells to pepper the trench. As we were turning to attack the trench again from the rear, we were hit by an enemy shell and had to abandon the tank. I was fired at by a German soldier as I left the tank but he fortunately missed both Roberts and myself. We only had revolvers and made a dash for the trench. Capt Wain was already there, with Corp Stower having got out on the port side. We were the only survivors. The Germans were in the long grass at the rear of the trench and they were being encouraged to rush us by a German N.C.O. who was in the trench. I pursued him down the dugout in the trench. In the meantime Capt. Wain was on the parados (rear wall of trench) and throwing enemy stick bombs he had picked up into the long grass. He was killed by an enemy bullet through his head and was later posthumously awarded the V.C. Roberts and myself then got a German machine gun across the trench and fired it into the long grass to stop the enemy rushing us. Corp Stower was rather badly wounded and took no part. We were eventually relieved by some infantry of the Newfoundland Regiment and I made a report to their officer. We were helped down the line and Corp Stower was carried by some R.A.M.C. Both Roberts and myself had quite a few superficial wounds and all we wore was a pair of shorts and a shirt, this was in November. We eventually got to a Field Ambulance Station and went by ambulance to a C.C.S. (Casualty Clearing Station). This was manned by Americans. Eventually I finished up in central France in an American hospital clad in a large blanket with a hole cut in the centre for my head. I was well cared for here and the American-Italian cook seemed to specialize in macaroni dishes. It was a welcome change from bully beef and crusts. I took the opportunity of sending home a field postcard to say I was wounded but OK. These cards had all the vital information printed on them (except 'I have been killed') and one just struck out the bits that didn't apply. Mary (my fiancée) received a letter to say I had been killed. This was from somebody in the Durham Light Infantry who had found my tunic beside one of the dead tank crew and I was buried in a 'nice grave' as he put it. Luckily Mary did not open this letter until she received the reassuring news that I was wounded. She had a feeling she must not open it as it was addressed to me. What luck! When I was discharged from the hospital I returned to the Tank Depot at Le Tréport and I joined the 10th Battalion just new from England. Most crews were provided with a member who had seen action and we did some training there. I became very friendly with a Danish lad, Jon Dan – correct name Aajee Lakke. His father was a major in the Danish Army and young Jon had run away to sea in 1912, deserted his ship in Algiers and joined the French Foreign Legion. When the war broke out he deserted the Legion, stowed away in a British ship and escaped reprisals. So he joined the Gloucester Regiment and got the Military Medal and Bar during the same battle. He eventually transferred to the tanks and was in 'C' Battalion until wounded at Cambrai. He was a character and if annoyed had the habit of pulling out a large seaman's spring knife.

After some training at Le Tréport, with plenty of time off to visit the cafés and estaminets on the quayside where we had marvellous meals of seafood, we moved up the line again back to the old Somme battlefield and we were near Havrincourt Wood and all billeted in Nissen huts on a secondary road. Our tanks were dispersed in various coppices about a mile away. This would be in January 1918 and we were there until the German attack and breakthrough on March 21st. On the morning of the 21st, at dawn, the enemy started a large-scale bombardment and shelled our camp and the coppices. A 5.9 shell demolished the officers' Mess, killing the Colonel and wounding and demoralizing a number of officers. We found that several of our tanks had been hit; however, as our tank was OK we moved up the line and were met by hundreds of our retreating infantry. We eventually joined in this retreat through Achiet-le-Grand, which incidentally was the depot for officers' food and drink. This place which had been abandoned

Appendix

was raided and looted by our troops and the job completed by the Germans next day. I'd never seen so much whisky and hams before, and the 51st Highland Division who had just done two days continuous fighting and retreating took full advantage of their good luck. We eventually moved further back and rested two days. On the third day, Easter Sunday, we were put into attack to recapture the ridge above Achiet-le-Petit. We had a replacement officer Lt. S. in charge and he unfortunately being quite new to the job in hand thought the half gallon of rum that each tank carried was specially there for his benefit and I personally had to restrain him and read him the riot act. When I returned to my battalion about two weeks later I was asked to make a report and was told he had been sent down the line with dyspepsia. To return to this attack, we were knocked out by mortars about half a mile from our objective but had time to get four Lewis Guns and one box of drums (ammunition) and retreated down the hill to a sunken road which was held by the Berkshire Regiment. A very large Brass Hat was there, the first I'd ever seen in the front line. He was, I gathered, General Ironside. On seeing the condition of Lt. S. he ordered him back to headquarters and said he could do with our Lewis Guns and ammo. I and the remainder of the crew were to fight with them for ten days during the rest of the retreat and eventually we made our way back to our Battalion. We went out on rest and awaited replacement tanks and men. I had a very happy time that spring. We were a long way back and were able to live off the land, so to speak. I will give one instance when four of us with the connivance of the company cook dined off duck, new potatoes and green peas at 1 a.m.

We eventually went up into the support line, that is to say behind the 18-pdr batteries but in front of the heavier stuff, again on the same ground we finished with in April. We took part in a few experimental day and night raids and the bulk of the crews slept in old German dugouts, but I preferred to sleep in the open by the tanks. It was lousy and airless in those old

263

dugouts and I had now reached the philosophy that if one had your name on it, that was that; dugout or no and the summer nights were marvellous, usually with a touch of early morning mist that made the groundsheet and blankets a necessity.

The big push came on August 8th, 1918, when we were to roll the Germans back. Our personal objective was the tank we had lost at Achiet-le-Petit. It was still there as the air photos showed. We attacked in a thick morning mist and when it lifted we were right on top of a battery of German field guns. Luckily they were firing in a different direction and at about 500 yards provided excellent target practice. The attack was called off before we reached our objective, and whilst we were crossing a ridge on the skyline we received our direct hit on the port side which burst in the engine and set us on fire. Three of the crew were killed and I got a superficial wound in my right shoulder. I endeavoured to put out the fire with a Pyrene extinguisher but we had to abandon the tank. I made my way back to the First Aid post to have my shoulder attended to and whilst there collapsed due to the Pyrene fumes. In fact, the first thing I knew about it was when I found myself in a Red Cross train attended by British nurses. We eventually made Rouen and to my great surprise I was admitted to No. 10 General Hospital on the racecourse – the hospital I had left over two years ago to join a Field Ambulance on the Somme. Owing to my right lung being affected (I still have the weakness), I was sent to a convalescent camp on the hill above Trouville on the Normandy coast. There I spent the month of August and had delightful times at Deauville and Trouville bathing, shrimping and playing tennis. My main memory of that place was my terrific appetite. I never could get enough to eat but we did find a friendly farmer's wife near the camp who used to put (my friend and I) us on lovely chicken dinners. Very cheap, they were wholesome. You may think I was fond of my victuals, well that is so; memories linger on but it must be remembered that a soldier in 1914 was fed the bare necessities. Bread, bully beef and Maconochie stew (in tins) and tea and the quantities provided depended on the ideas of too many Quartermasters and others. We were of course able to buy from the canteen if we were out of the line and if we had any money. After a payday we usually bought porridge oats and condensed milk after loading up with cigarettes. I have mentioned rest periods in this account. This was merely rest from the line and shellfire. These periods were usually full of hard work and discipline and getting ready for further fighting. Food was usually more plentiful at these times.

    I eventually found my way back to the Battalion via Le Tréport. They were then advancing a bit each day and forcing the Germans back. The end of the war was getting nearer. I was sent home on ten days' leave in September and had a grand time. My mother and sisters gave me a great welcome. I spent lots of my time boating on Talkin Tarn with them and Mary. I was held up about a week at Folkestone owing to German submarines in the Channel and had great difficulty in finding my Battalion which was now constantly on the move in the St Quentin area. The Germans put up a good rearguard action. Their tactics were to withdraw at night and leave well concealed and positioned machine-gun posts and it was our job to winkle out these places and allow the infantry to move in; nevertheless the infantry did suffer many casualties in these last weeks of the war. We were at the time supporting the Manchester Regiment (the old Regiment of Capt Wain of Cambrai fame). After many days of misses and near misses, we eventually finished up at the little town of Landrecies not far from Mons where the war started for Britain in 1914. It was during the period before arriving at Landrecies that one morning, when mopping up a M.G. post, we captured a live parrot in his cage. He had been the property of a German officer. He was taken over by a character in my tank named Darkie Carmen. He sent home for birdseed. Carmen was the Crown and Anchor expert and he and his chum used to visit American Army Units in the neighbourhood and he was reputed to send loads of money home. He did not make his fortune however, as several years after the war I met him in Derby where he was digging drains for the Corporation. He told me the parrot lived several years after he got home.

November 11th, 1918, 11 a.m. was Armistice Day, and we made what whoopee we could in Landrecies and we lit an immense bonfire that night of empty ammunition boxes. I moved down the line soon after this and was demobilized on January 13th, 1919, at Prees Heath in Shropshire. On looking back to fifty years ago, I suppose I was very lucky to get back; many of my friends never returned. Settling down to civilian life was a bit of a problem but the three and a half years of soldiering made one adaptable.

J. E. Mossman
January 1968

Joseph Mossman in later life

Bibliography

Aldous, J. W., *St. Bees School, Cumberland. The Roll of Honour & The Record of Old St. Beghians Who Served their King & Country in the Great War 1914–1919*, 1921.

Becke, Major A. F., *Gun Fire No. 47*, undated.

Bion, W. R., *The Long Week-end*, Karna Books, London, 1982.

Bristol Grammar School Chronicle, December 1916.

Brown, D. G., *The Tank in Action*, Leonaur, 2009.

Cooper, B., *The Ironclads of Cambrai*, Cassell, London, 1967.

Cooper, B., *Tank Battles of World War I*, Ian Allan Ltd., 1974.

De Ruvigny, *The Roll of Honour 1914–1918*, Uckfield, 2009.

Der Weltkrieg 1914–1918, Berlin, 1942.

Fletcher, D., *British Mark I Tank 1916*, Osprey, Oxford, 2004.

Fletcher, D., *British Mark IV Tank*, Osprey, Oxford, 2007.

Flight, 13 December 1917.

Gliddon, G., *VCs of the First World War, Cambrai 1917*, Sutton Publishing, Stroud, 2004.

Gibot, J-L. and Gorczynski, P., *Following the Tanks*, 1999.

Giese, Leutnant d. Res. Franz, *Geschichte des Reserve-Infanterie-Regiments Nr. 227 im Weltkrieg 1914–1918*, Berlin 1931.

Hammond, B., *Cambrai 1917*, Phoenix, London, 2008.

Hart, Liddell B. H., *The Tanks*, Cassell, London, 1958.

Hartley, J., *17th Manchesters*, Reveille Press, Brighton, 2012.

Hickey, Captain D. E., *Rolling Into Action*, Naval and Military Press, Uckfield, 2007.

Hicks, Dr J., *The Welsh at Passchendaele*, Y Lolfa, Talybont, 2017.

Horsfall, J. and Cave, N., *Cambrai, The Right Hook*, Pen and Sword, Barnsley, 1999.

Inglefield, Captain V. E., *The History of the Twentieth (Light) Division*, Nisbet and Co. Ltd., London, 1921.

John, S., *The Welsh at War. Through Mud to Victory*, Pen and Sword, Barnsley, 2018.

Lee, A. G., *No Parachute: A Fighter Pilot in World War I*, The Adventurers Club, London, 1969.

Ludendorff, General E., *My War Memories, 1914–1918*, Naval and Military Press, Uckfield, 2005.

McNab, C., *Cambrai 1917*, Spellmount, Stroud, 2012.

Miles, Captain W., *Military Operations, France and Belgium 1917 Volume 3*, Naval and Military Press, Uckfield, undated.

Moore, W., *A Wood Called Bourlon*, Pen and Sword, Barnsley, 1988.

Pope, S., *The First Tank Crews*, Helion and Company Ltd., Solihull, 2016.

Pries, Hauptmann d.R. Arthur, *Das Reserve-Infanterie-Regiments Nr. 90 1914–1918*, Oldenburg, 1925.

Pullen, R., *Beyond the Green Fields*, Tucann Books, Lincoln, 2008.

Pullen, R., *The Landships of Lincoln*, Tucann Books, Lincoln, 2007.

Rawson, A., *The Cambrai Campaign*, Pen and Sword, Barnsley, 2017.

Schwenke, Oberstleutnant a.D. Alexander, *Geschichte des Reserve-Infanterie-Regiments Nr. 19 im Weltkrieg 1914–1918*, Oldenburg, 1926.

Sheldon, J., *The German Army at Cambrai*, Pen and Sword, Barnsley, 2009.

Bibliography

Sheldon, J., *The German Army at Passchendaele*, Pen and Sword, Barnsley, 2007.

Smithers. A. J., *Cambrai, The First Great Tank Battle 1917*, Leo Cooper, London, 1992.

Smithson, J., *A Taste of Success*, Helion and Company Ltd., Solihull, 2017.

Strutz, Dr. G., *Die Tankschlacht bei Cambrai*, Didenburg, Berlin, 1929.

Swinton, E., *Eyewitness*, Hodder and Stoughton, 1932.

Tait, J. and Fletcher, D., *Tracing Your Tank Ancestors*, Pen and Sword, Barnsley, 2011.

Taylor, John A., *Deborah and the War of the Tanks 1917*, Pen and Sword, Barnsley, 2016.

The Tank Corps Honours and Awards 1916–1919, Midland Medals, Birmingham. 1982.

The Tank Corps Journal, Cambrai Anniversary Issue, 1922.

Thorne, R., *Penarth – a History of*, The Starling Press Ltd., Risca, 1975.

Victoria College Book of Remembrance, undated.

Von Watter, General O. F., *Dem Gedenken eines großen Soldaten von den alten Kameraden der 54. Infanterie-Division des Weltkrieges*, Berlag Broschef, Hamburg, undated.

Von Watter, General O. F., *Ein Gedenkbuch*, Berlag Broschef, Hamburg, undated

Watson, W. H. L., *With the Tanks*, Pen and Sword, Barnsley, 2014.

Williams-Ellis, C., *The Tank Corps*, G. H. Doran, New York, 1919.

Wilson, G. M. (ed.), *Fighting Tanks*, Seeley, Service and Co. Ltd., London, 1929.

Woollcombe, R., *The First Tank Battle*, Arthur Barker Ltd., London, 1967.

Acknowledgements

MY GRATITUDE TO each of the following for their assistance in producing this work:

Nigel Braybrook for the photograph of Harold Shouler.

Philippe Gorczynski for permission to use his photograph of the remains of Tank A.2 and the map in Chapter 12.

Ian Gumm of www.inthefootsteps.com for his maps of the Cambrai battlefield.

Simon Haynes for the photograph of Cecil Rich.

Eirian Jones of Y Lolfa for her editing and support.

Photograph of John Ehrhardt courtesy of King Edward's School, Birmingham

Jack Sheldon for his permission to quote from his books on the German Army at Cambrai and Passchendaele.

Feriel Small and Stuart Middleton for the material on Reginald Liles.

Rupert and Juliet Smith for permission to photograph The Knoll.

Katie Thompson of the Tank Museum at Bovington for her assistance with the primary sources.

Simon Toon for the photographs of, and information on, his grandfather Alexander Grove.

Nigel Williams and the Llantwit Major Local History Society for the photographs of the 7th Cyclist Battalion in Llantwit Major.

Acknowledgements

Anke Yee for her translations from the original German source material.

Radley College for the photograph of J. C. Tilly.

Tameside Local Studies and Archives Centre for the photograph of the 17th Manchester Regiment.

The descendants of Richard Wain V.C. for their encouragement and help.

I should especially like to thank my wife Wendy for her research, editing skills, her constant support and encouragement in the pursuit of my projects.

Ask for a print quote!
www.ylolfa.com